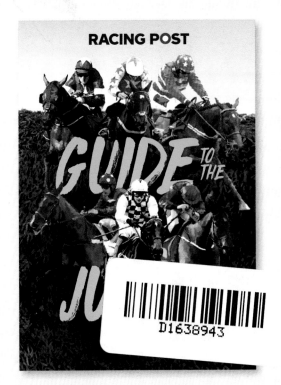

Edited and designed
by David Dew

Contributors

Richard Birch	Pietro Innocenzi	Justin O'Hanlon	Tom Ward
James Burn	David Jennings	Dave Orton	Nick Watts
Tom Collins	Paul Kealy	Tom Park	Robbie Wilders
Dave Edwards	Andrew King	Maddy Playle	Andrew Wilsher
Jonathan Harding	Steve Mason	Lewis Porteous	
Dylan Hill	Keith Melrose	Brian Sheerin	
James Hill	Ben Newton	Alan Sweetman	

Cover artwork by Samantha Creedon

Inside artwork by David Cramphorn, Liam Hill, Stefan Searle & Shane Tetley

Published in 2019 by Racing Post Books, Raceform, 27 Kingfisher Court, Hambridge Road, Newbury, RG14 5SJ

ISBN: 978-1839500121

Printed by Buxton Press Limited

LOWDOWN FROM THE TRAINERS

RACING POST EXPERTS

THIS SEASON'S KEY HORSES

THE LOWDOWN GORDON ELLIOTT

Roll on the spring and Tiger's bid for greatness

FEW horses in this modern era have captured the imagination quite like Tiger Roll. It says everything you need to know about the dual Grand National winner that his Aintree homecoming extended well into the summer months

and even featured an appearance on RTE's The Late Late Show.

Never one to concentrate on what's gone before, Gordon Elliott has his eyes fixed on equalling Red Rum's record of three Grand National successes with **Tiger Roll**, the undisputed star at Cullentra House Stables.

*Gordon Elliott with
Grand National
hero Tiger Roll*

WINNERS IN LAST FIVE SEASONS 177, 210, 193, 123, 92

"There's not a lot more I can say about Tiger Roll that hasn't been said already. He's an absolute legend of a horse. I've been lucky that, in a short space of time, we've come across a lot of nice horses but he's special," Elliott says.

On plans, he adds: "It'll be a very similar campaign to last season with him with all roads leading back to Aintree for the Grand National. The only thing we might do a bit differently is we probably won't go for the cross-country race at Cheltenham in November with him, as he'd have to carry a lot of weight. You'd be looking at the Boyne Hurdle at Navan, the cross-country race at the Cheltenham Festival and then, all being well, back to Aintree."

Galway Plate winner **Borice** will also be trained with Aintree in mind, as will 2018 Irish Grand National winner **General Principle**.

Tiger Roll (right) leads Apple's Jade and Samcro as they head towards the gallops

Elliott says: "Borice might be another for Aintree. I thought plenty of him last year but nothing really worked out with him. He won the Galway Plate well and we have the option of the Troytown at Navan, which I'd say is more likely at this stage, but he'll also be left in the Ladbrokes Trophy at Newbury.

"I'd be favouring having a whack at the Troytown because a big, galloping track like Navan would suit him well."

Elliott sent out 177 winners in Ireland last season, amassing over €4 million in prize-money and enjoyed a healthy Cheltenham Festival by sending out three winners.

The 41-year-old endured his fair share of low points along the way, and few horses frustrated quite like **Samcro**, who failed to fire in his three starts outside of novice company.

Elliott says: "He's had a wind operation after what was a really frustrating season. He scoped dirty all year so we decided to pull the plug as we never felt we had him fully right.

"He looks good at the moment, very strong, and the way things worked out, it might have been a blessing in disguise that he didn't go chasing last year because the ground was so good. The plan is to go chasing with him this season and I'd imagine we could start him off over fences at Down Royal in November."

Ten-time Grade 1-winner **Apple's Jade**, whose form tapered off in the spring, has also had her wind tinkered with.

Elliott explains: "She wasn't the same mare after Christmas last season and was very disappointing in the Champion Hurdle at Cheltenham. She's going to have a similar campaign this year, with the Lismullen Hurdle at Navan and the Hatton's Grace Hurdle at Fairyhouse the early targets. She's come back good and strong and she's had a wind operation."

Gold Cup ambition for Delta

Elliott knows what it takes to win the Cheltenham Gold Cup, having achieved the feat with Don Cossack in 2016, and if he's to win the great race for a second time, he believes **Delta Work** is the horse capable of doing it.

He says: "Delta Work isn't the biggest,

Ladbrokes
WHERE THE NATION PLAYS

strongest or most robust horse, but his last run was arguably his best run of the year when he won well at Punchestown. He's a triple Grade 1-winning novice chaser and he's probably gone under the radar a little bit as he doesn't get much appreciation.

"If I have a Gold Cup horse in my yard this season, Delta Work is the horse. He'll start off in the Ladbrokes Grade 1 Champion Chase in November."

Talented Duty on the way back

Death Duty was once talked about as a future Gold Cup horse and, despite the fact the eight-year-old hasn't been seen since falling in the Grade 1 Flogas Novice Chase at Leopardstown's 2017 Christmas festival, Elliott issues an upbeat bulletin on the returning chaser.

He says: "Death Duty is back cantering and looks great. He missed a year and a half but we've been delighted with him and he'll be aimed at Down Royal as well."

On the remainder of his older chasers worth watching out for this season, Elliott adds: "**Shattered Love** should have a good season. There's a good programme for mares and, while she might just be a grade below the top staying chasers, I think there should

be a lot of fun to be had with her this season.

"**The Storyteller** has been a great horse for us and, while he's just below that highest grade as well, he never runs a bad race and picks up plenty of prize-money. He's going for the American Grand National and might have a run beforehand somewhere.

"**Mengli Khan** has a massive engine but doesn't always turn up. He's got a lot of class and when he's good, he's very good. The second-season novice chase at Down Royal is the plan for him."

'Envoi Allen is very exciting'

It's no surprise Elliott believes he's working with the hottest bunch of youngsters he's ever had through his hands. Unbeaten Champion Bumper winner **Envoi Allen** heads a stellar cast, which also features top-notch prospects **Malone Road**, **Andy Dufresne** and plenty more.

On that terrific trio, Elliott says: "Envoi Allen is very exciting and we can't wait to start him off. We could look at a 2m4f maiden hurdle for him at Down Royal in November and take things from there. He doesn't do a whole pile at home but he does it on the track and he's come back in looking great.

Shattered Love leads Gordon Elliott's string up the gallops

GORDON ELLIOTT
LONGWOOD, COUNTY MEATH

ALL RACES	Races run	1st	2nd	3rd	Unpl	Per cent	Level stake
Non-hcp hurdles	2671	433	414	342	1482	16.2	-837.10
Hcp hurdles	1615	156	145	136	1178	9.7	-566.30
Non-hcp chases	1236	224	250	174	588	18.1	-249.73
Hcp chases	820	80	54	76	610	9.8	-244.49
Hunter chases	21	6	2	1	12	28.6	+1.61
NH Flat	798	181	146	96	375	22.7	-69.00
Totals	**7161**	**1080**	**1011**	**825**	**4245**	**15.1**	**-1965.01**

BY MONTH

	W-R	Per cent	Level stake
January	85-586	14.5	-178.66
February	95-557	17.1	-142.08
March	85-489	17.4	-132.02
April	73-701	10.4	-207.62
May	90-665	13.5	-181.85
June	73-477	15.3	-73.35
July	75-622	12.1	-309.22
August	81-625	13.0	-183.60
September	47-316	14.9	-94.44
October	119-538	22.1	-94.17
November	135-749	18.0	-128.44
December	122-836	14.6	-239.56

FIRST TIME OUT

	W-R	Per cent	Level stake
Non-hcp hurdles	87-598	14.5	-261.47
Hcp hurdles	18-241	7.5	-56.79
Non-hcp chases	36-196	18.4	+2.33
Hcp chases	12-119	10.1	+15.00
NH Flat	66-313	21.1	-15.16

FAVOURITES

	W-R	Per cent	Level stake
Non-hcp hurdles	226-530	42.6	-42.14
Hcp hurdles	67-284	23.6	-59.00
Non-hcp chases	123-275	44.7	-19.69
Hcp chases	39-122	32.0	+16.93
NH Flat	113-227	49.8	+20.58

Statistics relate to all runners in Ireland during the last five seasons

"Malone Road came back looking fantastic and he's very quick. He'd be one for the 2m novice hurdles. If you'd have asked me at the beginning of last season which horse would go on to win the Champion Bumper, I know I'd have told you Malone Road rather than Envoi Allen. He didn't get there in the end, but he's a horse I really like.

"Andy Dufresne won his bumper well. He didn't beat a whole lot but he did it well and he's still not the finished article. He's a big chaser for further down the line."

Land Rover bumper winner **Festival D'ex**, Grade 1 Punchestown Champion Bumper runner-up **Abacadabras** and **Thatsy** are three more exciting recruits to hurdles this season, according to Elliott.

He says: "Festival D'ex has got loads of scope for improvement and could be a nice horse. Abacadabras is another for the 2m novice hurdle bracket. He was second in the Champion Bumper at Punchestown and has plenty of pace.

"Thatsy pulled a muscle before Cheltenham, which is why he didn't run in the Champion Bumper, but he's got very strong over the summer and could be exciting."

Asked for some darker ones, Elliott adds: "**Daylight Katie** is a good mare. She jumps very well and could be one for the Mares' Novice Hurdle at Cheltenham.

"**Bigbadandbeautiful** finished second in the Grade 2 mares' bumper at Leopardstown before winning her bumper at Clonmel and we like her.

"I think, as a whole, we've got our nicest ever bunch of young horses. I could go on all day but two others who are worth following are **Feel My Pulse** and **Ard Abhainn**."

Strong novice chase team

Battleoverdoyen is reported to have done well during the summer and is likely to be a leading light in the novice chases.

Elliott says: "Battleoverdoyen is a big 3m chaser and looks really well. He was beaten after a hurdle at Cheltenham and, if you watch the rerun, he was changing his legs plenty and I think that inside track was too tight for him. Chasing will be his game."

Given it's Gigginstown House Stud's modus operandi to buy big horses with staying pedigrees at the store sales, it's no surprise to see Elliott well represented in this sphere, and **Champagne Classic**, **Felix Desjy** and **Cracking Smart** are put forward as leading prospects for the powerful owners.

Elliott says: "Champagne Classic is back cantering and he's still a novice this season which will be a help. My plan was to go for the National Hunt Chase at Cheltenham with him last season but he ended up pulling a muscle and he missed the rest of the season.

"He's a Cheltenham Festival winner and he won a Grade 1 as a novice hurdler – he's a classy horse. His legs look good and I think there's plenty to like about him this season. We've got a good team of novice chasers and he's one of a few we're looking forward to."

He adds: "Felix Desjy could be a very good horse over 2m this season. I was impressed with him at Aintree, where he galloped them into the ground, and he ran well back at Punchestown as well. I think he could be hard to beat from the front.

"Cracking Smart could be anything.

Nothing worked out for him last season. He got operated on for a kissing spine and it was halfway through the season when we got him going but he never looked right. This year, though, he looks brilliant and is cantering and we're really looking forward to him."

On **Vision D'honneur**, **Dortmund Park**, **Galvin** and **Chosen Mate**, Elliott adds: "Vision D'honneur disappointed me a bit last season but he's cantering so hopefully he can improve for fences.

"Dortmund Park has had three wind operations already. He's a Grade 1 winner and if his wind stands up he'll be a lovely recruit to chasing but he's a hard horse to keep right. Galvin stays and jumps while Chosen Mate could also go novice chasing."

Tintangle, **Black Tears** and **Surin** are three mares set to tackle the larger obstacles this season, and Elliott says: "Tintangle is definitely up to getting black type against her own sex. If you go back to her Cheltenham run, she was probably a little unlucky not to have finished closer than she did in the mares' novice hurdle as she was a bit far out of her ground.

"Black Tears also ran very well in the mares' novice at Cheltenham and she'll probably go chasing too.

"Surin looks great. We might rock on over

Labaik coasts home in the 2017 Supreme Novices' Hurdle at Cheltenham

SUPER STATS

Elliott enjoyed 55 winners in Britain last year – his highest total. That was aided by the **strength of his hurdlers**, who struck 38 times from 115 runs (33%, +3.88pt). Elliott's novice raiders in Britain also did the trainer proud (22-56, 39%)

The trainer's love of **Perth** is well documented and it's easy to see why with a 24-57 record (42%, +13.04pt). It's also worth taking the hint when Elliott has the occasional runner at **Sedgefield** (6-8, 75%, +6.11pt)

Richard Johnson is widely regarded as the best jumps jockey in the game right now, so it's only natural he would have a good rapport with a trainer like Elliott. Last season they had a record of 35-76 (46%, +21.63pt)

The trainer's partnership with **Jamie Codd** is also particularly fruitful – he rode 15 winners from 40 rides for Elliott in Ireland last season, returning an 8pt profit

Sligo proved a good hunting ground for Elliott last season with six winners from 15 runners and a healthy 25.23pt profit, which was boosted by his hurdlers doing the business (4-11, 36%, +14.40pt)

fences with her and take advantage of all those allowances. She looks like a 3m chaser and I think she could do well."

Labaik looking good

Something of a forgotten horse, 2017 Supreme Novices' Hurdle winner Labaik is back in full work and it's so far so good with the classy hurdler, who may come under consideration for a tilt at the Champion Hurdle, provided he stays sound.

"Labaik is cantering and looks great. If he stays in one piece, he could be a Champion Hurdle horse – he's very fast," says Elliott.

Cheltenham Festival winner **Sire Du Berlais** and **Coeur Sublime** are also given favourable mentions.

Elliott adds: "Sire Du Berlais is a good, staying horse. There's no decision made on what route we'll be going but he's a festival winner and exciting to have.

"Coeur Sublime tapered off a little last season but I think he was growing a little bit. He's a lot stronger this year and I'm thinking about keeping him over hurdles. He's got plenty of gears."

Interview by Brian Sheerin

It's all change but eyes fixed firmly on progress

HARRY FRY'S ascent to becoming a major force in jump racing should not be understated. Having held a licence for only seven years, there are few trainers who have established themselves so quickly and last season again proved fruitful for the yard.

Although the number of winners was slightly down on 2017-18, Grade 1 victories are what defines an operation and after a slight dip in the middle of the campaign two top-level triumphs came in the spring.

Emerging stayer If The Cap Fits landed the spoils in a rousing finish to the Ryanair Stayers Hurdle at Aintree before 11-year-old stalwart Unowhatimeanharry rolled back the years with a tear-jerking three-length success over Bacardys in the Champion Stayers Hurdle at Punchestown.

Reflecting on the last campaign, Fry says: "It ended on a real high and two Grade 1 victories can't be a bad year. We actually lost more horses last year than ever before as well, so it was an up and down season, really."

This season represents a changing of the guard for the team with Noel Fehily, who has been an integral part of the Seaborough trainer's success, retiring from the saddle and Sean Bowen assuming the role of stable jockey. However, Fehily will still have a major influence on the operation in a racing advisor capacity. Fry explains: "Noel has been a huge part of our success and will continue to be on the books as a racing advisor. He's in regularly – probably more regularly now than when he was riding for us

WINNERS IN LAST FIVE SEASONS 47, 53, 67, 54, 36

All smiles during morning work at Harry Fry's stables in Dorset

– passing on his thoughts and experience so he's very much still part of the team and will continue to be a big influence on what we do.

"He'll certainly be a big help to Sean as well, who won his first Grade 1 for us on If The Cap Fits which was an ideal start to a really exciting new partnership."

Stable star back for more

Unowhatimeanharry, despite advancing years, is still maintaining his appetite for the game. Fry says: "It's not getting any easier for Unowhatimeanharry but it was great at Punchestown to see him roll back the years to win that Champion Stayers Hurdle for the second time.

"He's come back in full of enthusiasm and owes us nothing. He's been the horse of a lifetime and as long as he continues to be competitive, we'll keep him in training. However, as soon as he starts to tell us he's had enough, that'll be the time to draw stumps. He certainly hasn't come back in looking like an 11-year-old on the gallops, probably the opposite. He's won the Long Distance Hurdle at Newbury twice and that

could be a starting point, or the bet365 Hurdle at Wetherby in November."

Top staying hurdles the plan

If The Cap Fits will embark on a similar campaign to his esteemed stablemate. The seven-year-old possesses great potential as a staying hurdler after scoring on his first try over 3m at Aintree and, although Paisley Park has asserted a stranglehold on the division, Fry believes the son of Milan could be the one to serve it up to Andrew Gemmell's pride and joy.

He says: "If The Cap Fits relished the step up to 3m at Aintree and did all he could to try and throw the race away at the last after making a bad mistake. He showed a great attitude to get up between two tough mares and we look forward to campaigning him in all the top staying hurdles.

"There's an impressive staying champion in Paisley Park and he'll be tough to knock off his perch, but someone has to serve it up to him. He's still fairly unexposed at the trip and we'll maybe look to start him off at Ascot in the Coral Hurdle over just shy of 2m4f, which he won last year. That will give us a

Happy scenes in the winner's enclosure at Punchestown

Ladbrokes
WHERE THE NATION PLAYS

HARRY FRY
SEABOROUGH, DORSET

	Number of horses	Races run	1st	2nd	3rd	Unpl	Per cent	£1 level stake
NH Flat	17	44	11	7	5	21	25.0	-5.25
Hurdles	44	131	22	17	13	79	16.8	-30.80
Chases	23	67	14	7	6	40	20.9	-8.50
Totals	74	242	47	31	24	140	19.4	-44.55
2017-18	71	239	53	34	34	121	20.9	-54.24
2016-17	87	284	67	42	33	141	23.6	+3.52

BY MONTH

NH FLAT	W-R	Per cent	£1 level stake	HURDLES	W-R	Per cent	£1 level stake
May	0-1	0.0	-1.00	May	2-8	25.0	+0.50
Jun	0-1	0.0	-1.00	Jun	0-4	0.0	-4.00
Jul	0-0	0.0	0.00	Jul	0-3	0.0	-3.00
Aug	0-1	0.0	-1.00	Aug	1-2	50.0	-0.75
Sep	0-0	0.0	0.00	Sep	1-4	25.0	+4.00
Oct	0-0	0.0	0.00	Oct	0-9	0.0	-9.00
Nov	1-7	14.3	-3.25	Nov	8-28	28.6	+8.32
Dec	5-12	41.7	+8.98	Dec	1-22	4.5	-19.38
Jan	0-2	0.0	-2.00	Jan	2-10	20.0	-4.63
Feb	2-8	25.0	-4.06	Feb	2-11	18.2	-2.50
Mar	3-9	33.3	+1.08	Mar	3-18	16.7	-7.38
Apr	0-3	0.0	-3.00	Apr	2-12	16.7	+7.00

CHASES	W-R	Per cent	£1 level stake	TOTALS	W-R	Per cent	£1 level stake
May	1-8	12.5	+3.00	May	3-17	17.6	+2.50
Jun	0-4	0.0	-4.00	Jun	0-9	0.0	-9.00
Jul	1-3	33.3	+0.50	Jul	1-6	16.7	-2.50
Aug	2-2	100.0	+5.41	Aug	3-5	60.0	+3.66
Sep	1-2	50.0	-0.86	Sep	2-6	33.3	+3.14
Oct	2-4	50.0	+10.50	Oct	2-13	15.4	+1.50
Nov	3-10	30.0	-2.80	Nov	12-45	26.7	+2.27
Dec	3-14	21.4	-3.00	Dec	9-48	18.8	-13.40
Jan	0-4	0.0	-4.00	Jan	2-16	12.5	-10.63
Feb	1-4	25.0	-1.25	Feb	5-23	21.7	-7.81
Mar	0-7	0.0	-7.00	Mar	6-34	17.6	-13.30
Apr	0-5	0.0	-5.00	Apr	2-20	10.0	-1.00

DISTANCE

HURDLES	W-R	Per cent	£1 level stake	CHASES	W-R	Per cent	£1 level stake
2m-2m3f	11-61	18.0	-17.95	2m-2m3f	3-16	18.8	-6.36
2m4f-2m7f	7-45	15.6	-6.60	2m4f-2m7f	8-33	24.2	+8.36
3m+	4-24	16.7	-5.25	3m+	3-18	16.7	-10.50

TYPE OF RACE

	NON-HANDICAPS			HANDICAPS		
	W-R	Per cent	£1 level stake	W-R	Per cent	£1 level stake
Nov hrdls	6-31	19.4	-13.25	0-4	0.0	-4.00
Hrdls	7-30	23.3	-7.05	8-63	12.7	-12.00
Nov chs	8-20	40.0	+4.00	0-1	0.0	-1.00
Chases	0-3	0.0	-3.00	4-39	10.3	-13.00
Sell/claim	0-0	0.0	0.00	0-0	0.0	0.00

Statistics relate to all runners in Britain from April 29, 2018 to April 27, 2019

month to the Long Walk back at Ascot before Christmas and thereafter the races pick themselves."

Christmas star again?

Hell's Kitchen can be a bit of a loose cannon with his running style and was another who dined at the top table last season, with a fourth to Altior in the Champion Chase the clear highlight.

Fry says: "Hell's Kitchen ran a career-best to finish fourth in the Champion Chase and he was highly tried after at Aintree and Punchestown, but admittedly he's probably not quite up to Grade 1 level. 2m2f is probably ideal for him and he always seems to come good around the festive period, having won over Christmas the last two years. There's no great plan, albeit we might look to start him off in the Haldon Gold Cup at Exeter.

"**Bags Groove** had a really good first season over fences winning two Grade 2s. The two occasions he ran in Grade 1s were my fault, really. In hindsight I shouldn't have run him at Huntingdon just over a fortnight before Kempton as that run left its mark on him for the Kauto Star, where he ran flat. He also didn't travel well up to Aintree on his last run of the season and probably shouldn't have taken part.

"It was a really productive campaign bar those two blips and we're looking forward to his second season over fences. I'd quite like to start him off at Ascot in the 1965 Chase, but the two highest rated horses in training are set to meet there and we might find something else. He's won over just short of 3m at Huntingdon and the Peterborough Chase could be an option.

"**Momella** was running an excellent race for us in the Long Distance Hurdle at Newbury but after jumping the second-last

Bags Groove landed a pair of Grade 2 novice chases last season

tripped herself up. I've never known a horse lose her confidence so much from something like that and it left its mark.

"She's had a good break now and hopefully can put that behind her. She'll probably have a run over hurdles to start, but we want to go chasing. She's schooled well over fences and hopefully will make a nice novice chaser.

Ready to land overdue success

"**Air Horse One** hasn't won in for what

seems like donkey's years now. It's taken him a really long time to drop to below his last winning mark, which was over two and a half years ago, so we're hopeful it will be his turn soon. He didn't stay the 3m at Punchestown so we'll bring him back in trip and he'll be remaining over hurdles because he's never taken to chasing at home.

"**Acting Lass**'s season didn't go to plan at all and when he was ready the ground went against him. It was way too quick when he ran at Punchestown but he's had a good break, he's come back in and hopefully his problems are behind him. We look forward to getting him out in 3m staying chases on slower ground.

"**Mr One More** didn't run last season but is back in training, He won his first three starts and actually beat Summerville Boy on his first try over hurdles. It'll be good to get

> ### DID YOU KNOW?
> Rock On Ruby might have won the Champion Hurdle for Paul Nicholls in 2012 but Harry Fry was actually training him by that time – and his wife Ciara continues to dote on him during his well-deserved retirement

SUPER STATS

Fry is a trainer to keep onside at **Exeter**. He has had 32 winners from 93 runners during the last five seasons – and a profit of 50.78pt.

The hint should be taken on the rare occasions Fry sends runners to **Stratford**, where he had two winners from three runners last season. Likewise, he did well in bumpers at **Uttoxeter** (2-3, 67%, +4.23pt)

Fry and **Sean Bowen** worked well together last season (8-34, +8.38pt)

Keep an eye on any **novice chasers** Fry has this season – he posted a 10-22 record last year and netted his followers a profit of 10.50pt. Races between 2m1½f and 2m3f also agreed with his runners (8-30, 27%)

him back on the racecourse in the autumn and we'll possibly think about a novice chasing campaign when he's ready.

"**Over To Sam** made a really encouraging return on his first start over fences when he jumped particularly well at Newton Abbot and we're looking forward to kicking on with him. He'll be a staying novice chaser to follow on slower ground this season.

Mares' chase targets

One of Fry's more interesting recruits in the past couple of seasons was the JP McManus-owned six-year-old mare **Dalila Du Seuil**, who has a Grade 1 fourth to De Bon Coeur at Auteuil to her name in 2017.

"Dalila Du Seuil won on her first start for

Dalila Du Seuil (right) will be campaigned in mares' chases

us and then didn't get very far on her second outing when she picked up an injury which curtailed her season," says Fry. "But we're looking forward to her second season over fences and there are some really nice mares' chases to campaign her towards.

"**Definitelyanoscar** won at Newton Abbot in August but was disqualified. A wind op really seems to have helped her. She's a winning pointer and will be another to go novice chasing with.

"There were a number of false starts at the Galway festival and when they did go **Ena Baie** dwelt and was playing catch-up from there on, but she didn't disgrace herself by finishing a never-nearer fourth. We have no choice but to campaign her in Ireland because the Irish handicapper put her back up 1lb for finishing fourth at Galway and the British handicapper thought it was worth an 8lb rise."

Queue one to look forward to

Last season shone light on an above-average crop of bumper performers for Fry, headed by the exploits of the unbeaten **Get In The Queue**, who provided Fehily with a fairytale ending to his glittering career by securing an emotional triumph in the valuable Goffs UK Spring Sale Bumper at Newbury on his final ride. The five-year-old suffered a minor setback that day but retains great potential in a strong team of novice hurdle prospects.

Fry says: "Get In The Queue was three from three in bumpers and memorably provided Noel with a winning last ride at Newbury, in a race we've won three years running.

"Unfortunately, he picked up a small injury that day which will rule him out until the second half of the season but we'll start off him off over 2m in novice hurdles and he'll tell us whether we need to step up in trip.

"He was particularly impressive when appearing out of the clouds to hose up at Exeter and the ground was a bit quicker at Newbury where he was less impressive. He prefers slower ground and he's certainly one to look forward to when he's back.

Misty an exciting prospect

"**Misty Whisky** scored in a Listed mares' bumper at Sandown in March, and it was probably just one run too many at Aintree after that. She comes from a really good family, being related to Air Horse One and One For Rosie. She's an exciting prospect who will go to war in mares' novice hurdles this season, probably over 2m4f.

"**Whitehotchillifili** wasn't disgraced in the same bumper when behind Misty Whisky having not had an ideal preparation. She had a flu jab in the lead-up to the race and finishing fourth was a very good effort.

"Again, it was probably one run too many after that – and she loves soft ground. She's another to look forward to when stepping up in trip in the mares' novice hurdle division.

"It's fair to say we have high hopes for **King Roland**. He was hugely impressive at Uttoxeter and then gave weight all round at Ffos Las on his second start.

"He's a winning pointer whom we have high hopes for in novice hurdles. He'll be ready to get out when we get some soft ground and we'll probably start over 2m and work our way up.

"**Ishkhara Lady** bolted up on her only start but suffered slightly from sore shins so we didn't rush her and gave her time to fully recover, which she has. She's another smart mares' novice hurdle prospect for us and could start off in the mares' Listed bumper at Cheltenham in November before going hurdling.

"**Fehily** is a lovely four-year-old to look forward to from what he's shown us and hopefully he can do the name justice.

"**Green Dolphin** won his bumper nicely at Wincanton on his second start and we probably ran him back too quickly at Newbury in a Listed bumper.

"We took a chance and it was clearly too soon, but he's maturing nicely and we're excited to go novice hurdling with him up in trip."

Interview by Robbie Wilders

Spectacular array of

NICKY HENDERSON might have last season surrendered the champion trainer title he won for the previous two years, but he remains at the very top of his game and has the most incredible amount of talent at his disposal that it would be no surprise to see him take the championship back from Paul Nicholls next April.

Top of the tree at Seven Barrows is the phenomenal **Altior** – winner of his last 19 races and four-time Cheltenham Festival winner, including the last two Champion Chases. He has had potential rivals running for cover for the past few seasons, and this time might well get the chance to try something different with a step up to 3m for a crack at the King George, for which he spent the summer as 3-1 ante-post favourite.

firepower

Henderson says: "He was great all the way through last season – I thought he was particularly brave at Cheltenham and back to his best at Sandown, winning the Celebration Chase for the third time.

"I know there is a lot of talk about the King George. I think a little bit further would help, but whether 3m is within his reach I don't know.

"Perhaps we could try further before the King George, but I'm not very keen on the Betfair Chase at Haydock, so maybe the 1965 Chase at Ascot in November is the best place to find out and try him over a little bit further."

Should Altior – who had a minor wind op during the summer – fail to stay the extra distance, a drop to 2m would be on the cards as would an attempt to become the first three-time winner of the Champion Chase since Badsworth Boy in 1985.

Henderson has sent out 64 winners at the Cheltenham Festival and his **Buveur D'Air** earned two of those successes with repeat wins in the Champion Hurdle. He might have failed last season in his bid for a hat-trick when falling, but he ended his campaign on a high note by landing the Grade 1 Punchestown Champion Hurdle, and his trainer has his eye on plenty more big days.

He says: "It was a fantastic performance at Punchestown and gave us all the clear encouragement we needed to know that he's still as good as ever.

"He suffered his first defeat since the 2016 Supreme Novices' at the hands of Verdana

The look of love: Nicky Henderson with Altior

Blue when she just pipped him in the Christmas Hurdle on what was unseasonably good ground – which she absolutely loves and it probably isn't his favourite.

"He won his preparation before Cheltenham very easily and we had hoped going into the festival that all was good and, although Supasundae touched him off in the Aintree Hurdle, it was just terrific to see him back to his very best at Punchestown.

"We'll have to, I suspect, continue down the same route and it would be surprising if it didn't begin with the Fighting Fifth and, I hope, lead into an attempt to regain his championship crown in March."

Ground the key to Verdana

Verdana Blue indeed stepped up considerably last season, winning four of her eight races over hurdles with the highlights being that defeat of Buveur D'Air at Kempton and success in the Scottish Champion Hurdle at Ayr.

The six-year-old is back for more this season and her trainer says: "She's been an absolute revelation and a pure joy for her very enthusiastic team.

"The secret to her is definitely the ground as she has to have it on the fast side – she'll virtually go on anything as long as the word 'soft' isn't near the description.

"She's had a nice break and is back in action for an autumn campaign on the Flat. We'll come back to the same hurdling campaign as last year."

That campaign is likely to take in the top 2m contests once again and the Champion Hurdle, for which she is a 33-1 chance.

Henderson, who has memorably patched up See You Then, Binocular and Sprinter Sacre, has not given up on 2018 Cheltenham Gold Cup runner-up **Might Bite**, who also won the King George that season, but he was disappointing last term, failing to fire on any of his three runs, including when pulling up in the Gold Cup following wind surgery.

The trainer says: "We've taken every nut, bolt, washer to pieces in an effort to find out why last season was such a disaster. He's summered exceptionally well and I know Nico [de Boinville] is keen to come back in trip a little. He's been a fantastic horse and it will be sad if we can't get back to those glory days.

With the jury out on whether Might Bite can be mighty again, RSA Chase runner-up **Santini** is potentially the stable's principal staying chaser this season, although **Ok Corral** and **Terrefort** also come into that category.

Santini may head for the Ladbrokes Trophy at Newbury in November, and Henderson says: "He came back from Cheltenham in great form after a preparation that was far from ideal and, although we were tempted to go on to Aintree, we decided to put him away and keep him for this season. He has enormous potential and we have to hope he could go to the very top."

Corral can bounce back

Ok Corral might have been disappointing in the NH Chase at Cheltenham following smooth novice chase victories at Plumpton and Warwick, but Henderson is confident normal service will be resumed this season, and says: "The flu vaccinations we had to administer due to the flu outbreak had quite a severe impact on him and his preparation for Cheltenham.

"This meant his performance was very much below par which was very frustrating. We had to put him away after that but he'll surely bounce back and still has an enormous future as a staying chaser, and will undoubtedly stay in excess of 3m."

Terrefort could have the Ladbrokes Trophy on his agenda in the first part of the season

Terrefort's season also ended on a low note when the six-year-old was pulled up in the Ryanair Chase, but again Henderson is optimistic for the months ahead: "He ran no race at the festival and we put him away for the year, but I'm sure the old Terrefort is still in there and that another big race will come his way this time."

His first main target might well be the Ladbrokes Trophy at Newbury – a race that could also come into the equation for **Brave Eagle**.

National treasure

Nine-year-old **Beware The Bear** had wind surgery last summer and went on to show the best form of his career. He followed a fourth place in the Ladbrokes Trophy on his return to action with success in a staying handicap at Cheltenham on New Year's Day and in the Ultima at the festival, where he stayed on well to beat Vintage Clouds.

If Henderson is ever to end his Grand National hoodoo, perhaps this tough stayer could be the one to do it.

The trainer says: "He was one of the stars of the year. Things didn't go quite so well at Sandown [pulled up in the bet365 Gold Cup] after having to miss the Scottish Grand National because the ground was simply too

firm. Anyway, he'll come back for all those sorts of races again and, having thought the Grand National wasn't his race, I get the feeling it might be on this year's agenda which is rather exciting."

Powerful novice chase team

Henderson's novice chase department looks formidable with no end of bright hopes, including the likes of **Adjali**, **Birchdale**, **Champ**, **Champagne Platinum**, **Dickie Diver**, **Downtown Getaway**, **Precious Cargo**, **Clarendon Street** and **Rathhill** on the teamsheet, while **Chantry House** could also come into that, although he has the option of novice hurdling, as do the exciting **Arturus**, **Shishkin**, **Mister Coffey** and **Jack Sharp**.

Henderson says: "Adjali enjoys soft ground and jumps very well, so it wouldn't be a surprise if we went over fences with him.

"Birchdale won his point-to-point in Ireland before joining us. I can easily see him making a high-class novice chaser.

"Champ has summered incredibly well and we're looking forward to his new career over fences in which he has every chance of being in the top level.

"I'd think Champagne Platinum is almost certain to switch to chasing this season and

I'll be very disappointed if he's not top class in that division.

"Dickie Diver finished a very honourable fourth in last season's Albert Bartlett Hurdle for a horse with very little experience. I'd be fairly certain that's the end of his hurdling career and he's something to look forward to over fences. He's a very exciting prospect.

"I'm pretty sure 3m will suit Downtown Getaway this year and he'll almost certainly go straight over fences."

'He could be really exciting'

"Precious Cargo looks like a big, staying type but in fact is far from it as he has bags of pace and needs a truly run 2m to see him at his best.

"I'm sure he'd get 2m4f but at this stage I'd be very happy to stay at the minimum distance and I think he could make a really exciting novice chaser this term.

"I'm looking forward to Clarendon Street enormously – as he has huge amounts of scope and, not to mention, a lot of ability."

And of Rathhill, the five-time champion trainer says: "He had a lameness issue that held us up last season and we drew stumps and put him away with a view to going straight over fences this season. He's a gorgeous-looking youngster and I think he has an enormous future."

Champion aspirations

Last season's star juvenile hurdlers **Fusil Raffles** and **Pentland Hills** will be trained with the Cheltenham 2m hurdling crown in mind, and Henderson says: "It's amazing to think Fusil Raffles managed to win two prestigious events from his only two starts with us.

"He wasn't healthy for much of the winter after arriving from Guillaume Macaire's last September and I was a bit surprised by the ease of his victory in the Adonis Hurdle at Kempton.

"It was a real shame he skinned his hind leg badly there as it ruled him out of Cheltenham and Aintree. However, after

The Henderson team on the Lambourn gallops at first light

constant lasering of the wound it closed up sufficiently to allow us to just about get to Punchestown, where Daryl Jacob gave him a super ride and pounced going to the last to win the Champion Four-Year-Old Hurdle in good style. I think there could be so much more improvement to come from him.

Pentland Hills won three out of three for the Seven Barrows team after being switched from a career on the Flat for Chris Wall, and followed an impressive success in the Triumph Hurdle with victory in the Anniversary Hurdle at Aintree three weeks later.

Henderson says: "For the time being we want to see how far he can go over hurdles as he undoubtedly enjoys jumping enormously and that has to be the reason for his transformation.

"He's very versatile and can go in soft ground – he could literally be anything and we have a lot to look forward to.

Recovery missions

Angels Breath, **Apple's Shakira** and **Mister Fisher** look to have unfinished business over hurdles.

Irish point-to-point winner Angels Breath

NICKY HENDERSON
UPPER LAMBOURN, BERKSHIRE

	Number of horses	Races run	1st	2nd	3rd	Unpl	Per cent	£1 level stake
NH Flat	34	51	10	8	6	27	19.6	-26.00
Hurdles	123	324	87	58	34	144	26.9	+35.75
Chases	52	168	43	23	15	87	25.6	-24.94
Totals	**174**	**543**	**141**	**89**	**55**	**258**	**25.8**	**-15.19**
2017-18	157	525	141	83	50	252	26.5	-82.18
2016-17	171	593	154	93	68	281	25.1	-105.47

BY MONTH

NH FLAT	W-R	Per cent	£1 level stake	HURDLES	W-R	Per cent	£1 level stake
May	2-12	16.7	-8.09	May	13-31	41.9	+17.18
Jun	1-1	100.0	+3.00	Jun	4-12	33.3	-0.67
Jul	1-2	50.0	-0.27	Jul	3-11	27.3	+2.70
Aug	2-2	100.0	+2.08	Aug	3-7	42.9	+2.63
Sep	0-0	0.0	0.00	Sep	0-7	0.0	-7.00
Oct	0-0	0.0	0.00	Oct	4-13	30.8	-2.54
Nov	0-2	0.0	-2.00	Nov	7-32	21.9	-0.56
Dec	0-5	0.0	-5.00	Dec	17-50	34.0	+16.62
Jan	0-3	0.0	-3.00	Jan	12-34	35.3	-10.14
Feb	0-4	0.0	-4.00	Feb	12-32	37.5	-3.79
Mar	4-12	33.3	-0.72	Mar	6-52	11.5	+20.75
Apr	0-8	0.0	-8.00	Apr	6-43	14.0	+0.57

Statistics relate to all runners in Britain from April 29, 2018 to April 27, 2019

CHASES	W-R	Per cent	£1 level stake	TOTALS	W-R	Per cent	£1 level stake
May	4-6	66.7	+3.72	May	19-49	38.8	+12.8
Jun	0-4	0.0	-4.00	Jun	5-17	29.4	-1.67
Jul	2-3	66.7	+1.44	Jul	6-16	37.5	+3.87
Aug	2-4	50.0	-1.14	Aug	7-13	53.8	+3.57
Sep	4-4	100.0	+18.37	Sep	4-11	36.4	+11.37
Oct	2-14	14.3	-11.52	Oct	6-27	22.2	-14.06
Nov	9-25	36.0	-7.89	Nov	16-59	27.1	-10.45
Dec	7-34	20.6	+10.44	Dec	24-89	27.0	+22.06
Jan	8-23	34.8	-1.00	Jan	20-60	33.3	-14.14
Feb	2-9	22.2	-4.90	Feb	14-45	31.1	-12.69
Mar	2-19	10.5	-6.64	Mar	12-83	14.5	+13.39
Apr	1-23	4.3	-21.83	Apr	7-74	9.5	-29.26

DISTANCE

HURDLES	W-R	Per cent	£1 level stake	CHASES	W-R	Per cent	£1 level stake
2m-2m3f	50-151	33.1	+32.72	2m-2m3f	15-33	45.5	-9.37
2m4f-2m7f	34-146	23.3	+14.28	2m4f-2m7f	13-71	18.3	-39.17
3m+	3-27	11.1	-11.25	3m+	15-64	23.4	+23.61

TYPE OF RACE

	NON-HANDICAPS				HANDICAPS		
	W-R	Per cent	£1 level stake		W-R	Per cent	£1 level stake
Nov hrdls	34-121	28.1	-38.69	Nov hrdls	1-9	11.1	+2.00
Hrdls	30-81	37.0	+29.03	Hrdls	20-108	18.5	+46.00
Nov chs	25-58	43.1	-7.07	Nov chs	2-9	22.2	-4.15
Chases	6-24	25.0	-15.13	Chases	7-65	10.8	+5.53
Sell/claim	0-0	0.0	0.00	Sell/claim	0-0	0.0	0.00

won last season's Supreme Novices' Trial at Ascot on his debut for the yard, but failed to score from three subsequent runs, including in the Supreme itself at Cheltenham. Henderson says: "I can't believe he won't be a better horse next time around. The only important thing is to see which road we want to go down as he'll make a high-class chaser at some stage."

Apple's Shakira won three juvenile hurdles on the bounce the season before last but pulled up on her return last season and could manage only sixth in the Coral Cup on her only other start. Henderson has not lost faith, however, and is hopeful the mare can resume winning ways this season.

Another winner of a Supreme trial last season was Mister Fisher, who scored at Haydock in January but was well beaten at the festival.

His trainer says: "He is still, in our opinion, a very high-class prospect and a really lovely individual who will go to the top in time. Sooner or later that will be over fences but I have a feeling that he has still got something

to prove over hurdles and maybe that is where we will stay for another year.

American dream

The talented **Brain Power** won the International Hurdle at Cheltenham last December but then pulled up in the Champion Hurdle and Scottish Champion Hurdle, leaving Henderson frustrated, but hopeful with a fascinating agenda mapped out for the eight-year-old.

"When everything is right he's a very good horse, but he can be a little bit unpredictable and genuinely is rather ground-dependent," says the trainer.

"Consequently, we're on an ambitious programme in that he had a short holiday and came back in earlier than the others. We're going to take him to America for their Grand National which is a 2m4f steeplechase at Far Hills in October so he is back in full work. We've tried this race before – it's worth a huge amount of money and nearly always run on fast ground over smaller fences than we have here, so it should suit him well."

Nicky Henderson organises his huge squad on the gallops during morning work in Lambourn

SUPER STATS

There was an element of deja vu to Henderson's season as last term he recorded **141 winners** – the exact same number he had in the 2017-18 campaign

It paid to follow hurdlers from Henderson's yard last season – they scored 87 times from 324 runs (27%, +35.75pt). It's also worth paying attention to those that the Seven Barrows trainer sends to **Newcastle**, where they have recorded a perfect four winners from as many runners

Warwick was another track at which Henderson did particularly well last season (15-36, 42%, +28.10pt). And the figures for his runners in chases at the course were even more impressive (4-4, 100%, +16.16pt)

Chases at Ascot also seem to work well for Henderson. He sent out four winners from ten runners in that sphere last season for a profit of 29.39pt

Returning from the injury list

Another horse who failed to go on as expected last season was **Call Me Lord**, who raced only twice and picked up an injury. Henderson says: "He incurred an injury in his last race that kept him out of what we were hoping was going to be a very lucrative spring campaign but he'll be back for more. We're confident the injury was not severe and his future still looks very bright."

L'Ami Serge was missing from the Seven Barrows team last season after picking up a tendon injury in the French Champion Hurdle. The good news is that he's back on the teamsheet and ready for action: "He seems in good nick and it's so far so good but we'll go steadily with him. I envisage us sticking to long-distance hurdles with his first main target likely to be the Long Walk Hurdle at Ascot."

With seven wins to his name over hurdles, a further three over fences and places in the RSA Chase and Ladbrokes Trophy to his name, **Whisper** is a real old favourite. He missed last season but returned to the track at Haydock in May for his first run in 18 months. Henderson says: "He came into training at the backend of last season and we just gave him one run over hurdles late on to get a run under his belt so that we could start this year with at least something achieved last time. The intention must be to go back chasing to see if we can pick up where we left off."

Interview by James Burn

29

Somerset maestro on the trail of another century

CONSISTENCY is king for Philip Hobbs. The trainer surpassed the magic 100-winner mark for the fifth time in six years last season and is hoping for more of the same this campaign.

He has been training since 1985 and with such experience follows realism. He is not one to get carried away with success or overestimate the ability of any horse at Sandhill Racing Stables.

"Our main thing is to have more than 100 winners and a million pounds in prize-money, and we achieved that last year," says Hobbs. "We're always in a rebuilding phase with young horses coming through. We'll hopefully have plenty of Cheltenham Festival runners again but realistically a few might be in handicaps."

The flagbearer last year was **Defi Du Seuil**, who hardly put a foot wrong with the

WINNERS IN LAST FIVE SEASONS 106, 63, 111, 113, 102

highlight being success in the Grade 1 JLT Novices' Chase in March.

It is likely the talented six-year-old will be aimed at a festival hat-trick, having won the 2017 Triumph Hurdle, and Hobbs says: "He couldn't have taken to fences much better and is very versatile. It's likely he'll be at Cheltenham but we'll have to see how he develops."

The trainer's fortunes are intrinsically tied with those of four-time champion jockey Richard Johnson, for whom he has provided more than 1,000 winners. "He's important to us," adds Hobbs. "Forget his riding ability, he's a great ambassador for the sport and our yard."

Options for stable star

Deciding where to campaign Defi Du Seuil this season is a nice headache for Hobbs to have and a number of cards remain on the table for the two-time Grade 1 winner.

After a tricky start to life over fences when fifth in the Grade 2 Arkle Trial at Cheltenham last November, Defi Du Seuil bounced back with his first novice chase victory at Exeter.

However, the season will be best remembered for his battles with the Colin Tizzard-trained and Gold Cup hope Lostintranslation, whom he beat in the Scilly Isles Novices' Chase at Sandown before powering clear of his rival at Cheltenham.

Demonstrating his versatility, Defi Du Seuil dropped back to 2m for the Ryanair Novice Chase at Punchestown and was second to Champion Chase contender Chacun Pour Soi.

"He's exciting but the plan is very flexible because he's versatile and we don't know what is likely to be his best trip," says Hobbs.

"Nothing is set in stone. His first target could be the Old Roan Chase at Aintree, the Haldon Gold Cup at Exeter or the Shloer Chase at Cheltenham's November meeting.

It depends on when he's ready and what the ground is like."

Thyme heading over hurdles

Hobbs had a strong Cheltenham Festival team last March and one to catch the eye was **Thyme Hill**, who finished third behind emerging Irish talents Envoi Allen and Blue Sari in the Champion Bumper under Richard Johnson.

Thyme Hill announced himself as a talented prospect when finishing six lengths clear of his rivals in a Worcester bumper last October and is set to go novice hurdling.

"His form in bumpers was good, particularly his placed effort in the Champion Bumper," says Hobbs, who won the race with Cheltenian in 2011.

"He'll want 2m4f over hurdles for sure and will probably start in a low-grade novice contest in October, then we'll up the ante. He

This season's plan is flexible for JLT Chase winner Defi Du Seuil

should have no problem over obstacles and I don't see why he can't get back to the festival."

Another who impressed at Cheltenham was the JP McManus-owned **Jerrysback**, a versatile chaser who stepped up more than a mile in trip to finish third in an attritional running of the four-miler behind Le Breuil and Discorama.

The son of Jeremy boasts top novice form over shorter distances too, having finished second to Vinndication and Castafiore in Grade 2s at Ascot and Haydock.

"He had very good novice form and is probably a better horse over 3m than over the longer trip," says Hobbs. "He'll be aimed at the decent handicap chases. He's versatile and should have a really good season."

McManus provided Hobbs with plenty of ammunition last season, including **No Comment**, who was fifth in the Kim Muir.

His third place behind Terrefort in the

Scilly Isles Novices' Chase reads particularly well, as he was just a neck behind Ascot Chase winner Cyrname.

"He's not won over fences yet so that gives him more options," says Hobbs. "He stays very well so 3m novice or handicap chases are the way forward for him."

Retrieval mission

The trainer has another interesting novice chase contender in **Crooks Peak**, but consistency will be key after the six-year-old finished down the field on his final two starts last season, including in the County Hurdle.

The six-year-old had arrived at the Cheltenham Festival in excellent form after winning three novice hurdles in a row at Exeter, Kempton and Newbury, but failed to make an impression in the Grade 3.

"There was plenty to take out of his performances last season but he's been rather

PHILIP HOBBS
WITHYCOMBE, SOMERSET

	Number of horses	Races run	1st	2nd	3rd	Unpl	Per cent	£1 level stake
NH Flat	27	47	4	5	7	31	8.5	-31.50
Hurdles	98	326	63	42	38	183	19.3	-9.04
Chases	58	188	39	27	25	96	20.7	+45.17
Totals	**143**	**561**	**106**	**74**	**70**	**310**	**18.9**	**+4.63**
2017-18	144	460	63	69	66	260	14.1	-152.70
2016-17	158	589	111	92	66	322	18.5	-97.28

BY MONTH

NH FLAT	W-R	Per cent	£1 level stake	HURDLES	W-R	Per cent	£1 level stake
May	0-3	0.0	-3.00	May	1-33	3.0	-30.13
Jun	0-1	0.0	-1.00	Jun	1-6	16.7	+3.00
Jul	0-2	0.0	-2.00	Jul	2-3	66.7	+0.63
Aug	0-2	0.0	-2.00	Aug	0-1	0.0	-1.00
Sep	0-0	0.0	0.00	Sep	3-4	75.0	+3.85
Oct	2-10	20.0	-3.50	Oct	6-38	15.8	-15.97
Nov	0-13	0.0	-13.00	Nov	11-51	21.6	+57.48
Dec	1-4	25.0	+2.00	Dec	11-52	21.2	-8.45
Jan	0-1	0.0	-1.00	Jan	6-40	15.0	-17.30
Feb	0-2	0.0	-2.00	Feb	3-23	13.0	+3.75
Mar	1-5	20.0	-2.00	Mar	14-50	28.0	+5.89
Apr	0-4	0.0	-4.00	Apr	5-25	20.0	-10.79

Statistics relate to all runners in Britain from April 29, 2018 to April 27, 2019

CHASES	W-R	Per cent	£1 level stake	TOTALS	W-R	Per cent	£1 level stake
May	3-11	27.3	0.00	May	4-47	8.5	-33.13
Jun	1-7	14.3	-3.25	Jun	2-14	14.3	-1.25
Jul	1-4	25.0	-1.38	Jul	3-9	33.3	-2.75
Aug	0-3	0.0	-3.00	Aug	0-6	0.0	-6.00
Sep	3-6	50.0	+14.13	Sep	6-10	60.0	+17.98
Oct	2-12	16.7	-8.55	Oct	10-60	16.7	-28.02
Nov	8-32	25.0	+9.25	Nov	19-96	19.8	+53.73
Dec	10-38	26.3	+68.28	Dec	22-94	23.4	+61.83
Jan	2-14	14.3	-5.00	Jan	8-55	14.5	-23.30
Feb	1-14	7.1	-9.50	Feb	4-39	10.3	-7.75
Mar	7-31	22.6	-8.81	Mar	22-86	25.6	-4.92
Apr	1-16	6.3	-7.00	Apr	6-45	13.3	-21.79

DISTANCE

HURDLES	W-R	Per cent	£1 level stake	CHASES	W-R	Per cent	£1 level stake
2m-2m3f	41-166	24.7	+50.40	2m-2m3f	13-51	25.5	+6.31
2m4f-2m7f	18-129	14.0	-41.94	2m4f-2m7f	15-67	22.4	+49.25
3m+	4-28	14.3	-14.50	3m+	11-70	15.7	-10.40

TYPE OF RACE

	NON-HANDICAPS				HANDICAPS		
	W-R	Per cent	£1 level stake		W-R	Per cent	£1 level stake
Nov hrdls	22-82	26.8	+43.19	Nov hrdls	1-10	10.0	-2.50
Hrdls	14-63	22.2	+1.91	Hrdls	26-168	15.5	-48.64
Nov chs	9-28	32.1	+52.52	Nov chs	2-11	18.2	+10.00
Chases	1-5	20.0	-3.38	Chases	23-118	19.5	-6.55
Sell/claim	0-0	0.0	0.00	Sell/claim	0-0	0.0	0.00

Springtown Lake could prove a force in decent handicaps at around 2m4f

inconsistent and I'm not entirely sure why," says Hobbs. "He seems to be better going fresh and I'd imagine he'll start in another handicap hurdle before going novice chasing."

Lake has more to give

Springtown Lake had a profitable season and was a respectable fifth behind runaway winner A Plus Tard in the Close Brothers Novices' Handicap Chase at the festival.

"He ideally wants to go right-handed, which makes his run at Cheltenham more impressive going the wrong way," says Hobbs. "He won well at Sandown at the start of the season and there's definitely room for improvement. He's probably best over a stiff 2m4f on soft ground."

Strong handicap hand

Hobbs had 56 handicap winners last season, accounting for a little over £800,000 of his total prize-money, and he has a strong hand this campaign.

The trainer has a useful blend of youth and

experience, which nine-year-old **Gala Ball**, who made two starts at Newbury last season, has in abundance. He had a light campaign, finishing second behind San Benedeto in the Grade 3 Greatwood Gold Cup in March before winning a handicap chase.

"He's not a young horse," says Hobbs. "He has to go up in the handicap for his win, so it's not going to be easy with him. He's got no set targets and I'm not sure about his trip. It's probably 2m4f, although he's effective over 2m on very soft ground."

It is hard to keep winning with any improving handicapper but Hobbs has high hopes for **Beau Du Brizais**, who he believes could be the ideal candidate for the bet365 Chase at Sandown in April.

The seven-year-old demonstrated his staying ability when 11th of 23 in the Scottish Grand National in April, which he followed with victory over 3m at Kempton and an end-of-season outing at Newton Abbot, in which he finished last of four.

"With any handicapper, if you win one a season you've done well," says Hobbs. "He's very tough and is possibly still an improver. He'll go as far as we want in terms of trip and is best right-handed. He can also go well on fast ground."

Deise looks on the up

Another going in the right direction is **Deise Aba**, who suffered one or two health issues

DISCOVER

—·—

Shared Racehorse Ownership

Search for your perfect ownership experience at

inthepaddock.co.uk

while novice hurdling last season. The six-year-old finished fourth in two starts at Ascot and Chepstow after making a big impression when winning his first outing at Chepstow last November.

"I'm sure he'll want 3m and soft ground in the end but he could improve a fair old bit on last year," says Hobbs. "We'll start low and go from there."

Reikers Island also showed plenty of promise last year, despite winning only once. The six-year-old was given some tough assignments, finishing sixth in the Listed Keltbray Swinley Chase at Ascot before being pulled up at the end of the season in the Grade 3 Betway Handicap Chase at Aintree.

"He's another who needs to go right-handed," says Hobbs. "He's only young and he's a handicapper, so it's not going to be easy to win with him, but at least he's going the right way and we think highly of him."

Novice chase possibilities

Defi Du Seuil stole the show for Hobbs last season with a near-perfect first season over fences and the trainer will be hoping for more of the same from the next wave of novice chasers.

Six-year-old **Cotswold Way** was prolific over hurdles last season, building to a mark of 140 with back-to-back victories at Huntingdon, Exeter and Leicester, followed by a 15-length demolition when beating Capitaine at Taunton in April.

He ended the season with a fourth-placed finish at Cheltenham and is versatile, with Hobbs suggesting the son of Stowaway will want further than 2m4f over fences.

"He was probably lucky to win last year but he goes on fast ground which is a help," says Hobbs. "His trip is probably 2m4f, although he'll want further eventually.

"He'll likely go straight over fences and we'll try to start him in a novice chase. The problem is he's rated 140, which is an inbetween mark. You need to be at least that to win a novice chase really."

Zanza also made a positive impression over obstacles in his debut season, winning two handicap hurdles and a novice contest in six starts for the trainer.

After finishing down the field in the Betfair Hurdle in February, the five-year-old bounced back with victory at Newbury in March and remains unexposed.

"He's going in the right direction," says Hobbs. "I'd imagine we'll probably start him in a handicap hurdle to give him a bit more experience before going novice chasing."

Truckin Away is owned by Brocade Racing, the partnership responsible for Gold Cup winner Native River, and his trainer believes he is well suited to longer trips.

He started the season with victory over Listed winner Acey Milan at Ffos Las but had a mixed time over hurdles, ending his campaign by finishing runner-up to the Paul Nicholls-trained Danny Whizzbang at Exeter.

"He'll stay very well and cope with soft

SUPER STATS

After a quiet 2017-18 campaign Hobbs bounced back to form last season with **106 winners** from 560 runners, returning a 5.63pt profit

November has been the strongest month for Hobbs over the past couple of seasons, and last year he had a 19-96 record (20%) to return a profit of 53.73pt

The trainer's runners appeared to agree with **Ludlow** best of all last season. He sent out nine winners from 22 runners for a profit of 35.90pt

Keep an eye out for when Hobbs has a rare runner at **Leicester**. Last season the trainer had his third profitable year in a row at the track (6-12, 50%, +8.92pt)

Last season Hobbs backers were in the black for runners racing between 2m and 2m6f, with those running between **2m3½f and 2m6f** serving up a tasty profit of 36.06pt

ground," says Hobbs. "I'd imagine he'll go novice chasing over three miles."

Another to end the season well was **Umndeni**, who remains unexposed after an encouraging hurdling campaign, which resulted in two victories at Fontwell and Taunton.

"There could still be plenty of room for improvement and he could go novice chasing," says Hobbs.

Interview by Jonathan Harding

Cotswold Way will be switched to novice chases this season after winning four times over hurdles

THE LOWDOWN ALAN KING

Fine mix of proven and unexposed performers

YOUTH is the order of the day at Barbury Castle. After a season in which stable star Sceau Royal was again consistent in top-level contests and the promising Talkischeap won the bet365 Gold Cup at Sandown, Alan King is placing his faith in a battalion of younger horses to supplement his stable's more established stars.

King's team returned to something near their best last season, following a down year in 2017-18, to record 91 winners – just the second time he has gone north of 90 in the ten previous seasons – and bring home over

WINNERS IN LAST FIVE SEASONS 91, 58, 104. 68, 75

£1 million in prize-money for the tenth time.

"We were pretty happy with last season," King says. "I said all the way through that we were struggling with our novice hurdlers and so we were very thin on the ground in that area – but any time we top £1 million I tend to be pretty happy.

"Sceau Royal did remarkably well, we managed to win the bet365 and we had 12 individual bumper winners so that indicates we have plenty of talent coming through."

When it comes to Grade 1s, King has been forced to revise his expectations somewhat. The trainer, whose last Grade 1 came thanks to Sceau Royal in the Henry VIII Novices' Chase at Sandown in December 2017, says: "I don't have the firepower to be consistently making the frame in Grade 1s. We just don't have the finances required to spend a fortune on horses and it's much more competitive than it used to be.

"We don't set any specific targets for the upcoming season, we just keep building and trying to win the odd good race along the way. Hopefully with the youngsters there might be one or two decent ones coming through; that's what I'm hoping for."

Sceau could step up in trip

Simon Munir and Isaac Souede's **Sceau Royal** is the yard's undoubted star. The seven-year-old was a Grade 2 winner last season and ended the campaign with a pair of excellent displays behind the sport's two-mile supremo Altior.

With that particular rival having vacated the two-mile chase scene for the time being, the opportunity for Sceau Royal to return to Grade 1 pre-eminence appears to have opened up once again.

King says: "There are plenty of youngsters coming through in the division, but he's in great form. The plan would be to have him ready to come back in the Shloer at Cheltenham and then will either go to the Tingle Creek – although he wouldn't want ground as testing as last year – or we could look at stepping him up to 2m4f in the Peterborough.

"He's a cracking little horse who just loves jumping a fence. Bar the Tingle Creek he really didn't run a bad race last year."

Grand National plan

Promising staying chaser **Talkischeap** retained a progressive profile throughout a novice season he rounded off with a dominant ten-length success in the bet365 Gold Cup at Sandown.

Now rated 157, the seven-year-old marked himself down as one of the top young chasers in Britain with that display and King's plan is to campaign him as such, with a trip to Aintree in April remaining very much a possibility.

He says: "We'd probably look at the Ladbrokes Trophy at Newbury but he would want a run beforehand. Long term, the owners are very keen on Aintree for him, so that's something we'll definitely be looking at as the season progresses. He's fairly ground-dependent – he's much better on good – and may be marginally better going right-handed."

Although arguably below the class of his two stablemates, **Dingo Dollar** retains plenty of ability and is being primed for another campaign based around some of Britain's top handicap chases.

Winless last season, he finished third in the Ladbrokes Trophy and was sent off favourite for the Listed Sky Bet Handicap Chase at Doncaster in January.

King says: "He ran very well in the Ladbrokes last year and although he didn't win he ran some solid races. I'd think the

DID YOU KNOW?
When out for the evening, King reveals that a Scotch and ginger ale is normally his drink of choice

ALAN KING
BARBURY CASTLE, WILTSHIRE

	Number of horses	Races run	1st	2nd	3rd	Unpl	Per cent	£1 level stake
NH Flat	32	65	12	18	6	29	18.5	+2.98
Hurdles	106	337	62	49	37	189	18.4	-119.90
Chases	28	93	15	17	17	44	16.1	-43.15
Totals	**139**	**499**	**91**	**84**	**60**	**262**	**18.0**	**-160.07**
2017-18	124	384	58	67	70	189	14.8	-133.86
2016-17	128	485	104	90	77	215	21.2	-67.25

BY MONTH

NH FLAT	W-R	Per cent	£1 level stake	HURDLES	W-R	Per cent	£1 level stake
May	2-7	28.6	+2.00	May	7-22	31.8	+3.07
Jun	0-3	0.0	-3.00	Jun	3-15	20.0	-10.38
Jul	1-2	50.0	-0.64	Jul	4-11	36.4	+1.68
Aug	0-0	0.0	0.00	Aug	6-13	46.2	+0.63
Sep	1-1	100.0	+0.33	Sep	2-8	25.0	-1.38
Oct	0-1	0.0	-1.00	Oct	4-27	14.8	-11.59
Nov	1-6	16.7	+11.00	Nov	15-67	22.4	-17.59
Dec	1-10	10.0	-5.67	Dec	6-61	9.8	-32.83
Jan	0-7	0.0	-7.00	Jan	2-25	8.0	-18.25
Feb	1-6	16.7	-1.67	Feb	3-30	10.0	-10.00
Mar	4-14	28.6	+10.61	Mar	5-32	15.6	-14.00
Apr	1-8	12.5	-2.00	Apr	5-26	19.2	-9.27

*Statistics relate to all runners in Britain
from April 29, 2018 to April 27, 2019*

CHASES	W-R	Per cent	£1 level stake	TOTALS	W-R	Per cent	£1 level stake
May	0-4	0.0	-4.00	May	9-33	27.3	+1.07
Jun	1-3	33.3	-1.56	Jun	4-21	19.0	-14.94
Jul	0-1	0.0	-1.00	Jul	5-14	35.7	+0.04
Aug	1-1	100.0	+1.63	Aug	7-14	50.0	+2.26
Sep	0-0	0.0	0.00	Sep	3-9	33.3	-1.05
Oct	0-1	0.0	-1.00	Oct	4-29	13.8	-13.59
Nov	1-10	10.0	-7.75	Nov	17-83	20.5	-14.34
Dec	4-19	21.1	-1.50	Dec	11-90	12.2	-40.00
Jan	1-12	8.3	-10.50	Jan	3-44	6.8	-35.75
Feb	2-12	16.7	-9.07	Feb	6-48	12.5	-20.74
Mar	3-20	15.0	-12.90	Mar	12-66	18.2	-16.29
Apr	2-10	20.0	+4.50	Apr	8-44	18.2	-6.77

DISTANCE

HURDLES	W-R	Per cent	£1 level stake	CHASES	W-R	Per cent	£1 level stake
2m-2m3f	43-213	20.2	-58.70	2m-2m3f	7-16	43.8	+5.35
2m4f-2m7f	15-98	15.3	-43.49	2m4f-2m7f	5-44	11.4	-31.50
3m+	4-26	15.4	-17.71	3m+	3-33	9.1	-17.00

TYPE OF RACE

	NON-HANDICAPS				HANDICAPS		
	W-R	Per cent	£1 level stake		W-R	Per cent	£1 level stake
Nov hrdls	17-92	18.5	-28.49	Nov hrdls	0-10	0.0	-10.00
Hrdls	25-85	29.4	-18.26	Hrdls	17-143	11.9	-61.33
Nov chs	4-21	19.0	-14.33	Nov chs	1-10	10.0	-6.25
Chases	1-5	20.0	-2.75	Chases	4-39	10.3	-16.70
Sell/claim	0-0	0.0	0.00	Sell/claim	0-0	0.0	0.00

Ladbrokes would be another target again for him this year and we might get one spin over hurdles into him beforehand.

"He's not really a winter horse and as such doesn't want it really testing. We would expect to head back to Doncaster at some point during the season and he could well turn into a Scottish National horse."

Who Dares Wins defines King's deserved reputation as one of Britain's top dual-purpose trainers having finished fifth in the Pertemps Final at the Cheltenham Festival in 2018 and won the Northumberland Plate at Newcastle in June.

"The plan is to send him chasing once he's come back from his holiday," King says. "If he got his ground he'd run in the Cesarewitch but he'll need some cut in the ground to line up for that."

King looks ideally positioned to take advantage of the expansion of Cheltenham's mares' programme this season, and says: "I very much welcomed the expansion. The programme for mares has been getting steadily better every year and this is very much a natural next step. It's extremely important we're encouraged to keep these good mares in training – it's good for the sport."

'We think the world of her'

Top bumper performer **The Glancing Queen** already has claims to be the most promising horse in the yard after her debut season concluded with a Grade 2 success at Aintree, and mares' novice hurdling now looks to be the order of the day for the five-year-old.

"She's very exciting," King says. "She was arguably a little bit unlucky not to be placed in the Champion Bumper at Cheltenham –

she just got shuffled back down the hill. We think the world of her and she's been schooling nicely of late. She'll start off in mares' novice hurdles."

More established is **Alsa Mix**, whose Grade 2 novice hurdle win at Sandown in December was the high point of a season that failed to reach similar heights in the spring.

Novice chasing is now the plan and King thinks he has his finger on why her downturn after Christmas occurred. He says: "She enjoyed a good season last year after winning a few early in the season, including the Graded race at Sandown. That probably took more out of her than we realised at the time – the ground was a bit testing and she was then a little bit disappointing on her next couple of starts. She's summered well and the plan is to send her novice chasing.

Passing Call started her chasing career at Worcester in September and will likely be aimed at the Listed mares' novice chase at Bangor in November. King is confident of more now she is faced with the larger obstacles and says: "We'll look at the mares' route with her and she could well be initially aimed at the Listed mares' novice chase at Bangor."

Glances looks one to watch

Giving Glances has been given a long break in order to prepare her for a full jumps campaign, and King says: "She had run all last Flat season and then went straight into jumping so she didn't have a holiday and I think she was a little over the top by spring.

"She's had a really good break now and will have a couple of runs on the Flat and

The Glancing Queen (left) heads over hurdles and is expected to do very well

then we'll go back jumping again. She might be well handicapped and one to watch."

Even without the services of the likes of Yanworth, Redicean and the injured Messire Des Obeaux, King's string remains strong throughout, bolstered by both proven operators and likely improvers.

Promising five-year-old **Ballywood** retained an excellent level of form last season with three wins in handicap chases as well as a good second in Grade 2 company at Doncaster.

"He should have strengthened again over the summer," King says of the 147-rated chaser. "He'll be one for all the good 2m handicaps at places like Ascot and he may, as the season goes on, step up to 2m4f."

Azzerti is another chaser who possesses obvious ability but whose temperament often gets the better of him on raceday. "He still has promise and was his own worst enemy for a long time as he was so highly strung and would often boil over at the races," King says.

"He got much better last season the more racing he did and I could see us starting him off at 2m4f before nudging up to 3m at the end of the season."

Fidux off to a flying start

After a good campaign over hurdles last season, **Fidux's** novice chase career started in the best possible manner with two victories on his first two starts this summer. A Listed hurdle winner in 2018, the five-year-old has taken to his job with aplomb despite his small physical stature.

King says: "He's a grand little horse. He won a big handicap hurdle at Ascot last year and the decision was made to send him chasing this season.

"He's not very big and I wasn't sure how he'd take to chasing but the first morning we

schooled him over fences he was excellent and he's now gone out and won his first two."

One horse King is not tempted to send over fences quite yet is **Harambe**. He showed marked progress over hurdles last season, ending with two wins and a good second to Getaway Trump on the final day of the jumps season at Sandown in April.

The six-year-old could be one to fully realise his potential over hurdles this season with the Greatwood Hurdle at Cheltenham an early target.

"He was a very good bumper horse a couple of years ago but then took a little bit of time to click over hurdles. He fell on his first start and then got beaten by a decent horse of Ben Pauling's but he then got his act together in the spring to win a couple.

"I was very pleased with his run at Sandown when he finished second in a valuable novice handicap. He's going to stay hurdling for the time being and could be aimed at the Greatwood."

'Lisp could be exciting'

Another intriguing novice chase prospect is **Lisp**, whose talent was clearly evidenced by good performances in major handicap hurdles last season – including the Betfair Hurdle and County Hurdle.

"He'll go novice chasing," King confirms. "We schooled him last spring and he jumped really well and he could be very exciting in that sphere this season."

While familiar stars have moved on in recent years, one returns this season with plenty to prove. **Elgin** was fifth behind Buveur D'Air in the 2018 Champion Hurdle, but has not been seen since finishing last in a Newmarket handicap in July 2018.

A Grade 2 winner over hurdles, Elgin's fans will have to wait until later in the season before he is seen on the track but needless to say King is delighted to have such a talented operator back in his ranks.

The trainer says: "He's back but he's just returned to light training at the moment so I imagine we won't see him until Christmas or

beyond. We'll look at some of the conditions races and see where we are with him."

After such a successful season in bumpers it is no surprise to see King once again laden with talented youngsters. One of them is **Wynn House**, and King says: "She's a Presenting filly who won well on debut at Uttoxeter despite being very green. She has never come off the bridle at home – she does everything very easily and is a lot stronger this season. I imagine we might stay down the bumper route for a whole year but I think she's very good."

Trevor Hemmings purchased **Major Dundee** after an impressive win at Southwell in May, and the four-year-old will go straight novice hurdling. Equally as promising appears to be JP McManus's **Heart Of A Lion**, about whom King make no secret of his excitement.

"He was very impressive when he won at Southwell a few months ago. Again, he's one who might stay down the bumper route but I think he's very smart."

Interview by Tom Ward

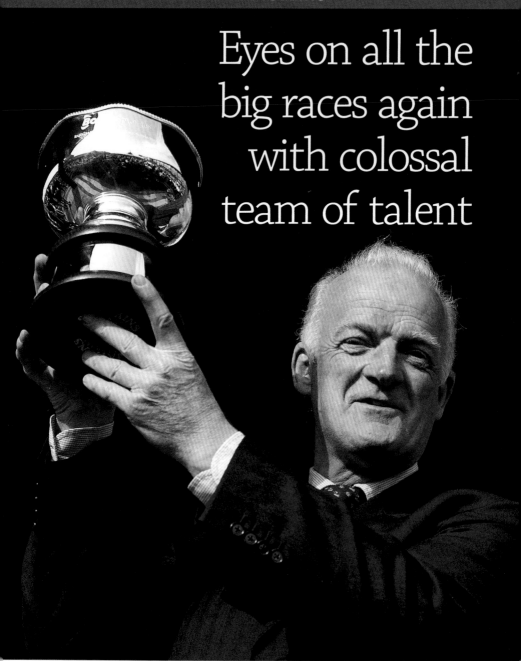

Eyes on all the big races again with colossal team of talent

WINNERS IN LAST FIVE SEASONS 207, 212, 180, 185, 187

AL BOUM PHOTO'S win in the Cheltenham Gold Cup at the Cheltenham Festival and Burrows Saint's victory in the Irish Grand National made the 2018-2019 season, another hugely successful campaign for Willie Mullins, an especially memorable one for Ireland's multiple champion trainer.

Despite years of trying, and many placed efforts, both races had eluded Mullins who derived considerable satisfaction from bagging both prizes in the spring of this year.

Al Boum Photo and **Burrows Saint** will form part of a strong team of staying chasers from Closutton stables this season.

Mullins says: "Al Boum Photo is going well and will be aimed at the top staying chases including the Gold Cup. He had a light campaign last season and didn't start off until he won at Tramore on New Year's Day. The plan is to get him started earlier this season, weather permitting."

Burrows Saint, too, appreciates plenty of cut in the ground and underfoot conditions will determine plans for the Irish National hero. "He's come back from summer grass looking very well. He'll be going for staying chases and we'll see if he might develop into a Gold Cup horse. He was fifth in the Grand Steeple-Chase de Paris in May and as that's a race we've yet to win he could go back to Auteuil for the 2020 running," Mullins says.

If Al Boum Photo landed the biggest prize of all last season, he was in many ways upstaged by stablemate **Kemboy**, a first-fence faller in the Gold Cup but winner of three Grade 1s – the Savills Chase at Leopardstown, the Betway Bowl at Aintree and the Coral Punchestown Gold Cup at the Punchestown festival in which he beat Al Boum Photo by two lengths.

Mullins says: "Kemboy's Punchestown win will live long in the memory as it was Ruby Walsh's final ride and brought his brilliant career in the saddle to a fitting end.

Celebrations in full swing as the locals come to see Cheltenham Gold Cup hero Al Boum Photo

WILLIE MULLINS

CLOSUTTON, COUNTY CARLOW

ALL RACES	Races run	1st	2nd	3rd	Unpl	Per cent	Level stake
Non-hcp hurdles	2704	876	525	342	961	32.4	-179.77
Hcp hurdles	756	88	67	54	547	11.6	-194.60
Non-hcp chases	1240	416	198	150	476	33.5	-75.62
Hcp chases	457	43	42	33	339	9.4	-140.89
Hunter chases	33	7	4	3	19	21.2	-7.29
NH Flat	1101	363	219	131	388	33.0	-43.48
Totals	**6291**	**1793**	**1055**	**713**	**2730**	**28.5**	**-641.65**

BY MONTH

	W-R	Per cent	Level stake
January	205-654	31.3	-62.63
February	183-609	30.0	+5.97
March	102-358	28.5	-14.51
April	190-952	20.0	+23.26
May	153-608	25.2	-142.37
June	58-211	27.5	-9.19
July	131-385	34.0	+4.56
August	140-492	28.5	-115.68
September	86-323	26.6	-59.06
October	91-309	29.4	-33.28
November	204-550	37.1	-28.58
December	250-840	29.8	-210.1

FIRST TIME OUT

	W-R	Per cent	Level stake
Non-hcp hurdles	274-688	39.8	-9.02
Hcp hurdles	18-200	9.0	-69.26
Non-hcp chases	84-283	29.7	-64.03
Hcp chases	10-111	9.0	-52.50
NH Flat	185-540	34.3	+8.36

FAVOURITES

	W-R	Per cent	Level stake
Non-hcp hurdles	653-1289	50.7	-52.66
Hcp hurdles	50-170	29.4	+1.90
Non-hcp chases	309-583	53.0	+49.36
Hcp chases	15-89	16.9	-25.89
NH Flat	278-655	42.4	-65.83

Statistics relate to all runners in Ireland during the last five seasons

Kemboy's achievements last season surpassed our expectations. He's back and going well."

Bellshill, another Grade 1 winner last season when he landed the Irish Gold Cup at Leopardstown, disappointed on his two subsequent starts and could reappear in the Ladbrokes Champion Chase at Down Royal on November 2.

"Bellshill didn't perform in the Cheltenham Gold Cup in which he was pulled up, but he's come back in very good order from his summer break and we're looking at the Grade 1 at Down Royal as maybe his starting off point," Mullins says.

Big player for Champion Chase

The revelation among the trainer's high-class team of chasers last season was **Chacun Pour Soi**, a name few were aware of at the start of the campaign. The seven-year-old French import had been off the track for three years before trouncing his rivals by 31 lengths on his first start for Mullins at Naas in March.

And he built on that impressive performance when landing the Grade 1 Ryanair Novice Chase at the Punchestown festival when beating Defi Du Seuil and Duc Des Genievres.

Mullins is a huge fan of the seven-year-old and says: "Chacun Pour Soi is very exciting and showed at Punchestown the sort of ability he had been showing us at home. To beat the JLT winner and the

Chacun Pour Soi (right) begins to pull away from Defi Du Seuil after the final fence at Punchestown

Arkle winner in the style he did was an exceptional effort. We'll probably stick to 2m or thereabouts with him and if all goes well then he'll be a serious contender for the Champion Chase."

Min, who has four Grade 1 victories to his name, delivered the performance of his career over 2m4f at Aintree in April when he trounced his rivals by 20 lengths in the Melling Chase.

"He's in great shape and will again be aimed at top races over 2m and 2m4f. He could start off in the Hilly Way Chase at Cork or maybe the John Durkan Memorial at Punchestown."

Mullins reports the ten-time Grade 1-winning chaser **Un De Sceaux** all set for another campaign. "He rounded off last season by winning the Champion Chase at Punchestown for the second consecutive year and, although he's rising 12, Virginie Bascop who rides him every morning tells me he feels more like a four-year-old. He's been a wonderful horse and has retained all his enthusiasm."

Douvan on his way back

Injury has interrupted **Douvan**'s career in recent seasons and the exceptionally talented nine-year-old has not run since finishing second to Un De Sceaux at Punchestown in April 2018.

"He's back and so far everything is fine with him but a lot will depend on how he gets on

SUPER STATS

Mullins will have plenty of friends in Britain, where he has recorded a level-stake profit over the past three years, including last season when he was up **19.38pt**

Mullins had just four winners from 61 runners at the **Cheltenham Festival** last season, but that didn't stop him returning a profit of 16pt

Clonmel was the track at which Mullins particularly flourished last season, notching 11 winners from 25 runners (44%) and giving punters a profit of 6.86pt

The trainer's hurdlers stamped their dominance at Sligo (8-13, 62%, +4.03pt) but it was when **Patrick Mullins** was in the saddle over those obstacles that he proved profitable (6-19, 32%, +26.85pt)

Paul Townend was the man to follow over fences for Mullins, posting a 29-83 record (35%, +8.69pt), while his novice chasers have a similarly impressive strike-rate of 16-48 (33%)

when we step up his training schedule."

Footpad, who excelled as a novice chaser, ran only three times last season and Mullins says: "We had a frustrating time with him last season but he seems to be back in good

GALLOP

WITH CONFIDENCE

form and it's possible we might step him up in trip."

Duc Des Genievres, winner of the Arkle at Cheltenham last season, has also won over 2m4f, and Mullins says: "He's done well and we might start him off in the Tingle Creek if not before."

Mullins believes Topham Chase winner **Cadmium** could make the transformation from handicapper to Graded company. "He's come back stronger from his summer break and we're hoping he'll be able to make an impact at a higher level this season."

Real Steel, twice a winner over fences last season, is likely to be aimed at races from 2m4f upwards, while **Voix Du Reve**, winner of the Grade 1 Ryanair Gold Cup over 2m4f at Fairyhouse, will be campaigned over that trip and possibly further.

"Voix Du Reve has done well since last season, while **Getabird** is another second-season chaser we think can improve on what he's done over fences so far."

All systems go for Champion

All roads will lead to the Champion Hurdle for last season's Supreme Novices' winner **Klassical Dream**. "He improved with every run last season," says Mullins. "We're hoping he'll improve again and he could start off in either the Morgiana at Punchestown or the WKD Hurdle at Down Royal."

The trainer adds that **Sharjah**, who achieved Grade 1 success in the Morgiana Hurdle and in Leopardstown's Ryanair Hurdle, has "summered very well and come back a stronger horse. I'm not sure whether he will stay hurdling or go novice chasing."

Another campaign over hurdles is on the cards for star stayer **Benie Des Dieux** who achieved Grade 1 success last season at the Punchestown festival and in the Grande Course de Haies d'Auteuil after falling at the last when looking set for a second OLBG Mares' Hurdle win at the festival.

"We have a lot of good chasers in the yard and, while Benie Des Dieux is three from three over fences and might mix hurdling

Arkle winner Duc Des Genievres (right) could start off in the Tingle Creek at Sandown

and chasing, I'd say it's more likely we'll keep her to hurdles with the big spring meetings in mind," Mullins says.

Dual Cheltenham Festival winner **Penhill** has not run since finishing second at Punchestown in 2018 and is set for a different type of campaign this season. "We'll start him off earlier this season and instead of waiting until the spring we're thinking in terms of the Hatton's Grace at Fairyhouse in December or maybe Leopardstown's Christmas meeting," Mullins says.

Novice chases for Melon

Melon, who was second in the 2018 Champion Hurdle and again last season, is going novice chasing: "We schooled him over fences towards the end of last season and were pleased with how he took to them. We'll be looking at races at around 2m."

Laurina, a six-time winner over hurdles who was fourth in the Champion Hurdle is another ready for fences: "She has the size and scope for chasing and that's the plan. She'll be aimed at races from 2m4f upwards."

Although he's rising 12, **Faugheen** will make a belated start as a novice chaser. "We probably should have sent him over fences

last season," says Mullins. "That's what he was originally bought for, but he took to hurdling so well that we went that route with him and persevered."

'We're looking forward to him'

Long-distance novice chases are the plan for **Allaho**, who was placed in Grade 1 3m novice hurdles at the Cheltenham and Punchestown festivals. "We're really looking forward to sending him over fences. We should be starting him in November or December.

"We think **Quick Grabim**, who won the Grade 1 Royal Bond Novice Hurdle last season, is a very good horse and we're thinking of going over fences with him. He can be very keen but is a good jumper. He could be one for the Arkle."

Carefully Selected and **Tornado Flyer** were among the better bumper horses two seasons back. Both won over hurdles last season and will be going chasing. Mullins says: "Carefully Selected looks every inch a 3m chaser. We're really looking forward to the season with him and with Tornado Flyer who has speed to go with stamina. He might be one for the Arkle."

Blackbow, another top bumper performer

in 2017-2018, missed all of last season but is back and set for a novice hurdle campaign.

Among other novice hurdlers Mullins is looking forward to are **Concertista**, **Blue Sari** and another French import **Ciel Du Neige**, who was having her first run for the yard when finishing third in the Boodles Juvenile Handicap Hurdle in March.

Mullins adds: "**Eglantine Du Seuil**, who won the Grade 2 Mares' Novices' Hurdle at Cheltenham, will be going for some of the good mares' races and, hopefully, might be one for the OLBG Mares in March.

"**Elimay**, who won twice for us over hurdles last season, is lovely and I'd imagine she'll be running in mares' novice chases."

Interview by Tony O'Hehir

DID YOU KNOW?

Willie Mullins was 63 on September 15. His new number-one rider Paul Townend was also celebrating that day, blowing out 29 candles on his cake. A racing super-power and Gold Cup-winning combination with the same birthday – at least they'll never forget to buy each other a present!

On the up and looking to hit next level with eyes fixed on century

IT'S a big year for Olly Murphy as he bids to build on the solid foundations laid last season – and the master of Warren Chase Stables near Stratford-upon-Avon has assembled a strong team over the summer months in a bid to deliver on that ambition.

In his first full season with a trainer's licence Murphy notched a very encouraging 82 winners but agonisingly missed out on a Cheltenham Festival winner last March as his three main contenders all finished in the money.

The trainer looks back on last term with bitter-sweet

WINNERS IN LAST TWO SEASONS 82, 47

Smart hurdler Thomas Darby (noseband) will be tackling novice chases this season

recollections and says: "The three horses we sent to Cheltenham in the spring did everything right barring win – Thomas Darby was second in the Supreme Novices' Hurdle and Itchy Feet finished third in the same race behind Klassical Dream.

"I was also keen on the chances of Brewin'upastorm in the Ballymore Novices' Hurdle and he ran his heart out to finish a close fourth, but the good thing is we have three high-class horses going forward into the core jumping season this October."

Novice chase plan

Looking ahead with **Thomas Darby**, Murphy reveals the six-year-old will now have his attentions switched to novice chasing: "He's a yard favourite for obvious reasons as he was one of our stars from last season and he'll now go over fences.

"We have a little plan with him and he'll start in a beginners' or novices' chase at Market Rasen in the third week of October as long as ground conditions are fine as I don't think at this stage of his career he wants it really testing.

"He handled the soft going at Cheltenham but I've always thought that the better the ground, the better he was. We're taking it one race at a time

RETURN OF THE JUMPS

BEER FESTIVAL
FRI 29 & SAT 30 NOV

FEATURING LIVE MUSIC BY
THE CHEAKY BLINDERS

doncaster-racecourse.co.uk

Terms and conditions apply. For full terms and conditions please visit our website.

OLLY MURPHY

WILMCOTE, WARWICKSHIRE

	Number of horses	Races run	1st	2nd	3rd	Unpl	Per cent	£1 level stake
NH Flat	28	35	14	2	3	16	40.0	+7.08
Hurdles	98	312	52	46	38	176	16.7	-85.93
Chases	33	82	16	14	11	41	19.5	-12.20
Totals	129	429	82	62	52	233	19.1	-91.05
2017-18	68	243	47	45	32	119	19.3	-54.39

BY MONTH

NH FLAT	W-R	Per cent	£1 level stake	HURDLES	W-R	Per cent	£1 level stake
May	2-3	66.7	+2.75	May	3-22	13.6	+16.46
Jun	0-1	0.0	-1.00	Jun	2-25	8.0	-17.38
Jul	2-4	50.0	+7.25	Jul	3-17	17.6	-7.75
Aug	1-3	33.3	0.00	Aug	6-21	28.6	-3.13
Sep	1-2	50.0	+0.25	Sep	3-9	33.3	+3.90
Oct	1-2	50.0	-0.17	Oct	7-30	23.3	+0.18
Nov	2-4	50.0	+1.17	Nov	2-35	5.7	-26.00
Dec	1-4	25.0	-1.50	Dec	10-41	24.4	-5.84
Jan	0-2	0.0	-2.00	Jan	5-30	16.7	-11.47
Feb	2-3	66.7	+0.08	Feb	2-21	9.5	-9.00
Mar	1-3	33.3	+0.25	Mar	5-35	14.3	-18.40
Apr	1-4	25.0	0.00	Apr	4-26	15.4	-7.50

CHASES	W-R	Per cent	£1 level stake	TOTALS	W-R	Per cent	£1 level stake
May	1-5	20.0	-2.50	May	6-30	20.0	+16.71
Jun	1-4	25.0	-0.75	Jun	3-30	10.0	-19.13
Jul	1-5	20.0	-1.75	Jul	6-26	23.1	-2.25
Aug	2-8	25.0	+11.50	Aug	9-32	28.1	+8.37
Sep	0-3	0.0	-3.00	Sep	4-14	28.6	+1.15
Oct	4-6	66.7	+3.73	Oct	12-38	31.6	+3.74
Nov	1-5	20.0	-2.50	Nov	5-44	11.4	-27.33
Dec	1-13	7.7	-1.00	Dec	12-58	20.7	-8.34
Jan	3-10	30.0	+3.91	Jan	8-42	19.0	-9.56
Feb	0-8	0.0	-8.00	Feb	4-32	12.5	-16.92
Mar	1-7	14.3	-5.94	Mar	7-45	15.6	-24.09
Apr	1-8	12.5	-5.90	Apr	6-38	15.8	-13.40

DISTANCE

HURDLES	W-R	Per cent	£1 level stake	CHASES	W-R	Per cent	£1 level stake
2m-2m3f	24-163	14.7	-44.86	2m-2m3f	4-18	22.2	-7.56
2m4f-2m7f	25-118	21.2	-22.67	2m4f-2m7f	9-33	27.3	+19.26
3m+	3-30	10.0	-17.40	3m+	3-31	9.7	-23.90

TYPE OF RACE

	NON-HANDICAPS				HANDICAPS		
	W-R	Per cent	£1 level stake		W-R	Per cent	£1 level stake
Nov hrdls	25-107	23.4	-8.06	Nov hrdls	2-12	16.7	+4.00
Hrdls	10-44	22.7	-8.30	Hrdls	10-126	7.9	-73.32
Nov chs	3-14	21.4	-3.44	Nov chs	3-10	30.0	+3.66
Chases	2-3	66.7	+1.98	Chases	7-48	14.6	-19.40
Sell/claim	5-16	31.3	+5.63	Sell/claim	1-8	12.5	-4.00

Statistics relate to all runners in Britain from April 29, 2018 to April 27, 2019

Itchy Feet has been sparkling in his work at home

at this stage but obviously we all hope he progresses and can become a live contender for the Arkle Chase at Cheltenham in March."

Itchy Feet has the option of staying over hurdles or making his debut over fences this autumn with Murphy keeping an open mind. He says: "He had a long season last year and ran below par at Aintree in April, but he's been showing us all his old sparkle at home.

"He could start off in the Welsh Champion Hurdle at Ffos Las or a Listed hurdle at Kempton in mid-October. If he runs well we then have the option of staying over hurdles but he's more likely to go chasing as I've always considered that would be his future. We're keeping plans fluid with him until after he's run over hurdles."

Ready to cause a storm

Murphy has given **Brewin'upastorm** a breathing operation over the summer and explains: "He's a lovely horse and did everything but win a Grade 1 last season when fourth at Cheltenham before finishing runner-up at Aintree and we felt he wasn't quite seeing out 2m5f because of his wind.

"He'll now be tried over fences, possibly at Warwick in the middle of October, and after that we have the choice of stepping him back

up in trip if necessary. At this point I'm not scared of running him over the 2m trip as he has plenty of pace."

Return of an old favourite

And Murphy can barely conceal his delight that **Hunters Call**, who gave him his first big-race success when landing a very valuable handicap hurdle at Ascot in December 2017, is on the way back as the nine-year-old has been sidelined with a tendon problem.

He says: "It's fantastic to have him back in training. It's been difficult since he won the Grade 3 at Ascot as he's not been the easiest to train – all credit to everybody at the yard for all the hard work and patience. He's probably one of the best-handicapped horses in training if he stays sound.

"We have to take it one day at a time with him due to his fragile nature but he'll be aimed at all the big handicap hurdles when conditions are right and there's a real chance he might try to win the Ascot Hurdle [formerly the Ladbroke] for the second time come December."

Being a protege of Gordon Elliott has stood Murphy in good stead and, like his old boss, he is not one to sit on his hands and has been busy alongside his bloodstock agent father Aiden Murphy adding new blood to

Brewin'upastorm (left) could make his chase debut at Warwick

his already standout team of young horses.

Some of the new arrivals at the yard will not make their debuts until after Christmas and, apart from those with proven form, Murphy will rely on a number of horses who will be making their debuts over hurdles in the coming months having graduated from bumpers or novice hurdles in the spring.

Brunel ready to show his mettle

Of those coming through the ranks Murphy is very keen on **I K Brunel** progressing this season and says: "We like him a lot as he won a bumper at Carlisle and then went on to run well behind Elixir De Nutz at Cheltenham last December. He ran down the field at Kempton but that was trainer error in retrospect as it was the wrong trip.

"He's had a long break since then and has strengthened up a lot so is one to look forward to in novice hurdles. He could be anything and it will be interesting finding out just how far he can progress."

At this early stage Murphy is also keen on the likes of **Gunsight Ridge**, **Finawn Bawn** and **Dundrum Wood** flying the flag for Warren Chase over the coming months and says: "Gunsight Ridge bolted up in his point-to-point in Ireland and was later bought privately. He'll make his bumper debut for the stable in November.

"Finawn Bawn is a gorgeous type who ran well in a Grade 2 novice hurdle at Warwick and ended up with a handicap mark of 136. He wants 3m and a fence so hopefully he can become an RSA Chase contender.

"Every trainer has their knock-backs and I honestly couldn't believe Dundrum Wood got beaten on his bumper debut at Warwick. I went there thinking he'd win convincingly as he'd been doing everything so easily at home but he ended up running green and getting beaten. However, he continues to show a good attitude and should put matters right over hurdles."

Smart novice hurdle prospects

Others catching Murphy's eye when going through their paces are fellow youngsters **Overthetop**, **Nickolson** and **Blazer's Mill**.

The trainer says: "Overthetop came to us after winning a point in Ireland and duly won his bumper at Warwick in April. He's another who has prospered from his summer holiday and should be suited by hurdling.

"Nickolson is the first horse owner Tim Syder has had here in his own right and I'm pleased to say he overcame plenty of greenness to win a bumper at Ayr and looks just the type to make it in novice hurdles.

"Blazer's Mill had to do it the hard way from the front on his bumper debut at Fontwell but got the job done and is another who will go down the novice hurdling route."

Murphy has such a wealth of potentially smart equine talent on his hands that he is very hopeful of bettering last year's total and posting a century in just his second full season.

He concludes: "Many people ask me for a horse to follow but it's difficult singling any individual out as they all look good at this

SUPER STATS

Murphy proved his consistency last year in only his second season training. He had 82 winners and recorded a **19% strike-rate** – the same as in his debut season

Murphy and jockey **Gavin Sheehan** were a top partnership in races over fences last season. They notched five winners from seven runners together and returned a profit of 13.73pt

Fergus Gregory was the man to follow in bumpers for the trainer, striking six times from 11 rides. Murphy proved himself particularly adept in this field, with a record of 14-37 and earning his followers a profit of 5.08pt

It's worth keeping an eye on Murphy at **Newton Abbot**. He had five winners from 11 runners at the track last season (+15.25pt). His runners at **Warwick** also returned a strong profit for punters (+26.88pt)

stage. However, I must admit I'm quite keen on the chances of **Fusionice** as he was the subject of plenty of whispers before his point-to-point debut in Ireland but finished only fourth. I hope those people are going to be proved right as he's a lovely-looking type and will make his bumper debut for us in late October or early November."

Interview by Andrew King

Hunters Call has been absent since scoring at Ascot in December 2017 – but he is due to return to action this season

'We have the strongest batch we've seen since the golden era'

WINNERS IN LAST FIVE SEASONS 135, 127, 171, 122, 124

PAUL NICHOLLS took the trainers' championship back off Nicky Henderson last season after beginning the campaign as underdog. It was a mammoth 11th title for the Ditcheat maestro, and he admits it came as something of a surprise, saying: "Even I was gobsmacked by the improvement some of the horses showed.

"I could never have predicted the likes of Frodon and Clan Des Obeaux would win those big Grade 1s [the Ryanair and King George]. It is the culmination of many years' hard work.

"It was always going to be near impossible to replace the likes of Kauto, Denman, Big Buck's and those other good horses. But the ones we have for this season look the

strongest batch we've seen at Ditcheat since that golden era."

The star of the show at Manor Farm Stables last term was **Cyrname**, whom the trainer has pencilled in for the 2m5f Christy 1965 Chase at Ascot in November, when we could see a head-to-head with the mighty Altior.

"He clearly loves Ascot and that race is a perfect trial for his first big objective, the King George VI Chase," says Nicholls.

"I understand Altior also goes there so it's going to be very interesting – the handicapper reckons there's a pound difference between them, with Cyrname one ahead on 176.

"Our horse is in grand order. He had a breathing operation two years ago, so we re-

cauterised his palate over the summer. That's a standard procedure we do every two years following a breathing operation."

Cyrname earned his lofty rating with last season's standout display over fences in Britain in the Ascot Chase and, looking back at his 17-length demolition, Nicholls concedes: "There's a chance his mark might flatter him, but then the fourth-placed Politologue came out and ran second in the Champion Chase, so the form looks sound.

Asked whether he was daunted by the prospect of taking on Altior, Nicholls adds: "While I respect Altior enormously – he's a great horse – we won't be frightened of him."

All the Gold Cup qualities

It has been ten years since Nicholls won the Cheltenham Gold Cup but he believes he has the ideal candidate in **Topofthegame**.

The champion trainer reveals last season's RSA winner will be aimed at the Ladbrokes Trophy at Newbury on November 30 and believes the seven-year-old could have a serious chance at the festival.

"He strikes me as an ideal Gold Cup horse," Nicholls says. "We'll train him with that race in mind. He travels beautifully, jumps and stays, and those are the qualities you need."

The unexposed stayer looks to have done exceptionally well over the summer, and the trainer adds: "We had a few little problems with him last season and he's not been easy to train. Obviously it wasn't the plan to take him to the festival without a win over fences under his belt, but we just ran out of time. He beat Santini fair and square there, and

the third has since boosted the form, so the first three at Cheltenham all look top-class.

"And look at his earlier form. Any horse capable of giving Defi Du Seuil the best part of 25 lengths start, as Topofthegame did at Exeter, and then getting within four lengths of him, must be a serious horse.

"The one day I want him at his very best this season will be Gold Cup day in March. I'll also aim to get him spot-on for his first big objective, the Ladbrokes Trophy.

Clan heading back to Kempton

While Nicholls considers Topofthegame to be his number one Gold Cup hope, the trainer said he is expecting improvement from last season's Gold Cup fifth **Clan Des Obeaux**.

"He was bang there jumping the last in March, but didn't quite get up the hill," he says. "As soon as the rain arrived on the morning of the race it had me worried. But if we go back there next spring, on different ground, who knows?"

Clan Des Obeaux had put up a career-best performance when winning the King George and Nicholls adds: "All roads in the first half of the season will lead back to Kempton on Boxing Day. For his first run we're aiming to take him to Down Royal for the JNwine Champion Chase on November 2. Although he's won going both ways, his best form has come going right-handed, so Down Royal should be ideal."

Could Frodon go for gold?

Nicholls has an embarrassment of riches in the staying chase department and the remarkable **Frodon** could enter the Gold Cup mix, although he will more likely bid for another Ryanair.

The seven-year-old's glorious association with Bryony Frost lit up last season from October to March. Their brilliant victories in the Old Roan, Caspian Caviar Gold Cup, Cotswold Chase and Ryanair led to ecstatic scenes every time and captured the imagination of a wider audience, to the extent Frost has become one of the most

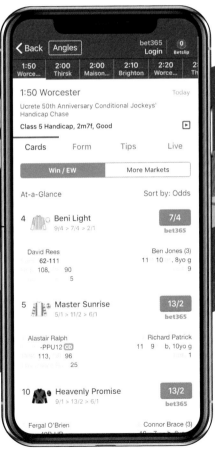

recognisable faces in racing after Frankie Dettori.

Nicholls reveals: "He'll go to Aintree on October 27 for the Old Roan Chase again. His rating of 169 is 11lb higher than when he won it last year, so it won't be easy giving weight away, but at least it's a limited handicap.

"Aintree fits in nicely as the race I think is made for him is the Betfair Chase four weeks later. He'll love the flat track at Haydock."

Breathing op for tough grey

The consistent **Politologue** will attempt to repeat his 2017 Tingle Creek Chase victory and Nicholls says: "He's come back from a wind op. His breathing has been an issue on occasions, so we got it sorted this summer.

"He'll probably come back in the Shloer Chase at Cheltenham in November. For whatever reason he hasn't always run up to his best there but I was immensely proud of his effort in the Champion Chase last season when he was second to Altior."

Black Corton put up another career-best performance when making a gallant attempt to defy top weight in the Galway Plate. He has been runner-up five times in his last eight starts and his trainer explains: "That's going to happen with a chaser like him who is around 12lb shy of top class – these sorts of horses aren't easy to place. I suspect he'll go back to Wetherby for the Charlie Hall, in which he finished second last year. His last two runs suggest he's improving."

Dolos was another to put up a career-best when winning a valuable chase at Kempton in May. He's pencilled in for the Haldon Gold Cup, which could also come into consideration for much-improved **Capeland**.

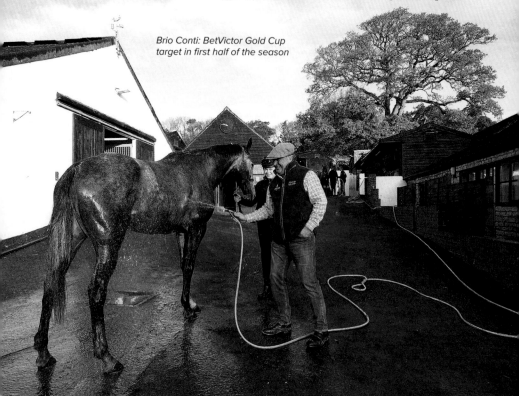

Brio Conti: BetVictor Gold Cup target in first half of the season

Hat-trick hero?

Present Man will attempt to become the first three-time winner of the Badger Ales Trophy on November 9, and Nicholls says: "He'll be 4lb higher than last year but seems to come alive at Wincanton and is mustard there."

Another possible contender for the race is **Give Me A Copper**. Highly rated this time last year, the lightly raced nine-year-old disappointed at times last season but Nicholls warned against giving up on him, and said: "There's still a decent staying handicap chase to be won with him. He possibly wants a flat track."

Brio Conti is being targeted at the BetVictor Gold Cup at Cheltenham. His trainer says: "He was one from one over fences before suffering a tendon injury nearly two years ago, but he came back as good as

ever over hurdles, running a really good fourth in the Coral Cup. He's hard to get fit, so providing I can get a run into him beforehand I'd like to take him for the BetVictor in November."

The JP McManus-owned **Le Prezien**, **Brelan D'As**, who goes particularly well for Harry Cobden, and **Kapcorse** are all more than capable on their day and should pop up in a decent handicap.

Magic Saint is also decent at his best, despite not quite producing the performances his trainer expected last season.

"He was troubled by his breathing so has been operated on over the summer," says Nicholls. "That should help him relax better."

Romain De Senam is on a break but has big targets later on. "He'll return for what I still call the Racing Post Chase at Kempton in February, then he'll be trained for the

PAUL NICHOLLS

DITCHEAT, SOMERSET

	Number of horses	Races run	1st	2nd	3rd	Unpl	Per cent	£1 level stake
NH Flat	26	49	16	5	9	19	32.7	+3.77
Hurdles	87	284	63	53	31	137	22.2	-37.22
Chases	69	255	56	53	27	119	22.0	-17.76
Totals	161	588	135	111	67	275	23.0	-51.21
2017-18	153	573	127	91	74	282	22.0	-136.34
2016-17	161	657	171	89	78	320	25.9	-65.39

BY MONTH

NH FLAT	W-R	Per cent	£1 level stake	HURDLES	W-R	Per cent	£1 level stake
May	1-4	25.0	-1.00	May	3-19	15.8	-6.50
Jun	0-0	0.0	0.00	Jun	0-6	0.0	-6.00
Jul	0-0	0.0	0.00	Jul	1-5	20.0	-3.38
Aug	0-0	0.0	0.00	Aug	0-0	0.0	0.00
Sep	0-0	0.0	0.00	Sep	0-1	0.0	-1.00
Oct	3-3	100.0	+11.00	Oct	5-23	21.7	-3.20
Nov	3-7	42.9	+3.75	Nov	9-41	22.0	-17.26
Dec	2-8	25.0	-3.33	Dec	13-43	30.2	+18.37
Jan	0-5	0.0	-5.00	Jan	4-26	15.4	-14.53
Feb	3-7	42.9	+1.45	Feb	11-49	22.4	+17.83
Mar	1-8	12.5	-4.50	Mar	10-41	24.4	-12.71
Apr	3-7	42.9	+1.40	Apr	7-30	23.3	-8.83

CHASES	W-R	Per cent	£1 level stake	TOTALS	W-R	Per cent	£1 level stake
May	2-19	10.5	-15.17	May	6-42	14.3	-22.67
Jun	1-6	16.7	-0.50	Jun	1-12	8.3	-6.50
Jul	0-9	0.0	-9.00	Jul	1-14	7.1	-12.38
Aug	0-1	0.0	-1.00	Aug	0-1	0.0	-1.00
Sept	0-0	0.0	0.00	Sep	0-1	0.0	-1.00
Oct	5-19	26.3	-0.13	Oct	13-45	28.9	+7.67
Nov	9-46	19.6	-2.22	Nov	21-94	22.3	-15.73
Dec	11-41	26.8	+29.13	Dec	26-92	28.3	+44.17
Jan	4-22	18.2	-10.40	Jan	8-53	15.1	-29.93
Feb	11-33	33.3	+2.26	Feb	25-89	28.1	+21.54
Mar	6-32	18.8	+0.23	Mar	17-81	21.0	-16.98
Apr	7-27	25.9	-10.95	Apr	17-64	26.6	-18.38

DISTANCE

HURDLES	W-R	Per cent	£1 level stake	CHASES	W-R	Per cent	£1 level stake
2m-2m3f	38-163	23.3	-19.37	2m-2m3f	15-66	22.7	-18.20
2m4f-2m7f	19-87	21.8	-19.59	2m4f-2m7f	24-98	24.5	+16.28
3m+	6-34	17.6	+1.75	3m+	17-91	18.7	-15.84

TYPE OF RACE

	NON-HANDICAPS			HANDICAPS		
	W-R	Per cent	£1 level stake	W-R	Per cent	£1 level stake
Nov hrdls	29-101	28.7	-17.57	Nov hrdls	4-9	44.4	+23.25
Hrdls	16-59	27.1	-15.85	Hrdls	12-108	11.1	-27.75
Nov chs	15-41	36.6	+5.41	Nov chs	1-12	8.3	-9.00
Chases	10-47	21.3	-9.32	Chases	25-134	18.7	+0.68
Sell/claim	0-2	0.0	-2.00	Sell/claim	0-0	0.0	0.00

Statistics relate to all runners in Britain from April 29, 2018 to April 27, 2019

Grand National," says Nicholls. "He wants good ground and a flat track, so Aintree might be ideal."

Aintree will once again be on the agenda for **Warriors Tale**, who will try to repeat last season's win in the Grand Sefton in December.

Adrien Du Pont is quite hard to predict as he wants holding up and therefore needs luck in running, but his trainer hopes there is a decent staying handicap in him if he can learn to relax a bit more.

Tactics are equally important for **Secret Investor**, who showed improvement over fences when positively ridden. He could be off to Down Royal for the Grade 2 Skymas Chase in November.

Truckers Lodge has had only one run over fences, when runner-up at Newton Abbot in May, but will be targeted at the Welsh Grand National.

Nicholls says: "He'll stay as far as you want him to, loves Chepstow and loves the mud, so the Welsh National could be ideal. We need to get two more runs over fences into him to qualify for the race."

SUPER STATS

The optimal distance for Nicholls-trained runners last term was chases between **2m7f** and **3m2½f**, at which there were 19 winners from 86 runners and a profit of 14.56pt

Nicholls saddled **16 bumper winners** from 50 runners last season (32%, +2.77pt)

Ascot was the most profitable track for Nicholls backers last season (+37.65pt), but the trainer's runners at **Fontwell** should also come into consideration – he recorded eight winners from 18 last season (44%)

Bryony Frost has a great relationship with Frodon and Black Corton, which helped the rider to a tremendous record for Nicholls last season (18-71, 25%, +31.88pt)

October has consistently been a good month for backing Nicholls runners, with a profit of 17.18pt since 2015

Getaway Trump (left): smart novice hurdler last season will tackle fences this term

This time last year there was some head-scratching over **Getaway Trump**, who had looked distinctly moderate in two bumpers.

By the end of the season he had improved into one of Britain's leading novice hurdlers and a decision had to be made on whether to keep him hurdling or set him off on a career over fences.

"He goes chasing," says Nicholls. "He'd have to improve another stone to be a genuine Champion Hurdle horse, and he's always looked an exciting prospect for novice chases this winter.

Grand hopes for Sancy

There is strength in depth in this division and **Grand Sancy** is another highly rated hurdler switching codes. "It was a good bit of placing to win the Kingwell Hurdle at Wincanton, but he was never going to make up into a Champion Hurdle horse this season, so it's sensible to go chasing, where he could be very good," says Nicholls.

Hopes are high **Posh Trish** can make a major impact, and not just against her own sex. "She's a big, strong mare who could prove high-class over fences," says the champion trainer.

"I'm really excited to see what she can achieve and we might take her to Chepstow in October for the 2m3f chase we've started a number of good horses in down the years.

"Then we could go on to the Rising Stars at Wincanton. I'd have no hesitation taking on geldings in receipt of 7lb. Those sorts of races don't get many runners and she loves dominating in a small field."

Southfield Stone surprised his trainer with his improvement last season. He went from winning a Taunton bumper to placing in the Grade 1 Tolworth Hurdle in the space of a month, and has the size and scope to do well over fences.

Big improvement is expected from **Trevelyn's Corn**, who ran too free in the Grade 1 novice hurdle at Aintree over three miles. His trainer explains: "A lot of horses who struggle with their breathing can run

like that, so he's had an op over the summer and looks and works like a different animal.

"As he's a novice over hurdles until October 31, he'll start off in the Persian War at Chepstow and then go chasing. There'll be a lot more to come from him."

Malaya took time to click last winter before winning the Imperial Cup at Sandown in March. Expect to see this talented mare ply her trade round the smaller tracks over fences to begin with, then work her way up as her confidence grows.

If You Say Run showed very useful form in mares' hurdles but connections are undecided whether she stays hurdling or switches to fences. She has plenty of scope for chasing.

Heading off the injury list

Nicholls issues a positive update on **Dynamite Dollars**, who had been a leading Arkle fancy before sustaining an injury after winning a Grade 2 at Doncaster in January:

"We'll make a decision whether he comes back into training on October 1 and is aimed at the Tingle Creek, or as seems more likely, we give him a bit more time and get him ready for the Game Spirit Chase in February as a stepping stone to the Champion Chase."

Master Tommytucker was considered one of the stable's brightest novice chase prospects a year ago but suffered a knee injury when falling on his debut over fences at Chepstow.

"He's fine but will need a bit more time than the others so we won't see him before November," says Nicholls.

As De Mee has been off since damaging a tendon last February but it is all systems go with this useful handicap chaser. He has shown a liking for the Aintree fences, completing three times in four attempts, including when winning the 2016 Grand Sefton, so he will be trained for the big one in April after the Becher Chase.

Sametegal has not had much luck with injuries and has been off for 18 months. "He's fine at the moment and we're trying to get him ready for the Listed handicap chase at Wetherby's Charlie Hall meeting," says Nicholls. His first-time-out record is 21112.

The lightly raced but talented **Diamond Guy** suffered a small tendon injury last autumn. The time off has not done him any harm and connections are going to try their luck over fences.

Brewers Project, a costly purchase last year after winning an Irish point-to-point, sustained a hairline fracture of the pelvis while schooling. "The time off won't be lost on him and after possibly one bumper he'll go novice hurdling," says Nicholls.

The ex-French-trained **Tamaroc Du Mathan** had been working well before a small tendon injury ruled him out last season. Although lacking experience, he is expected to make his mark in handicap hurdles on soft ground.

McFabulous a class act

If there is a potential star novice waiting in the wings at Ditcheat then it must surely be **McFabulous**. The half-brother to Waiting Patiently has looked a class act since day one and enhanced his reputation when winning three bumpers, including a Grade 2 at Aintree.

Nicholls says: "He came back with sore shins after suffering his only defeat at Cheltenham in November. He jumps really well and is very much one to look forward to in novice hurdles."

Enrilo was another member of last season's rich bumper crop. He was still green when making it two from three at Kempton in February and was arguably unlucky when beaten at Ascot. An athletic sort, he should improve for hurdles.

Eritage boasts an identical two-from-three record if you include his French bumper win. He is getting his act together schooling-wise and can only improve.

Ecco, who showed good Flat form in Germany, must be one of the best maiden hurdlers in training having finished sixth in the Triumph on only his second run over obstacles.

Nicholls reports he is a different horse for having a summer breathing operation. He had taken a long time to get over being gelded so big improvement might be forthcoming.

The trainer has long had a soft spot for **Ask For Glory**, who finished down the field in the Champion Bumper, and smart prospect **Silver Forever**. She could start off in the mares' novice hurdle at Chepstow in October the yard won last year with Posh Trish.

One place behind Ask For Glory in the Cheltenham Festival bumper was **Flic Ou Voyou**, another dual bumper winner. "He's by Kapgarde, a sire I love, and has been jumping for the best part of two years so won't lack for experience," says Nicholls.

It is early days for

sorting out any pecking order among the bumper horses, but one who will command plenty of interest is **Bravemansgame**.

Flat owner John Dance forked out £370,000 at the sales for the four-year-old, whose impressive victory on his only start made him the highest-rated point-to-pointer of his age in Ireland last season.

Cue Card's half-brother **Hugos Other Horse** was not considered a natural bumper horse so pleased his trainer with his Fontwell win. He's doing very well physically.

Carry On The Magic, runner-up in an Irish point-to-point last winter, was considered too green to run in the spring but is progressing well, and another who will step up considerably is **Zyon**.

Nicholls says: "We've given this lovely five-year-old plenty of time and I'm sure he's going to repay us."

Normally, an Irish point winner like **Young Buck** would be seen in bumpers this season, but Nicholls believes they might prove an insufficient stamina test for him and that he can show his potential in a novice hurdle over three miles on soft ground.

Smart recruits from France

The JP McManus-owned **Mick Pastor** created a good impression when successful on his juvenile hurdling debut at Auteuil in May, with the runner-up winning a Grade 3 next time.

The owner's silks will also be carried by **Nimix De Juilley**, a winner on his hurdling debut at Strasbourg last autumn. He'll have to go into handicaps with limited experience but looks interesting.

Fidelio Vallis boasts an eyecatching piece of Auteuil form. He shaped with promise when chasing home a Grade 1 bumper winner in April and was bought for John Hales.

Amateur champion David Maxwell has snapped up three French chasers. All had very useful form in their homeland, notably **Cat Tiger**, who was not far behind the best four-year-old chasers in France last year.

Maxwell teamed up with his new purchase to win the Grade 3 Prix Morgex at Auteuil last November, but the five-year-old is still a maiden over hurdles so Nicholls intends to go down that route.

Staying novice hurdles are expected to suit **Saint Xavier**, whose only win over fences came in a valuable Grade 3 handicap at Auteuil last October, while four-time chase winner Bob And Co was bought for Maxwell to partner in hunter chases.

Cap Du Mathan showed promise in two starts over hurdles at Auteuil last year, notably when second to Finale Hurdle third Arverne. He is one of eight youngsters bought recently by long-standing owner Andy Stewart, who has reinvested heavily after a couple of quiet seasons.

Interview by Ben Newton

McFabulous (left): three-time bumper winner could prove a big hit in novice hurdles

Exciting times as rebuilding mission well under way

IT IS all change at Jackdaws Castle this season, with new owners, new horses and a new sponsor giving Jonjo O'Neill reason for optimism as he plots his path back to the top.

By his own high standards, the Gold Cup and Grand National-winning trainer has had a lean couple of years, with last season's total of 56 winners his lowest since the turn of the millennium.

However, O'Neill is hungrier for success than ever and, after waving goodbye to many of the stable's stalwarts over the past few seasons, the rebuilding process is well on the way.

"We have about 40 four-year-olds and they're lovely horses, with new owners," says O'Neill. "It's a whole new system here and it's so exciting. We'll take our time with them but in the next three to five years I think we're in for a great time.

"I think the idea that it's a closed shop has gone out of the window and everyone knows they can have a horse here. We've worked hard at it and we're delighted to have a lot of new owners and nice horses. It's really exciting and I'm like a kid with a new toy – I can feel good vibes."

With his son Jonjo jnr making a big splash

WINNERS IN LAST FIVE SEASONS 56, 64, 78, 81, 104

in the saddle and younger brother AJ also a big part of the Jackdaws team, O'Neill snr says his enthusiasm for training has never been stronger and re-establishing the yard rather than retirement is top of his agenda.

"The two boys are interested and that gives you a buzz," he says. "We've got a real good, young team of staff here and I won't be giving up for a long time yet."

After 13 years, the Wasdell Group takes over from Jewson as backers of the yard and Wasdell chairman Martin Tedham has made a significant investment in horses as well as sponsorship at Jackdaws Castle.

Tedham forked out a Goffs UK Aintree Sale record of £440,000 for winning pointer **Papa Tango Charly** in April and O'Neill is confident that will prove money well spent.

"He's a gorgeous horse," says the trainer. "You can't just go and buy Gold Cup horses but he looks like that type. We might start in a bumper before embarking on a novice

hurdle campaign but we won't rush him. We're delighted to have him here at Jackdaws."

Sticking with youth, O'Neill is predicting a good season for bumper winner **Arrivederci**, who will kick on over hurdles.

"We've always thought plenty of him," he says. "We'll head straight over hurdles where I think he'll flourish and he's very much one to look forward to."

Another four-year-old with a seemingly bright future is **Adicci**, who hails from the same family as Jackdaws favourite Black Jack Ketchum.

"He showed a huge amount of potential to finish second on his debut at Warwick in what was a warm bumper for the time of year," says O'Neill. "I may look to give him another bumper run before he goes over jumps. He has plenty of size about him and we look forward to him novice hurdling."

Carys' Commodity was another to finish

second in a bumper on his debut and O'Neill says: "We bought him as a store and loved him from day one. We took him to Newton Abbot for a bumper in May and he ran a cracker coming second. He'll probably have another run in a bumper in the autumn before going novice hurdling."

Smart novice hurdle prospects

Garry Clermont and **Lunar Baby** have already won bumpers for the yard and are further evidence of the talent coming through the ranks.

Their trainer says: "We purchased Garry Clermont at the Cheltenham sales having been impressed with his point debut win. We took him to Aintree for a bumper for his first run for the yard where he won well. He's going to make some chaser in the long term but in the meantime we'll start over hurdles this season and he's a lovely prospect.

"Lunar Baby made a winning debut at

SUPER STATS

Stratford was good to O'Neill and his followers last season with five winners from 28 runners and a profit of 8pt. His chasers also went well when they ran at **Warwick** (3-9, +17pt)

Punters will be hoping O'Neill can match last season's achievements between **2m3½f and 2m6f** – he returned a profit of 59.50pt with his runners over those distances

O'Neill had a good record in **bumpers** last year, highlighted by his level-stake return of 20pt

It is worth taking note of when O'Neill has **Aidan Coleman** booked to ride for him in chases (12-58, 21%, +16.38pt)

He might not have had as many **handicap hurdle winners** as he would have liked, but that didn't stop O'Neill doing his supporters a favour last season (28-192, 15%, +34.70pt)

Warwick in November. That was a fair performance over 1m6f, especially as she's bred to excel when tackling a trip and the plan is to go mares' novice hurdling now."

A year older at five, **Orrisdale** has a lovely National Hunt pedigree and it was a bonus that the son of Oscar was able to land a bumper at Bangor when last seen in April.

"He quickened up nicely there and held on well when challenged. He's going straight to novice hurdling."

It is not all about the youngsters, though, and some big-race plans are already being hatched for the leading lights from last year.

Aintree plan for Cloth Cap

The Randox Health Grand National may well end up as the target for **Cloth Cap**, who carries the colours of Aintree fanatic Trevor Hemmings and signed off last season with a close third in the Scottish Grand National.

"We're a long way from the National but he's going the right way," says O'Neill. "He likes good ground and is a grand jumper. He'll need to win a couple of good races first to get his handicap up but Aintree might be where we're heading."

Sky Pirate, who travelled well before faltering late on in the Kim Muir at the Cheltenham Festival in March, is likely to drop in trip this season, with the BetVictor Gold Cup back at Cheltenham in November among his early targets.

"The early meetings at Chepstow and Wetherby might be where we start and the BetVictor could be a race for him if he goes up a few pounds," says the trainer.

Lithic was rarely out of the money last season and is described as a Saturday horse for the year ahead.

"He's a sound horse who really thrives on his races," says O'Neill. "We ran him seven times last season and he finished in the first three on four occasions. He jumps well and always travels beautifully into his races."

Staying chases are also on the agenda for **Mustmeetalady**, who got back to winning ways at Perth in August.

We rise to your risks.

Speak to your broker about Markel International
A winning name in equine insurance

"That was a valuable chase and there's an excellent staying chase programme for us to target with him this season."

The last of the old guard who has served the stable so well in the past is 2017 Gold Cup runner-up **Minella Rocco**, who will have his sights lowered this year.

"He needs good ground to show his best form and a real test of stamina," says his trainer. "The handicapper is likely to show him some leniency now following last season which is going to help."

Annie Mc was a big improver for the yard last season, culminating in a Grade 2 success in the final of the mares' novice hurdle series at Newbury and she will likely embark on a chasing career at some stage this season.

"What a star she has been," says O'Neill. "She won impressively at Chepstow in January and it was then we decided to train her for the big mares' final at Newbury. The plan came together and she won easily under top weight. She has plenty of size about her, so chasing is going to be where she excels but we could have a look at some of the valuable mares' conditions races over hurdles first."

'He'll make a smashing chaser'

Django Django is another who could start over hurdles before tackling fences and, like Arrivederci, is one for owner Martin Broughton and friends to get excited about.

O'Neill says: "We kept him over hurdles last season and it culminated in him winning the stayers' final at Haydock. He could still have some unfinished business in staying hurdles so we will look at those before going over fences, as we have always felt he will make a smashing chaser."

His Dream fits a similar mould and it is a matter of 'when' rather than 'if' with regards to switching to fences according to his trainer.

"He's won twice in the past year and both times showed plenty of stamina and courage," he says. "He has more races to win over hurdles but will come into his own when we go staying chasing with him.

"We also have the option of sending **Knight Destroyer** chasing now and that should see him back in the winner's enclosure. He was unlucky not to win on his penultimate start and showed real flair with his jumping that day."

Ready And Able, who carries the colours of the Coolmore partners, was a big improver over hurdles last season and is described as having "an awful lot of ability" while **Tedham** (no prizes for guessing his owner) is another O'Neill is quick to get excited about.

The trainer continues: "Going over fences was always going to be Ready And Able's game and he proved that at Southwell on his chasing debut in July.

"We plan to bring Tedham back for the Silver Trophy at Chepstow in October and then,

2017 Gold Cup runner-up Minella Rocco will have his sights lowered this season

JONJO O'NEILL

CHELTENHAM, GLOUCESTERSHIRE

	Number of horses	Races run	1st	2nd	3rd	Unpl	Per cent	£1 level stake
NH Flat	14	22	5	3	2	12	22.7	+20.00
Hurdles	80	257	28	18	41	170	10.9	-30.29
Chases	62	193	23	25	21	124	11.9	-52.75
Totals	**125**	**472**	**56**	**46**	**64**	**306**	**11.9**	**-63.04**
2017-18	146	552	64	52	54	382	11.6	-197.26
2016-17	156	685	78	84	75	449	11.2	-214.08

BY MONTH

NH FLAT	W-R	Per cent	£1 level stake	HURDLES	W-R	Per cent	£1 level stake
May	1-3	33.3	+10.00	May	2-31	6.5	-8.50
Jun	0-1	0.0	-1.00	Jun	3-15	20.0	-1.75
Jul	0-0	0.0	0.00	Jul	5-22	22.7	-1.75
Aug	0-0	0.0	0.00	Aug	1-13	7.7	-5.50
Sep	0-1	0.0	-1.00	Sep	1-13	7.7	+13.00
Oct	0-1	0.0	-1.00	Oct	2-29	6.9	+10.00
Nov	1-2	50.0	+7.00	Nov	4-24	16.7	-1.17
Dec	1-2	50.0	+2.00	Dec	2-26	7.7	-12.50
Jan	0-1	0.0	-1.00	Jan	2-25	8.0	-16.50
Feb	1-5	20.0	+2.00	Feb	0-18	0.0	-18.00
Mar	0-3	0.0	-3.00	Mar	3-23	13.0	+19.00
Apr	1-3	33.3	+6.00	Apr	3-18	16.7	-6.63

Statistics relate to all runners in Britain from April 29, 2018 to April 27, 2019

CHASES	W-R	Per cent	£1 level stake	TOTALS	W-R	Per cent	£1 level stake
May	4-28	14.3	+12.50	May	7-62	11.3	+14.00
Jun	5-18	27.8	+0.38	Jun	8-34	23.5	-2.37
Jul	3-19	15.8	+10.50	Jul	8-41	19.5	+8.75
Aug	1-12	8.3	-9.75	Aug	2-25	8.0	-15.25
Sep	2-13	15.4	-5.75	Sep	3-27	11.1	+6.25
Oct	1-21	4.8	-12.50	Oct	3-51	5.9	-3.50
Nov	3-22	13.6	-5.13	Nov	8-48	16.7	+0.70
Dec	1-20	5.0	-16.50	Dec	4-48	8.3	-27.00
Jan	0-8	0.0	-8.00	Jan	2-34	5.9	-25.50
Feb	1-6	16.7	-0.50	Feb	2-29	6.9	-16.50
Mar	0-12	0.0	-12.00	Mar	3-38	7.9	+4.00
Apr	2-14	14.3	-6.00	Apr	6-35	17.1	-6.63

DISTANCE

HURDLES	W-R	Per cent	£1 level stake	CHASES	W-R	Per cent	£1 level stake
2m-2m3f	5-100	5.0	-87.38	2m-2m3f	8-40	20.0	-1.63
2m4f-2m7f	13-100	13.0	+37.25	2m4f-2m7f	5-65	7.7	-3.50
3m+	10-57	17.5	+19.83	3m+	10-88	11.4	-47.63

TYPE OF RACE

	NON-HANDICAPS			HANDICAPS		
	W-R	Per cent	£1 level stake	W-R	Per cent	£1 level stake
Nov hrdls	0-39	0.0	-39.00	Nov hrdls	3-14	21.4	+4.00
Hrdls	0-22	0.0	-22.00	Hrdls	25-178	14.0	+30.71
Nov chs	0-7	0.0	-7.00	Nov chs	3-18	16.7	-6.00
Chases	0-2	0.0	-2.00	Chases	17-141	12.1	-33.75
Sell/claim	0-0	0.0	0.00	Sell/claim	0-0	0.0	0.00

all being well, the Betfair Stayers' Handicap Hurdle at Haydock at the end of November. He's going to be a chaser long term and it could be we go that way after Christmas."

Strong young team

In the juvenile division, Jackdaws has a nice blend of horses with Flat and jumping pedigrees and this could be an area where the stable makes an impact.

O'Neill says: "**Extreme Force** has had a couple of runs on the Flat for us since arriving from Sir Michael Stoute's yard and he'll be going over hurdles in the autumn. He should make up into a nice juvenile.

"I think **Harry The Norseman** will continue to improve as he goes up in trip on the Flat, which bodes well with a view to him ultimately going juvenile hurdling.

"**Mondesca** is a fantastic mover and light on his feet for a big horse. He looks exciting and should have plenty of speed.

"**Pop The Cork** is going to make a smashing hurdler in time and I'm looking forward to him jumping obstacles, while **Prefontaine** is a lovely addition to the team. He had some strong Flat form for Roger Varian and has the potential to make up into a smart juvenile hurdler this season."

O'Neill is increasingly looking to buy two-year-olds to run on the Flat before progressing to hurdling as he further strengthens the foundations for the future, and **Imperial Command** is a name to look out for from the yard in the dying embers of the Flat season before he unleashes a team of more than 100 horses over jumps.

Interview by Lewis Porteous

77

THE LOWDOWN DAN SKELTON

Quality over quantity the way forward after reaching landmark

FRESH from becoming just the second trainer in history to notch 200 winners in a British jumps season, Dan Skelton has his eyes set on another stellar campaign but admits he won't be putting a specific numerical target in place for this year.

Instead, the main target is to cement himself as a Grade 1 trainer after tasting his first success at the top level in March thanks to Roksana's success in the OLBG Mares' Hurdle at the Cheltenham Festival.

"Last year we started out with a good summer – we always planned that, it wasn't a

WINNERS IN LAST FIVE SEASONS 205, 156, 118, 104, 73

surprise – and to get those types of numbers is what you dream of. We started only six years ago and to record 200 winners in a season so quickly has been remarkable – it's only thanks to the owners, staff and suppliers.

"We gave the landmark 200 winners a go last year when we knew it was achievable but there won't be a number to track this year. It's going to be natural and the final number of winners is what it is.

"The aim is to get more horses into Graded races," adds Skelton. "Our first Grade 1 winner had been a long time coming given how many runners we've had, but it just shows that to compete at the highest level you can't fake it.

"Good horses are really hard to come by and it's a hard job keeping them sound and productive, but we want to get more horses there and I want to cement myself as a Grade 1 trainer. It's an exciting year as I can see the raw ingredients we have got.

Skelton's upward trend of runners and

winners per year has been nothing other than impressive and he is known for shrewdly taking advantage of smaller fields and nice ground over the summer, most prevalent when recording a whopping 71 winners between the months of June and August last year.

However, those numbers have fallen this campaign and despite the fact he still leads the trainers' title at this early stage and boasts a good strike-rate, Skelton saddled only 106 runners during those three months compared

to 229 last year. He says: "We haven't had as many runners through the summer this time around as to have a productive summer you have to plan it nine or ten months in advance," he explains. "We knew that wasn't the plan this year, but what we have got is a higher quality of winter horse, which is what you're always trying to do."

All roads lead back to festival

Skelton will be hoping **Roksana** will continue to fly the flag in the big races, and a structured plan has been laid out for her, with the OLBG-sponsored Mares' Hurdle set to be her spring target once again.

"We had a little hold-up with her in the autumn last year which probably counted towards her good season in the end – it meant we didn't overdo it. If at any point we think to ourselves this year that we're doing too much too soon then we'll wait. I don't want to overrace her and then arrive in the spring with half of what we should have.

"We had a bit of luck at Cheltenham as well as had Benie Des Dieux jumped the last, we would have probably finished second. However, she proved with a good run at Aintree that she's a Grade 1 horse."

Roksana's starting point this campaign is pencilled in at Aintree at the start of November, which would see her drop in trip to 2m4f before competing in a couple of 3m mares' races at Kempton and Ascot before Christmas.

Ch'tibello (left) jumps away from the final flight before winning last season's County Hurdle

BetVictor tilt on the cards

Another horse who will be targeted at Cheltenham contests is the improving **Spiritofthegames**, who has gone close to winning on all four starts at the Cotswolds track and was last seen finishing fifth in a Grade 1 at Aintree. A recent visit to the vets may be the catalyst to future success.

"He raced a little awkwardly so we gave him a wind operation over the summer and maybe there is some more improvement to come from him," Skelton says.

"We'll start him off in the BetVictor Gold Cup at Cheltenham. He's won on his reappearance the last two seasons and, given he's good when fresh and loves the track, it's something we're looking forward to."

When you ask Skelton which race at the Cheltenham Festival he has a soft spot for, it doesn't surprise that the County Hurdle ranks high on his list. A Grade 3 handicap hurdle over 2m1f wouldn't often feature among the favourites, but when you have trained three of the last four winners – including the last two – it's hard to argue with his logic.

Eight-year-old **Ch'tibello** was the most recent inmate to take home the coveted prize

for the Skelton team following a highly successful plan that enabled him to drop into handicap company, and Skelton describes him as "brilliant" last year.

"He had a tough season in 2018 against the best 2m hurdlers – The New One and Yanworth – and he wasn't quite that grade at the time. It took him a while to find his feet in handicaps as he had a lot of hard races but he had a good day at Cheltenham."

Connections are toying with the Fighting Fifth or International Hurdle as his first target, which would be viewed as "a test to see if his confidence has grown", but Skelton asserts that this season could prove tough should the handicapper not relent.

"Horses like him only have so much to do with training," says Skelton. "A lot of their success is when the handicapper lets them win."

The same applies to 2018 County Hurdle winner **Mohaayed**, who finished a valiant seventh behind Ch'tibello in a bid to retain his crown last season off a much higher mark.

Early season targets are not the be-all-and-end-all as the reliable stalwart has proved rather unpredictable on his returns from a long break.

"He's been a remarkable horse – he won the County Hurdle and then the Ladbroke. He's fantastic to have about, but the handicapper has a grip on him and he's just below Grade 1 standard.

"Hopefully he'll have another day in the sun at some point, but what I've noticed is that he takes a run or two to kick into gear as he's got older and I couldn't say when his next big day could be."

As much as Cheltenham is at the forefront of Skelton's mind, it has not always proved a happy hunting ground and it is a track that can catch out younger horses early in their careers.

Ready to prove the real deal

One of those who has been unable to put it together at the track is the highly touted **Born Survivor**, a prolific winner on flat tracks but winless in three attempts at Cheltenham and unlikely to run at the venue again.

The future looks bright for the unexposed chaser, though, and Skelton says: "He doesn't get on well with Cheltenham but he really got his stuff together last year and maybe it's taken him time to fully mature. He wants a flat track and decent ground and after Christmas I can see us looking at races like the Topham at Aintree for him.

"Before then we'll start in the Old Roan or the race he won at Wetherby last year, just as a starting point before going for a nice race at the Ladbrokes Trophy meeting at Newbury."

Skelton is far from shy when discussing big-race plans for his stable stars and the majority have already had their next 12

months planned out with a fine-tooth comb. That skill will have been learned when he was assistant to Paul Nicholls, as well as other talents that include finding future chasing stars who excel when tackling the bigger obstacles.

Two horses who took their form to a different level last year when sent over fences were **Molly The Dolly** and **Hatcher**. The duo have completely contrasting racing styles but are equally effective in getting the job done.

The former, who at eight clearly remains unexposed and has been given plenty of time by Skelton, won three of four starts in novice chases last season and suffered her sole defeat when pitched into Listed company.

However, it was the rich series final at Ayr that proved to be her target and she lived up to the billing with a near four-length win.

"I kept her fresh for a long time before Ayr and I fancied her for that race, so I'm glad she came good," says Skelton, who wants to have a crack at the big stage with the four-time winner.

"We're going to try the Charlie Hall as she's good when fresh, likes the trip and why not? We might as well give it a go. We're clearly biting off a lot but if she's ever going to do it I think it will be in this race."

Hatcher's plans are not so lofty, however, despite a brilliant last 12 months that has seen him notch six victories, two of which were over fences.

"He's been great. We were holding him up and trying to settle him but I said to Harry [Skelton, brother and regular rider] that he should just let him go one day last summer and he broke the track record at Stratford.

"We're going to start him off in a novice chase, but life will be hard for him when he moves into handicaps. I think he'll be made to pay for his success."

Hopes high for smart Beakstown

Skelton will be hoping for much of the same this year with his young horses who are transitioning to fences after promising and

DAN SKELTON
ALCESTER, WARWICKSHIRE

	Number of horses	Races run	1st	2nd	3rd	Unpl	Per cent	£1 level stake
NH Flat	37	58	12	7	10	29	20.7	-22.78
Hurdles	171	618	116	99	64	338	18.8	-102.23
Chases	90	310	76	39	41	154	24.5	+35.07
Totals	244	986	205	145	115	521	20.7	-89.94
2017-18	215	800	156	121	123	400	19.4	-153.85
2016-17	201	696	118	134	99	345	17.0	-257.57

CHASES	W-R	Per cent	£1 level stake	TOTALS	W-R	Per cent	£1 level stake
May	10-29	34.5	-2.67	May	30-99	30.3	+25.61
Jun	7-24	29.2	+3.07	Jun	17-69	24.6	+0.36
Jul	9-18	50.0	+11.58	Jul	24-61	39.3	+6.78
Aug	4-14	28.6	-3.53	Aug	11-55	20.0	-24.30
Sep	3-14	21.4	-2.43	Sep	6-44	13.6	-23.98
Oct	7-32	21.9	+24.25	Oct	15-99	15.2	-4.62
Nov	8-52	15.4	-5.19	Nov	18-132	13.6	-47.32
Dec	6-33	18.2	+16.25	Dec	16-104	15.4	+34.05
Jan	4-15	26.7	+4.00	Jan	12-55	21.8	-1.50
Feb	2-18	11.1	-11.09	Feb	7-61	11.5	-33.72
Mar	5-33	15.2	-11.17	Mar	24-113	21.2	-11.82
Apr	11-28	39.3	+12.00	Apr	24-94	25.5	-9.49

BY MONTH

NH FLAT	W-R	Per cent	£1 level stake	HURDLES	W-R	Per cent	£1 level stake
May	1-3	33.3	+3.50	May	19-67	28.4	+24.78
Jun	1-2	50.0	+0.63	Jun	9-43	20.9	-3.34
Jul	1-1	100.0	+0.50	Jul	14-42	33.3	-5.30
Aug	2-2	100.0	+0.43	Aug	5-39	12.8	-21.20
Sep	0-0	0.0	0.00	Sep	3-30	10.0	-21.55
Oct	0-8	0.0	-8.00	Oct	8-59	13.6	-20.87
Nov	1-7	14.3	-2.50	Nov	9-73	12.3	-39.63
Dec	0-7	0.0	-7.00	Dec	10-64	15.6	+24.80
Jan	1-2	50.0	+3.00	Jan	7-38	18.4	-8.50
Feb	0-3	0.0	-3.00	Feb	5-40	12.5	-19.63
Mar	3-12	25.0	-3.00	Mar	16-68	23.5	+2.35
Apr	2-11	18.2	-7.33	Apr	11-55	20.0	-14.16

DISTANCE

HURDLES	W-R	Per cent	£1 level stake	CHASES	W-R	Per cent	£1 level stake
2m-2m3f	57-342	16.7	-105.08	2m-2m3f	31-111	27.9	+10.90
2m4f-2m7f	47-217	21.7	+4.06	2m4f-2m7f	25-119	21.0	-17.69
3m+	12-58	20.7	-0.22	3m+	20-80	25.0	+41.87

TYPE OF RACE

	NON-HANDICAPS			HANDICAPS		
	W-R	Per cent	£1 level stake	W-R	Per cent	£1 level stake
Nov hrdls	25-135	18.5	-35.44	7-26	26.9	+23.25
Hrdls	20-97	20.6	-35.63	62-340	18.2	-37.82
Nov chs	12-40	30.0	+7.28	12-38	31.6	+12.95
Chases	1-8	12.5	-6.50	43-191	22.5	-0.44
Sell/claim	0-5	0.0	-5.00	0-4	0.0	-4.00

Statistics relate to all runners in Britain from April 29, 2018 to April 27, 2019

beneficial hurdling exploits, and he believes he has a couple of smart sorts on his hands in a talented squad headed by **Beakstown**.

Skelton has always had a lofty opinion of this son of Stowaway and believes there was a viable excuse for his disappointing effort when pulled up in the Ballymore Novices' Hurdle last time.

"The ground was all wrong at Cheltenham," Skelton says. "He won a Grade 2 last year and broke the track record at Warwick. He's a very big horse who I can see improving this year for a fence.

"He's probably a finished physical specimen now so there shouldn't be any excuses on that part. He goes chasing at the perfect time to suit him and I'd like to think he will be a very smart novice."

Graded races are clearly on the agenda for Beakstown should things go to plan and the tone in which Skelton talked about another smart novice, **Destrier**, you would imagine his plan will be similar.

More to come from Destrier

"He needed time, he's a very big horse and carries quite a lot of weight but I really like him. He's probably at his best around Aintree and Newbury and going right-handed might not be best for him."

Patience may well prove key with Destrier, though, as Skelton adds: "We're going to wait with him but when the right race comes along he's got improvement in him."

Two other chasers worth following could be **Tommy Rapper** and **Longhouse Sale**.

"Tommy Rapper ran really well at Aintree and we'll go chasing with him now," Skelton says. "He's needed time but looks the finished article now.

Molly The Dolly comes home in good style to score at Ayr

"Longhouse Sale is going for a Listed novice hurdle at Kempton in October before potentially having the winter off. He needs good ground and we'll go novice chasing with him in the spring. He's been magic."

Promising new recruits

Skelton spent much of the summer purchasing and learning about his new recruits, two of whom have garnered his attention with their early work.

"**Defining Battle** is a tough, hardy horse who I think will be a nice juvenile hurdler," says the trainer who does so well with stable-switchers.

"**Interconnected**, who cost a lot of money at the sales, has impressed me so far. Whatever he does over hurdles will be a bonus as he's a proper, big horse and will be better over fences. He's going to win one or two over hurdles because he's good, but how high he goes we don't know."

Interview by Tom Collins

SUPER STATS

Skelton made headlines as he recorded a phenomenal 205 winners last season, but the trainer also hit his **highest strike-rate** yet, coming in at 21%

Last season the trainer had **76 wins in chases** from 310 runners (25%, +35.07pt), with his novices particularly doing well (29-103, 28%, +35.84pt)

Uttoxeter suited Skelton's runners well, and punters even more so (44-111, 40%, 60.38pt). **Leicester** was also a happy hunting ground (7-14, 50%, +13.33pt)

Supporters of Skelton's **Southwell chasers** would have enjoyed last season, with a 63% strike-rate and a profit of 17.64pt

Backing Skelton's runners last season between **2m7f and 3m2½f** would have produced a profit of 72.47pt (49-188)

THE EXPERTS

Get ready for another thrilling campaign with excitement all the way

LOOKING BACK

The 2018-19 Irish jumps season didn't lack for much in terms of excitement. A riveting domestic campaign came to a crescendo at the Punchestown festival, while Irish-trained horses secured two of the most coveted prizes in jumps racing, the Cheltenham Gold Cup and the Grand National at Aintree.

There was a healthy spread of Irish-trained winners at the Cheltenham Festival. Willie Mullins finished top of the pile with four strikes, including a breakthrough Gold Cup triumph with Al Boum Photo, closely followed by his great rival Gordon Elliott, who sent out three winners at the festival.

Joseph O'Brien, who enjoyed his best domestic jumps season with 88 winners, sent out two winners at the festival, as did Henry de Bromhead, who also enjoyed his best season on home soil with 98 winners.

Collectively, it was a solid performance from the Irish at Cheltenham, with Ted Walsh, Martin Brassil and Gavin Cromwell also sending out a winner apiece.

At home, there was no titanic tussle to the trainers' championship as Willie Mullins waltzed to his 11th consecutive title. Ireland's dominant handler held Elliott in prize-money – €6,262,160 to €4,184,127 – and numerically as Mullins sent out 30 more winners.

Mullins recorded 207 winners, which worked out at a strike-rate of 24 per cent compared to Elliott's 177 successes.

Noel Meade [62 winners] and Jessica Harrington [47 winners] enjoyed typically solid campaigns while Cromwell, who broke the sound barrier at Cheltenham when claiming the Champion Hurdle with the sadly ill-fated Espoir D'Allen, continued to make waves with 33 winners in Ireland.

The riders' championship was slightly more competitive, with Paul Townend eventually seeing off Rachael Blackmore by a score of 109 to 90 winners, with the Cork native securing his second championship.

Fitting that Townend, the new number one at Mullins' legendary Closutton stables, should be crowned champion in a week in which Ruby Walsh, famous for his association with horses like Hurricane Fly, Hedgehunter, Annie Power, Big Buck's and Kauto Star exited the stage on a big winner.

Walsh, arguably the greatest jumps rider to ever pull on a pair of silks, announced his immediate retirement shortly after riding Mullins' Kemboy to victory over stablemate Al Boum Photo in the Punchestown Gold Cup.

TIGER ON THE VERGE OF HISTORY

Tiger Roll will be hard to knock off his perch at Aintree and his date with destiny

will be eagerly anticipated. In leading home an Irish-trained one-two-three in the great race, with **Magic Of Light** finishing second and **Rathvinden** third, Tiger Roll became the first horse since Red Rum to win back-to-back Nationals.

Connections of the modern-day phenomenon, who has also won four times at the Cheltenham Festival, will be planning their season with one day in mind as the people's horse tries to equal Red Rum's record of three Nationals.

Elliott could have an interesting supporting squad in the race, with Galway Plate hero **Borice** and 2018 Irish Grand National winner **General Principle** one of a number

of horses the 41-year-old will be teeing up for the unique spectacle.

Burrows Saint, who provided Mullins with a breakthrough Irish Grand National success at Fairyhouse last Easter, would be an ideal horse for the race while Tony Martin's **Anibale Fly** is likely to be trained with Aintree in mind again.

BOUM BACK FOR MORE

The Gold Cup was a race that eluded Mullins for too long. Mullins had finished second in the Cheltenham Festival showpiece six times before **Al Boum Photo**, one of four horses the champion handler ran in the race last

Al Boum Photo powers towards the winning line to give Willie Mullins a first victory in the Cheltenham Gold Cup

season, came storming up the hill under Townend.

Al Boum Photo may have been beaten by his stablemate **Kemboy** in the Punchestown equivalent but remains the standard-setter for the big one next March.

Presenting Percy turned out to be one of the major disappointments of the season but, if the 2018 RSA Chase winner could recapture his form, he could have a big year ahead of him.

Due to unseasonably quick ground, Presenting Percy was given an unorthodox preparation for the Gold Cup by his trainer, the charismatic Galway-based Pat Kelly.

After winning the Red Mills Hurdle at Gowran Park, his only run of the season before tackling the Gold Cup, Presenting Percy was sent off a 100-30 favourite but could finish only eighth. It later transpired he had suffered a bone bruise but is understood to have recovered well.

Elliott, who managed Don Cossack to a memorable Gold Cup triumph in 2016, has gone on the record to say if he has a potential winner of the race in his Cullentra House Stables, **Delta Work** could be the one. Meanwhile, it's interesting that **Death Duty**, once talked about as a potential Gold Cup horse before suffering an injury, is back in training and is reported to be doing well by the trainer.

Chacun Pour Soi (right) puts in a fine leap before scoring at Punchestown

Samcro, who had the world at his feet this time 12 months ago, has undergone a wind operation after a bitterly disappointing campaign and is set to go novice chasing this term, adding yet more interest to a fascinating season.

STARS OF THE FUTURE

There are few more exciting young chasers around than Mullins' **Chacun Pour Soi**. Clearly not the easiest horse to keep sound, Chacun Pour Soi returned from a 1,089-day absence to win a 2m chase at Naas before blowing his rivals away in the Grade 1 Ryanair Novice Chase at Punchestown.

There is an air of invincibility about Altior, but perhaps Mullins has unearthed a horse who could give that great champion something to think about.

Mullins and Elliott have an extraordinary depth of talent to work with this season. The champion trainer will be hopeful of recording a fifth Champion Hurdle success with last season's Supreme Novices' Hurdle winner **Klassical Dream**, while stablemate **Saldier** could be a potential dark horse in that category.

Elliott freely admits he is working with the best bunch of youngsters he has ever trained, and unbeaten Champion Bumper winner **Envoi Allen**, **Malone Road** and **Andy Dufresne** are likely to make up what looks like a fantastic bunch of novice hurdlers for the trainer.

Mullins looks well represented in that discipline, too, with **Carefully Selected**, **Colreevy** and **Blue Sari** in line to go novice hurdling.

While a large proportion of the talent resides between the top two trainers, there are a number of high-class prospects shared equally between a number of other stables.

Gypsy Island, arguably one of the best bumper horses from last season, could provide shrewd operator Peter Fahey with a season to remember and would look an obvious contender for the mares' novice hurdle at Cheltenham even at this early stage.

Dlauro and **Midnight Run** are exciting novice hurdlers for O'Brien, while it remains to be seen if **Le Richebourg** will make a return to the track for the young handler this year.

Sixshooter is an exciting novice hurdler for Noel Meade while Martin Brassil's Ballymore Properties Novice Hurdle winner **City Island** is set to embark on a career over fences.

Henry de Bromhead has no shortage of talent either, with Cheltenham festival winners **A Plus Tard** and **Minella Indo** set for a big season, while the mares **Honeysuckle** and **Minella Melody** have a bright future for the Knockeen-based handler.

ANTE-POST ANALYSIS NICK WATTS

Saldier a Champion bet at 20-1

CHAMPION HURDLE

The Champion Hurdle has already had its first shake-up after the sad death of last season's hero Espoir D'Allen. That has meant a promotion to favouritism for Klassical Dream who had an extremely impressive spring, winning consecutive Grade 1 hurdles at the Cheltenham and Punchestown festivals.

He is the rightful favourite but, as ever,

ante-post is all about price and he does not appeal from that perspective as he is already around 3-1 in most books.

So where does the value lie? Possibly with Willie Mullins. That might seem an odd statement as most of the Mullins horses are routinely short prices for festival races whether they deserve to be or not.

However, in the case of **Saldier** there might be some mileage in his price of 20-1.

He is still something of an unknown quantity as he has raced only five times in Ireland and has been beaten on three of those occasions. However, he did win a Grade 1 hurdle at Punchestown in April 2018 and, eyecatchingly, could well have taken the scalp of Espoir D'Allen at Naas last November but for falling at the last.

He wasn't seen after that so his wellbeing has to be taken on trust, but the vibes at this stage from Closutton are positive.

CHAMPION CHASE

Mullins also has some interesting options for the Champion Chase – a race he has yet to win – especially with reigning champ Altior possibly vulnerable this season.

That might appear a strange notion given Nicky Henderson's ace has won his last 19 races, but he never looked particularly impressive last season and might well go up in trip with a crack at the King George the plan in the first half of the season.

Even if he did run in the Champion Chase again in a bid for the hat-trick, it is worth bearing in mind that only two of the last 20 winners have been his age and younger legs may get the better of him over a trip that might now be a bit short for him.

Mullins has Min, Chacun Pour Soi and Cilaos Emery to go to war with – but I wonder if this is the season when **Sceau**

Fighting out the finish to last season's RSA Chase

Royal will win the big one his consistency deserves.

The Alan King-trained chaser should be in his prime next year as an eight-year-old and he wasn't far off Altior last season in this very race – beaten just three and a half lengths having looked massively dangerous at the last fence.

The soft ground wouldn't have played to his strengths so his effort can be marked up a bit and I wouldn't be too concerned about his late-season defeat at Sandown (again to Altior) as you're never quite sure what kind of form a horse will be in at that late stage.

He can be backed at 20-1, is a likely runner, a genuine two-miler, and a very good one at that when he gets his ground.

STAYERS' HURDLE

Last year's winner Paisley Park will have strong claims of doing the double, following in the footsteps of Baracouda, Inglis Drever and Big Buck's, of whom he does a very passable impersonation – hitting a flat spot before coming on strong in the last couple of furlongs. That is a deadly weapon. The strongest part of his race is from the last to the line and once he gets on a roll he is mighty hard to stop.

The only angle here is to side with 12-1 **If The Cap Fits**, who is still unexposed over staying trips.

He improved plenty for the step up to 3m at Aintree in April, beating Roksana and Apple's Jade in a thrilling Grade 1. Although that bare form needs improving upon, it can be given time and experience.

Harry Fry's seven-year-old has a bit of speed to go with his stamina, and as the intention is to stay hurdling this season we can be pretty sure he will line up in this contest if his season goes according to plan.

CHELTENHAM GOLD CUP

Reigning champion Al Boum Photo will surely go for the race again, but I can see him struggling to follow up and Mullins has better prospects with Kemboy, who beat his stablemate at Punchestown.

That, and his performance at Aintree, proves conclusively he does stay and he is a better horse than Al Boum Photo. He gives the Irish maestro a great chance of winning the race again, but there is another strand of form that should stand up to scrutiny this season.

In last season's RSA Chase at Cheltenham Topofthegame narrowly edged out **Santini** with Delta Work in third – and all three will be a potent force this season.

Of the trio, I prefer Nicky Henderson's gelding, as he had an injury-interrupted season and still ran Topofthegame mighty close at the festival. That, on just his third chase start and his first since Christmas, was an enormous effort and bodes well for his second season.

I would fancy him at Cheltenham – a course at which he excels – to get the better of Topofthegame and confirm the form with Delta Work. Whether that is enough to beat Kemboy who knows, but he is double the price so I would prefer him out of the pair.

GRAND NATIONAL

It is very early to be talking about the Grand National, but I would give a nod to the Caroline Bailey-trained **Crosspark** were he to go for the race. An unfashionable stable maybe, but Bailey's father Dick Saunders rode Grittar to victory in 1982 so the family have history with the race, and Crosspark boasts some great staying chase form.

Last season the nine-year-old won the Eider Chase and was runner-up in the Scottish National to Takingrisks. He is on a mark of 146 and, while he wouldn't want to drop too much from there if he is to get a run, Bailey might decide to preserve that mark until the weights are out before unleashing him. He is a tough, sure-footed stayer who thrives in big fields and over long distances. What's not to like?

Four riders it can pay to watch closely this season

MOST professional jump jockeys will enjoy a number of days during any given season where they ride well and are rewarded with winners.

However, it's much more difficult – even among the top tier – to find riders who maintain a high level of consistency on a day-to-day basis throughout the season.

As a punter with over 35 years' experience of watching racing it's not difficult to spot the jockeys who produce the goods day in, day out.

Multiple champion Richard Johnson is the prime example. It doesn't matter whether he is competing at Fakenham on a wet Monday or Cheltenham on Gold Cup day, he always gives his horse a proper ride.

Those comments apply equally to Sam Twiston-Davies. Day in, day out, he gets his horses perfectly placed and into a proper rhythm.

It was interesting to see an interview Twiston-Davies gave to At The Races during the summer when asked about the mental health of riders.

He emphasised how lucky he was to still live at home, and have his mum Cathy look after him in terms of meals and washing.

The inference was that other riders – particularly those who come over from Ireland – have to fend for themselves and deal with all kinds of pressures that arise from being a professional jockey. Being looked after at home makes him immune to some of those difficulties.

They include the daily grind of driving up and down Britain's ridiculously congested motorways endeavouring to get to a meeting on time.

Not many riders – jumps or Flat – have a full-time chauffeur, and have to drive themselves.

There is also the mental and emotional stress for many riders at not being able to eat proper meals in order to make the required weight.

And then there is the relatively new phenomenon of riders being hammered and criticised on social media whenever a disgruntled punter loses money.

Owing to a combination of these and other factors, it is no surprise that many jockeys do not ride to their optimum on every day of the year and, as a punter, I would rather back a hungry, talented young conditional who is claiming 7lb over most fully-fledged, more experienced riders – Johnson and Twiston-Davies being two exceptions. There are others, but the number does not reach double digits.

Four young riders who will play a significant part in my punting operation this winter are Danny McMenamin, Jack Tudor, Jonjo O'Neill jnr and Rex Dingle.

McMenamin, who is attached to Nicky Richards, celebrated 16 winners from 141 rides last season, including a big-race breakthrough aboard Nietzsche for Brian Ellison in Cheltenham's Greatwood Hurdle.

While he impressed many observers on the big stage that day, it was his victory on Millie The Minx in a Class 4 handicap hurdle at

JUMP SEASON OPENER

THE SEASON STARTS HERE...
PERSIAN WAR SILVER TROPHY

FRIDAY 11TH & SATURDAY 12TH
OCTOBER 2019

AT CHEPSTOW RACECOURSE

Oktoberfest OVER THE 2 DAYS

UNIBET

CHEPSTOW
RACING & EVENTS

chepstow-racecourse.co.uk | 01291 622260

Sedgefield in November which marked him down for me as a young pilot going places.

Millie The Minx is by no means straightforward as a string of subsequent defeats illustrates, but McMenamin made things look easy.

Always perfectly positioned, he got the mare, who had been backed from 7-2 to 6-4 favourite, jumping beautifully.

Upsides the leader at the second-last, McMenamin pushed his mount firmly into the lead approaching the last, and she stayed

Riding stars of the future (from top): Danny McMenamin, Jack Tudor and Rex Dingle

on strongly to beat Ninepointsixthree by four and a half lengths.

The 7lb claimed by McMenamin that day was clearly punting gold dust and, with the backing of Richards and other northern trainers this season, he is expected to take another significant step forward in what could prove to be an exciting career.

Richly talented teenager Jack Tudor had five winners from ten rides during the 2018-19 season, and looks an exceptional prospect.

Tudor's first winner, Uno Mas at Fakenham last November, was achieved at the tender age of 16, and here's what his boss Christian Williams said about him in a Racing Post interview that month.

"I've a young boy in the yard who's an exceptional rider and I'm trying to find runners for as many amateur races as I can to give him experience."

Ironically, I latched on to Tudor several months after that when he rode me a loser, Fifty Shades, in a 3m handicap chase at Fakenham in June.

Fifty Shades finished second that day, beaten a length and a half by the prolific Hepijeu, but I am adamant the quirky grey would have got nowhere near the winner if ridden by a world-weary jockey without a 7lb claim.

Tudor conjured some fabulous leaps from Fifty Shades in an attacking ride from the front, full of intent and vigour.

His efforts deserved more, but the horse

Passing the crowds in the Punchestown handicap won by Musical Slave and Jonjo O'Neill jnr

could not be cajoled into going through the pain barrier once Hepijeu came upsides rounding the final turn.

Wales has provided a fruitful source of top-class riders in recent years, with the Bowen brothers, Sean and James, two of the best in the business, and Tudor looks the next conditional superstar from that part of Britain. His claim this season will be a huge weapon for punters in the battle with the bookmakers.

Jonjo O'Neill jnr and Rex Dingle both excelled last season, with 30 and 32 winners in Britain respectively.

If you want to see what O'Neill is all about then just watch the video of his victory at the Punchestown festival aboard the JP McManus-owned Musical Slave.

With the eyes of the racing world on him, the youngster produced Musical Slave with an ice-cool, exquisitely timed challenge in a 24-runner handicap hurdle to beat Conron by a length and a quarter.

O'Neill received plenty of plaudits last season – deservedly so – but I felt Dingle was at least his equal.

The partnership he struck up with the tricky, Jeremy Scott-trained mare Bonza Girl, lit up many a bleak midwinter afternoon.

Dingle and Bonza Girl combined for five wins, including a head success over Big Man Clarence at Lingfield which owed almost everything to the skill of the rider in keeping his mount fully focused after the final flight.

He'll find life more difficult without a claim, but has the ability to make the adjustment.

Jonjo O'Neill jnr arrives in the winner's enclosure after his Punchestown masterclass

DOZEN TO FOLLOW DAVE ORTON

Darasso can prove up to Champion Chase class

ABACADABRAS

A classy bumper performer last term, Abacadabras ought to be capable of having a big say in the novice hurdle division for Gordon Elliott. He is bred to enjoy stepping up beyond the minimum trip and, while winter ground shouldn't pose an issue, the five-year-old does seem particularly happy on a sound surface.

BENTHAM

This unexposed performer took time to come good, but it became clear when he landed a second bumper at Killarney in the summer that a sound surface was the key. He's bred to make his mark over hurdles and, while he needs early experience of jumping during the winter, he's definitely one to keep tabs on for handicaps when the ground dries up.

DARASSO

Although it was clear he was a smart sort, it seemed as though this ex-French performer could prove tricky to place after his first two outings as a hurdler for Joseph O'Brien. However, a return to fences really paid off as he subsequently won a Grade 2 contest over 2m, taking his chasing record to three from three. This season he can prove a surprise package in the Champion Chase division for leading owner JP McManus. He acts on good to soft, but excels when the mud is flying.

DLAURO

It's fair to say legendary Australian owner Lloyd Williams had to be patient after signing the docket for £410,000 to snap up Dlauro. The scopey gelding easily won an Irish point in early 2018, but it wasn't until the following year's Punchestown festival that he made his rules debut, and the signs that day weren't great as he proved friendless in the betting. However, Dlauro slammed some fair rivals by 11 lengths and confirmed himself as being out of the ordinary. This season he could go right to the top as a novice hurdler.

DUC DE GRISSAY

This work in progress showed just ordinary form in Irish points before making his hurdling debut for Sandy Thomson after a long layoff. He was sent off at 40-1 in a 2m contest at Hexham in September and, awash with sweat, he got behind early and clouted a few, looking sure to finish tailed off. However, as the leaders began to wane he found his feet and finished strongly to grab third. Thomson excels with stayers and Duc De Grissay ought to come into his own when stepping up in trip as he matures.

ELYSEES

This four-year-old enjoyed a fair time of it as a juvenile hurdler last season, winning twice. However, this winner at 1m6f on the Flat has been crying out for a real test over jumps and will now get his chance to shine with races opening up to him beyond the intermediate distance. A mark of 134 should prove well within his compass and he's capable of holding his form well.

FAST BUCK

After this two-time French Flat winner chased home smart Fakir D'oudairies on his hurdling debut for team Mullins, when conceding the best part of a stone, Fast Buck looked a surefire winner. However, he flopped next time out and it wasn't until the summer that he made the breakthrough. That success came in an ordinary maiden, but he showed his true colours when following up at the Galway festival and should be interesting to follow. He could well be one for a big handicap.

FLOORING PORTER

This son of Yeats failed to achieve a great deal in his first four starts as a novice hurdler. However, it all clicked into place at Bellewstown in August when he came from out of the clouds to win by a comfortable seven lengths. His dam won a point and he's crying out for a step up beyond the minimum. Expect him to win more than his share when connections allow him to do so.

JON SNOW

Having got off the mark at the third time of asking over 1m4f on the level in France, Jon Snow was subsequently gelded and snapped up for a hurdling campaign in the famous silks of Susannah and Rich Ricci, under the expert tutelage of Willie Mullins. Out of a

half-sister to Champion Hurdle winner Binocular, he should stay no bother and winter ground isn't expected to pose any issues.

MOUNT WINDSOR

Defying a penalty in bumpers is no mean feat, especially for one housed outside of a powerhouse operation, and so it's no surprise that Mount Windsor is the apple of trainer Chris Gordon's eye. The trainer endured a frustrating time last season, but the horses came good again towards the backend and this four-year-old impressed when winning twice in May. His hurdling debut is eagerly anticipated.

Fast Buck jumps to victory at Galway and could be one for a big handicap hurdle

PAPA TANGO CHARLY

This French-bred four-year-old caused quite a stir when comfortably landing an Irish point at Liscarroll in March and was subsequently snapped up for a whopping £440,000 to join Jonjo O'Neill for a campaign under rules. He hails from a successful jumps family and will be expected to win a bumper at least before connections then decide whether to crack on over hurdles. Soft ground is no problem and he'll appreciate a decent test.

WARTHOG

A return of just one success from 11 outings since joining David Pipe in 2018 is admittedly poor. However, we've definitely not seen the best of this late-maturing grey and it is this season as a handicap chaser that he is expected to belatedly deliver. He'll begin the campaign off an attractive mark of 132 and is versatile regarding underfoot conditions.

FESTIVAL FANCIES PAUL KEALY

A dozen names to help lock in a profit

ANDY DUFRESNE

There's not too much to say about Andy Dufresne as he has run only twice, winning a maiden point-to-point in Ireland and then a bumper by ten lengths on his debut for Gordon Elliott.

He put up quite a performance there and the runner-up won his next two, so it's clear he's very promising for this season and his trainer indicated as much, saying: "We think he's as nice as any of the good bumper horses we've run all year."

That's fair praise from the man who saddled the first and fourth in the Champion Bumper at Cheltenham and it will be interesting to see what the plans are, although given he'll be six in January you'd be surprised if he stayed down the bumper route for too long.

ANGELS BREATH

Looked like a potential star when winning a Grade 2 novice hurdle on his debut under rules and for Nicky Henderson at Ascot in December and, while that remains his sole victory to date, he still remains of immense promise.

Angels Breath had only four hurdles to jump at Ascot, but it wasn't a lack of fluency that was his problem after that as he refused to settle, which is a surprise for a horse bred to get further than 2m. Although beaten when odds-on for the Dovecote at Kempton, he was giving the winner 5lb so emerged with plenty of credit, although he was well below that form when well fancied for the Supreme Novices' Hurdle.

He was a bit keen until getting outpaced there and did his best work late, so was moved up to 2m4f for a Grade 1 at Aintree, where his free-going tendencies again proved his undoing and he finished third to Reserve Tank. His trainer is reportedly thinking of running him in a hood, which is certainly worth a try, but if he does learn to settle he will surely improve in leaps and bounds.

An official mark of 146 is begging to be taken advantage of over hurdles, but Angels Breath is built to be a chaser and it won't be a surprise if fences make a man of him. He has already won a point.

CHACUN POUR SOI

Assuming Altior makes his long-awaited move up in trip this season there could be a big gap to fill in the 2m division and the one who makes most appeal to fill that space has to be Chacun Pour Soi.

Of course, he is going to need to stay sound, so hardly appeals as an ante-post proposition for the Champion Chase at this stage as he missed three whole years before his return to the track in March. However, to reach the level he did in just two chase outings for Willie Mullins after his long absence when trained in France was astonishing and an official mark of 167 already puts him high up the list of 2m chasers.

His return win at Naas in March was fully expected as he went off at 4-9 and coasted

Andy Dufresne could prove a major force over hurdles

home by 31 lengths, putting in some prodigious leaps along the way, but it was still a big ask for him to be pitted into Grade 1 company on his next outing in the Ryanair Novice Chase at Punchestown, a race which featured the Arkle and JLT winners.

Chacun Pour Soi proved well up to the task, though, always travelling strongly and, while he wasn't always as fluent as he had been on his debut, his jumping still held up well given the company and he scored in commanding fashion from Defi Du Seuil with Duc Des Genievres another 16 lengths away.

I always worry that we can tend to over-rate post-Cheltenham form, but Chacun Pour Soi gives the impression he's the real deal and let's hope so as he could be the one to give Willie Mullins a first Champion Chase.

CYRNAME

A horse who has seemingly annoyed a lot of jumps fans by daring to put up a performance that led to the official handicapper rating him 1lb superior to unbeaten 2m superstar Altior.

However you rate him, and most won't have it at all, it's simply impossible to argue that he didn't put up two incredibly high-class performances on his final two starts of the 2018-19 season at Ascot. The seven-year-old won a 2m5f handicap by 21 lengths off a mark of 156 and then thrashed Waiting Patiently by 17 lengths in the Grade 1 Ascot Chase over the same course and distance.

The winning times for both races were exceptional, but the doubters will argue he never looked like doing anything like that before and therefore has a lot more to prove than Altior, particularly when moving away from Ascot. They would have a point, but Cyrname was a pretty high-class novice (best RPR 162) and it might be that at the age of seven he has improved dramatically as some horses do.

I'm a big fan anyway because his jumping was electric for those two victories and I can't wait to see him in action again.

Paul Nicholls has pinpointed the 1965 Chase at Ascot as a starting point en route to the King George over a trip he looks likely to stay, and that was the race originally mentioned for Altior's first foray beyond 2m, although you'd have to doubt whether Nicky Henderson would want him to go head-to-head in a prep.

The prospect of those big guns clashing is obviously mouth-watering, but even if it doesn't happen (and I very much doubt it will), Cyrname is a serious horse and I expect him to prove it again this season. He's said to need to go right-handed, but his best novice form left-handed wasn't that far off his best right-handed, so let's hope he's given another chance to prove himself.

KLASSICAL DREAM

If there might be a gap in the 2m chase division there most definitely is one over that distance over hurdles following the sad death in the summer of Champion Hurdle winner Espoir D'Allen. The bookmakers reacted by making Willie Mullins' Supreme Novices' winner Klassical Dream favourite to give the trainer a fourth individual Champion Hurdle winner after Hurricane Fly, Faugheen and Annie Power – and it's hard to disagree given the way he dismantled the opposition in the Supreme in March.

Klassical Dream had already shown his willingness for a battle when overcoming stablemate Aramon on his second run for the yard in a Grade 1 at Leopardstown in February, but he took his form to a new level at Cheltenham and then again at Punchestown as he reeled off a Grade 1 treble.

He travels powerfully, stays exceptionally well and jumps slickly, so there doesn't seem to be much in the way of a negative and I wouldn't be surprised if, injuries and hold-ups aside, he ends up a warm favourite for the big one next spring.

RoR
Retraining of Racehorses

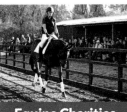

MISTER FISHER

At a Cheltenham Festival preview last year, Nicky Henderson's assistant trainer Toby Lawes was quite vociferous in his view that Mister Fisher was at least as promising as Angels Breath if not more so.

There wasn't that much between them, but they could manage only seventh and eighth, a long way behind winner Klassical Dream in the Supreme Novices', so it's hard to draw too many conclusions there. Mister Fisher again failed to deliver when sent handicapping for the Swinton at Haydock in May (only seventh when favourite) but he made a couple of costly errors and I think that is easy enough to forgive.

As a five-year-old with only five hurdles runs under his belt, he might just have needed a bit more time and it will be bitterly disappointing if he can't land a decent hurdles prize off a mark of just 144 this term.

ONE FOR ROSIE

One For Rosie made a winning debut in a bumper in October 2017, but must have had some sort of setback as he wasn't seen again until November last year, when he also made a winning debut over hurdles.

And quite an impressive debut it was, too, as he cruised past subsequent high-class novice chaser Glen Forsa on his way to a five-length win on good ground.

Connections thought an odds-on defeat next time out at the same track may have been down to the soft ground, but it seems more than likely it was just a blip as following a good-ground win at Warwick in February, One For Rosie went down by only a short head in the 18-runner Grade 3 EBF Final at Sandown on his handicap debut off a mark of 138.

He dipped his toes into Grade 1 company next time, dead-heating for third with Angels Breath behind Reserve Tank at Aintree. There might be more to come from him over hurdles and his useful half-brother Air Horse One never ran over fences, but One For Rosie is surely built for them and I hope that's the route he takes.

PROSCHEMA

As a horse who is rated above 100 on the Flat, goes on any ground, is tough and stays well, Proschema must be one of the most interesting horses to go hurdling from the Flat this season – and if new trainer Dan Skelton can teach him to jump he could go a long way in his novice season.

Proschema may have won only twice on

One For Rosie (right) looks built for fences and could take high rank in the novice chase division

the Flat, but he earned a high rating early in his three-year-old season thanks to two soft-ground victories and his list of places in quality staying handicaps is long and impressive.

He was third in last year's Melrose off a mark of 100 and then second in another valuable York handicap that October off 105, after which he was gelded. When he returned he took time to warm up, but he was third again off 103 at Newmarket in July and then ran third off the same mark in the Northumberland Plate at Newcastle, where he did remarkably well to finish so close given he came from miles off the pace.

Not all Flat horses transfer their ability to hurdles, but he has the right credentials to develop into a festival contender.

SAMS PROFILE

Sams Profile won only once over hurdles last season, but he was highly tried once he'd won his maiden at Cork and he has two runner-up spots to his name in Grade 1s – the first when second to Battleoverdoyen at Naas in February and then when beaten half a length by Reserve Tank at Punchestown in May, having in between been fifth to City Island in the Ballymore at Cheltenham.

However, despite compiling a pretty impressive CV in a first season over obstacles, I still got the impression he wasn't quite living up to his potential and was a bit babyish. I hope that is the case anyway as another summer on his back can only have done him the world of good and he should improve in leaps and bounds this term. He's a big horse who will probably be very effective on soft ground, but he handles good well enough and it's fences that are going to make a man of him.

SIXSHOOTER

It's often tempting to focus solely on Willie Mullins and Gordon Elliott when it comes to looking for future stars over jumps in Ireland, but Noel Meade has had his share of decent performers and he seems to think a fair amount of Sixshooter, who was unbeaten in two bumpers in the spring.

He has not put up the massive performances of some in the bumper division, but he did turn over a Mullins hotpot at the Punchestown festival and his trainer reports that he jumps well and is a nice novice to look forward to. He was still pretty green on his second outing, too, which is hardly surprising given he is only four, so hopefully there will be a lot more to come yet.

SOUTHFIELD STONE

This six-year-old wouldn't be the most obvious inmate of Paul Nicholls to turn into a star, especially given the trainer said he

wouldn't dream of running him in the Supreme Novices' Hurdle even after he'd beaten Angels Breath in the Dovecote at Kempton.

He certainly didn't run his race when last of seven in the 2m Grade 1 Aintree in April but, as the old cliche goes, whatever he has done over hurdles is a bonus and this is a horse begging for fences. He was Grade 1 placed over hurdles (third in the Tolworth), but he is going to stay well as he progresses (his dam was a 2m4f bumper winner) and I see him as a potential JLT or RSA horse if he takes as well to fences as I think he might. He was a 33-1 chance for the former and wasn't even quoted for the latter in the autumn, which gives you an idea of how much he needs to progress to challenge the best of last season's novice hurdlers set to go chasing, but he is one to keep an eye out for all the same.

TOPOFTHEGAME

Ask a big group of punters who they think will turn out the best from the first three home in last season's RSA Chase and you'd

RSA Chase ace Topofthegame should prove a live Gold Cup contender

probably get a fairly even split of those in favour of Topofthegame, Santini and Delta Work. All three are exciting chasers heading into their second seasons and any one of them could finish the season as a Gold Cup winner, but I'm all in favour of Topofthegame, not least because Paul Nicholls is the master trainer when it comes to 3m chasers – in Britain at the very least.

Topofthegame won only once last year, but he ran a blinder on his debut when losing 20 lengths at the start before running second to Defi Du Seuil over an inadequate 2m3f at Exeter on his chase debut in December and it was arguably rider error that cost him in the Feltham at Kempton.

Harry Cobden gave him a crack with the whip as he was about to rise at the second-last, which caused him to balloon it. He still finished in front of Santini. And he beat Santini again in the RSA, Cobden this time giving him a peach of a ride to produce him after the last and win by half a length.

Nicholls said at his September owners' day he believes Topofthegame is an ideal horse for the Gold Cup, and it will be disappointing if he doesn't turn up at Cheltenham in March as a realistic contender.

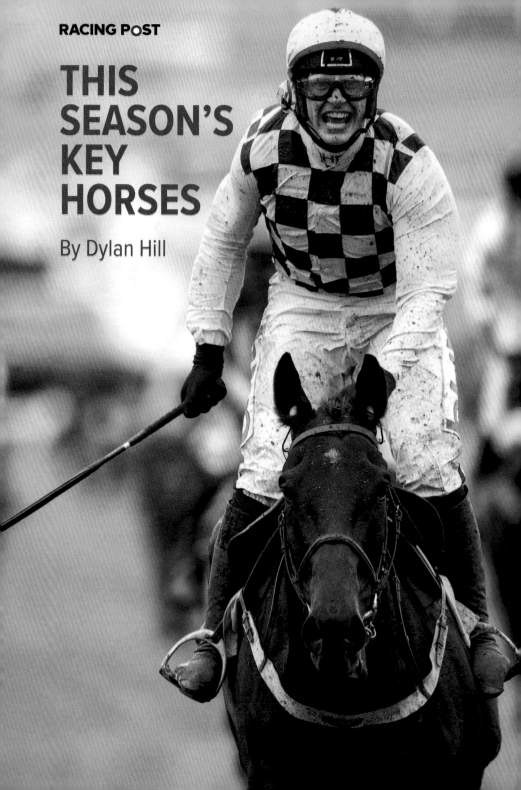

RACING POST

THIS SEASON'S KEY HORSES

By Dylan Hill

A Plus Tard (Fr)

Breeding: 5 b g Kapgarde - Turboka (Kahyasi)

Trainer: Henry de Bromhead (Ir) **Owner:** Cheveley Park Stud

PLACINGS: 12231/2121-3   RPR **165**+c

Starts	1st	2nd	3rd	4th	Win & Pl
10	4	4	2	-	£134,900
144	3/19	Chel	2m4f Cls1 Nov List 138-145 Ch Hcap soft		£39,389
	12/18	Naas	2m3f Ch yield		£7,904
0	4/18	Autl	2m2f List Hdl 4yo Hcap heavy		£39,823
	10/17	Sbri	2m2f Hdl 3yo gd-sft		£6,974

French recruit who quickly proved a very smart chaser last season and ran away with the novice handicap at the Cheltenham Festival by 16 lengths; looked a Grade 1 horse that day but didn't stay 3m in that grade at Punchestown, though he didn't look a match for Delta Work anyway.

Abacadabras (Fr)

5 b g Davidoff - Cadoubelle Des As (Cadoudal)

Gordon Elliott (Ir)   Gigginstown House Stud

PLACINGS: 1O4-2   RPR **132**b

Starts	1st	2nd	3rd	4th	Win & Pl
4	1	1	-	1	£26,543
	10/18	Gway	2m¹/₂f NHF 4yo soft		£5,451

Among last season's leading bumper performers; would have finished a good second to Envoi Allen at Leopardstown but for running out on the run-in and was fourth behind the same rival at Cheltenham; second behind Colreevy in a Grade 1 at Punchestown on final run.

Acapella Bourgeois (Fr)

9 ch g Network - Jasmine (Valanjou I)

Willie Mullins (Ir)   Slaneyville Syndicate

PLACINGS: 1/4F341165/F2P/013-0   RPR **154**c

Starts	1st	2nd	3rd	4th	Win & Pl
23	7	2	3	2	£151,512
	3/19	Clon	2m4f Ch good		£9,712
	2/17	Navn	3m Nov Gd2 Ch sft-hvy		£21,432
	1/17	Navn	2m4f Ch soft		£6,833
	3/16	Fair	2m4f Nov Gd2 Hdl yield		£19,522
	2/16	Thur	2m4f Nov Gd2 Hdl soft		£19,522
	12/15	Leop	2m4f Mdn Hdl heavy		£6,953
	10/14	Rcpp	1m4f NHF 4-5yo gd-sft		£4,167

Unlikely to fulfil potential of front-running novice chase wins in early 2017 but did much better in second season for Willie Mullins last term; got back to winning ways at Clonmel (first chase in more than a year) and followed up with a fine third in the Irish Grand National.

Acting Lass (Ire)

8 b g King's Theatre - Darrens Lass (Montelimar)

Harry Fry   Nigel & Barbara Collison

PLACINGS: 124/1119/P   RPR **154**c

Starts	1st	2nd	3rd	4th	Win & Pl
8	4	1	-	1	£69,716
143	1/18	Asct	2m5f Cls2 133-143 Ch Hcap soft		£47,571
141	1/18	Leic	2m4f Cls3 Nov 127-141 Ch Hcap soft		£8,295
135	11/17	MRas	2m5¹/₂f Cls3 Nov 125-135 Ch Hcap gd-sft		£7,988
	11/16	Hrfd	2m3¹/₂f Cls4 Nov Hdl soft		£3,639

Missed last season through injury but had taken really well to fences two seasons ago, winning first three chases including an open handicap at Ascot on soft ground; reportedly unsuited by good ground when a disappointing favourite in the Betdaq Chase at Kempton (also first run beyond 2m5f).

Activial (Fr)

9 gr g Lord Du Sud - Kissmirial (Smadoun)

Tom George   R S Brookhouse

PLACINGS: 49213/U5/0/83212660-   RPR **156**+c

Starts	1st	2nd	3rd	4th	Win & Pl
23	4	4	5	1	£136,863
	11/18	Hayd	2m5¹/₂f Cls2 Ch good		£31,714
	1/16	Extr	2m3f Cls4 Ch heavy		£3,899
	2/14	Kemp	2m Cls1 Gd2 Hdl 4yo soft		£15,661
	9/13	Stra	1m4f NHF 3yo		£4,878

Lightly raced for his age having been plagued by injuries since looking set for big things as a youngster; got back on track last season when showing smart form in graduation chases; found it harder in handicap company but not beaten far when sixth in the Ultima at Cheltenham.

Adjali (Ger)

4 b g Kamsin - Anabasis (High Chaparral)

Nicky Henderson   Simon Munir & Isaac Souede

PLACINGS: 21/312374-   RPR **139**h

Starts	1st	2nd	3rd	4th	Win & Pl
8	2	2	2	1	£69,511
	12/18	MRas	2m¹/₂f Cls4 Hdl 3yo gd-sft		£4,549
	4/18	Comp	2m Hdl 3yo v soft		£20,389

French hurdles winner who hacked up by 13 lengths on British debut last season but didn't quite live up to lofty expectations after that; beaten favourite the next twice before finishing seventh and fourth behind Pentland Hills in top juvenile hurdles at Cheltenham and Aintree.

Adrien Du Pont (Fr)

7 b g Califet - Santariyka (Saint Des Saints)

Paul Nicholls   Mrs Johnny De La Hey

PLACINGS: 1/43UP/13232F/47130-   RPR **156**+c

Starts	1st	2nd	3rd	4th	Win & Pl
20	6	3	4	2	£174,436
144	12/18	Kemp	3m Cls2 120-144 Ch Hcap gd-sft.........£31,280
	10/17	Font	2m5¹/₂f Cls4 Nov Ch good.........£4,549
139	4/16	Asct	1m7¹/₂f Cls2 116-139 Hdl 4yo Hcap gd-sft.........£25,024
	1/16	Chep	2m Cls1 Gd1 Hdl 4yo heavy.........£28,475
	10/15	Chep	2m Cls4 Hdl 3yo good.........£3,899
	4/15	Engh	2m¹/₂f Hdl 3yo v soft.........£17,860

Became slightly disappointing as a novice chaser two seasons ago but did better when stepped up in trip last term, winning a 3m handicap at Kempton; looked likely to flourish over further again when staying on into third in a valuable contest over that course and distance in February.

Agrapart (Fr)

8 b/br g Martaline - Afragha (Darshaan)

Nick Williams   Gascoigne, Brookes & Barker

PLACINGS: 16/74139/77212/49P7-   RPR **153**h

Starts	1st	2nd	3rd	4th	Win & Pl
20	4	3	2	2	£210,617
	1/18	Chel	3m Cls1 Gd2 Hdl heavy.........£34,170
	1/17	Chel	2m4¹/₂f Cls1 Gd2 Hdl soft.........£22,887
137	2/16	Newb	2m¹/₂f Cls1 Gd3 128-153 Hdl Hcap heavy.........£88,273
	12/15	Aint	2m1f Cls3 Nov Hdl soft.........£6,279

Has twice won Grade 2 hurdles at Cheltenham, outstaying the opposition in testing conditions both times, most recently in the 2018 Cleeve Hurdle; less effective on quicker ground and only

subsequent win came on soft ground on the Flat at Ascot in May.

Al Boum Photo (Fr)

7 b g Buck's Boum - Al Gane (Dom Alco)

Willie Mullins (Ir)   Mrs J Donnelly

PLACINGS: F/3115/1F2F1O/11-2   RPR **178**+c

Starts	1st	2nd	3rd	4th	Win & Pl
14	6	2	1	-	£526,696
	3/19	Chel	3m2¹/₂f Cls1 Gd1 Ch gd-sft.........£351,688
	1/19	Tram	2m5¹/₂f List Ch soft.........£16,622
	4/18	Fair	2m4f Nov Gd1 Ch sft-hvy.........£52,212
	11/17	Navn	2m1f Ch sft-hvy.........£8,950
	4/17	Fair	2m4f Nov Gd2 Hdl sft-hvy.........£21,432
	1/17	Thur	2m Mdn Hdl 4-5yo yld-sft.........£5,256

Clearcut winner of last season's Cheltenham Gold Cup and ran equally well in defeat when a close second to Kemboy at Punchestown; would also have won two Grade 1 races as a novice but for being infamously steered around the last at Punchestown in 2018.

Al Dancer (Fr)

6 gr g Al Namix - Steel Dancer (Kaldounevees)

Nigel Twiston-Davies   Walters Plant Hire

PLACINGS: 2314/11110-   RPR **152**+h

Starts	1st	2nd	3rd	4th	Win & Pl
9	5	1	1	1	£72,590
141	2/19	Asct	1m7¹/₂f Cls1 Gd3 125-145 Hdl Hcap gd-sft.........£47,830
129	12/18	Chel	2m1f Cls3 116-137 Hdl Hcap good.........£9,747
	11/18	Ffos	2m Cls4 Nov Hdl soft.........£4,159
	10/18	Carl	2m1f Cls4 Nov Hdl gd-sft.........£4,549
	3/18	Bang	2m¹/₂f Cls5 Mdn NHF 4-6yo soft.........£2,395

High-class novice hurdler last season; completed

Altior stalks Saint Calvados before winning the Champion Chase for the second time

a four-timer with a smooth success in the rearranged Betfair Hurdle at Ascot off 141 having earlier won at Cheltenham; only tenth when joint-favourite for the Supreme Novices' Hurdle; has plenty of scope for fences.

Allaho (Fr)

5 b g No Risk At All - Idaho Falls (Turgeon)

Willie Mullins (Ir)				Cheveley Park Stud
PLACINGS: 2/413-2				RPR **148**h

Starts	1st	2nd	3rd	4th	Win & Pl
5	1	2	1	1	£65,416
	2/19	Clon	3m Nov Gd3 Hdl gd-yld		£21,261

French recruit who made a winning start over hurdles in Ireland, claiming the scalp of Minella Indo in a Grade 3 at Clonmel; unable to confirm that form in two subsequent runs at Grade 1 level but still ran well when third at Cheltenham and second at Punchestown.

Alpha Des Obeaux (Fr)

9 b g Saddler Maker - Omega Des Obeaux (Saint Preuil)

Gordon Elliott (Ir)				Gigginstown House Stud
PLACINGS: 486/2414646F/521422-				RPR **168**c

Starts	1st	2nd	3rd	4th	Win & Pl
33	6	11	2	5	£298,200
	11/18	Thur	2m6f List Ch gd-fm		£15,511
	11/17	Clon	2m4½f Gd2 Ch sft-hvy		£25,299
	11/16	Cork	2m4f Nov Gd3 Ch good		£17,353
	10/16	Thur	2m6f Ch good		£4,974
	1/16	Gowr	3m Gd2 Hdl heavy		£18,750
	11/14	Punc	2m4f Mdn Hdl 4yo yield		£5,750

Became slightly disappointing when trained by

Mouse Morris but put together a fine series of runs for Gordon Elliott last season; won only a Listed chase at Thurles but also finished second behind Kemboy and Rathvinden either side of another second under top weight in the Thyestes.

Altior (Ire)

9 b g High Chaparral - Monte Solaro (Key Of Luck)

Nicky Henderson				Mrs Patricia Pugh
PLACINGS: 11/1111111/111/11111-				RPR **180+**c

Starts	1st	2nd	3rd	4th	Win & Pl
22	20	-	1	-	£1,234,751
	4/19	Sand	1m7½f Cls1 Gd1 Ch good		£85,425
	3/19	Chel	2m Cls1 Gd1 Ch soft		£225,080
	1/19	Asct	2m1f Cls1 Gd1 Ch gd-sft		£85,425
	12/18	Kemp	2m Cls1 Gd2 Ch gd-sft		£56,950
	12/18	Sand	1m7½f Cls1 Gd1 Ch soft		£84,405
	4/18	Sand	1m7½f Cls1 Gd1 Ch gd-sft		£74,383
	3/18	Chel	2m Cls1 Gd1 Ch soft		£228,872
	2/18	Newb	2m1½f Cls1 Gd2 Ch soft		£28,475
	4/17	Sand	1m7½f Cls1 Gd1 Ch good		£71,188
	3/17	Chel	2m1f Cls1 Nov Gd1 Ch gd-sft		£99,663
	2/17	Newb	2m1½f Cls1 Gd2 Ch soft		£28,475
	12/16	Kemp	2m Cls1 Nov Gd2 Ch good		£22,780
	12/16	Sand	1m7½f Cls1 Nov Gd1 Ch gd-sft		£25,628
	11/16	Kemp	2m2f Cls4 Nov Ch soft		£4,549
	3/16	Chel	2m1½f Cls1 Nov Gd1 Hdl gd-sft		£68,340
	12/15	Kemp	2m Cls2 Nov Hdl good		£11,696
	11/15	Chel	2m1½f Cls1 Nov Gd2 Hdl gd-sft		£17,286
	10/15	Asct	1m7½f Cls3 Nov Hdl good		£7,798
	10/15	Chep	2m Cls4 Nov Hdl good		£3,899
	5/14	MRas	2m7½f Cls6 NHF 4-6yo good		£1,560

Legendary chaser who has won a record 19 successive jump races and never been beaten over hurdles and fences; took his Cheltenham Festival tally to four with a second successive Champion Chase last season; strong stayer at 2m and likely to step up in trip in future.

Angels Breath (Ire)

5 gr g Shantou - Mystic Masie (Turgeon)

Nicky Henderson — Walters Plant Hire & Ronnie Bartlett

PLACINGS: 1/1273- RPR **148+**h

Starts	1st	2nd	3rd	4th	Win & Pl
4	1	1	1	-	£35,078
	12/18	Asct	1m7¹/₂f Cls1 Nov Gd2 Hdl soft		£19,933

Made a big impression when winning a Grade 2 novice hurdle at Ascot on rules debut but that form suspect (four hurdles omitted and beaten horses achieved little) and failed to win again; seventh in the Supreme at Cheltenham and third when stepped up to 2m4f at Aintree.

Anibale Fly (Fr)

9 b g Assessor - Nouba Fly (Chamberlin)

Tony Martin (Ir) — John P McManus

PLACINGS: 112P142/591F34/6225- RPR **174**c

Starts	1st	2nd	3rd	4th	Win & Pl
24	7	5	2	3	£543,108
148	12/17	Leop	3m¹/₂f 126-150 Ch Hcap yield		£94,017
	1/17	Naas	3m Nov Gd3 Ch yld-sft		£22,692
	11/16	Navn	2m1f Ch yld-sft		£7,235
135	4/16	Punc	2m4f 125-149 Ch Hcap yield		£43,382
	12/15	Navn	2m Mdn Hdl heavy		£7,488
	4/15	Fair	2m NHF 4-7yo soft		£7,221
	3/15	Navn	2m NHF 5-7yo heavy		£4,814

Tough staying chaser who has been placed in the last two runnings of the Gold Cup, chasing home Al Boum Photo last season, and has gone on to run big races in the Grand National both times; yet to win above Grade 3 level, though, and without a win at all since December 2017.

Annamix (Fr)

6 gr g Martaline - Tashtiyana (Doyoun)

Willie Mullins (Ir) — Mrs S Ricci

PLACINGS: 2/21- RPR **117+**h

Starts	1st	2nd	3rd	4th	Win & Pl
3	1	2	-	-	£12,092
	3/19	Clon	2m Mdn Hdl gd-yld		£6,105

Early ante-post favourite for the last two runnings of the Supreme Novices' Hurdle having been talked up by connections but missed one season through injury and was beaten first time out last term before winning his only subsequent run at Clonmel; trainer keen to get him over fences.

Annie Mc (Ire)

5 b m Mahler - Classic Mari (Classic Cliche)

Jonjo O'Neill — Coral Champions Club

PLACINGS: 2/2324151- RPR **143+**h

Starts	1st	2nd	3rd	4th	Win & Pl
6	2	1	1	1	£33,752
127	3/19	Newb	2m4¹/₂f Cls1 Nov 107-127 Hdl Hcap gd-sft		£24,760
118	1/19	Chep	2m3¹/₂f Cls3 117-129 Hdl Hcap gd-sft		£6,238

Progressed with every run last season bar one flop at Exeter, bouncing back in the EBF Mares' Final at Newbury when storming home by eight lengths; was due to step up to Grade 1 level at Fairyhouse only to be withdrawn over a vaccination error; could go novice chasing.

Another Crick

6 b g Arcadio - Suetsu (Toulon)

Noel Williams — David Sewell

PLACINGS: 4/564235/82211- RPR **140+**c

Starts	1st	2nd	3rd	4th	Win & Pl
12	2	3	1	2	£24,607
124	2/19	Kemp	2m4¹/₂f Cls3 109-132 Ch Hcap good		£8,447
117	12/18	Newb	2m1¹/₂f Cls3 Nov 113-125 Ch Hcap gd-sft		£8,058

Sharply progressive when sent novice chasing last season, climbing 26lb in just four races and finishing with handicap wins at Newbury and Kempton (most impressive when stepped up to 2m4f); strong traveller and seen by trainer as the type to go well in top handicaps.

Any Second Now (Ire)

7 b g Oscar - Pretty Neat (Topanoora)

Ted Walsh (Ir) — John P McManus

PLACINGS: 113U/22238/52531F- RPR **154+**c

Starts	1st	2nd	3rd	4th	Win & Pl
15	3	4	3	-	£110,030
143	3/19	Chel	3m2f Cls2 133-144 Am Ch Hcap gd-sft		£41,510
	1/17	Punc	2m Nov Gd2 Hdl soft		£22,440
	12/16	Navn	2m Mdn Hdl 4yo yld-sft		£5,426

Hugely impressive winner of last season's Kim Muir at Cheltenham; hadn't won in two seasons over fences prior to that but had run in several good Graded races and relished going up in distance; fell early when well fancied for the Irish Grand National.

Apple's Jade (Fr)

7 b m Saddler Maker - Apple's For Ever (Nikos)

Gordon Elliott (Ir) — Gigginstown House Stud

PLACINGS: 21211/11133/111163-5 RPR **168+**h

Starts	1st	2nd	3rd	4th	Win & Pl
23	14	4	3	-	£743,241
	2/19	Leop	2m Gd1 Hdl gd-yld		£89,077
	12/18	Leop	3m Gd1 Hdl gd-yld		£52,212
	12/18	Fair	2m4f Gd1 Hdl good		£65,265
	11/18	Navn	2m4f Gd2 Hdl good		£22,190
	12/17	Fair	3m Gd1 Hdl soft		£42,863
	12/17	Fair	2m4f Gd1 Hdl soft		£50,427
	11/17	Navn	2m4f Gd2 Hdl sft-hvy		£21,432
	4/17	Punc	2m4f Gd1 Hdl gd-yld		£50,427
	3/17	Chel	2m4f Cls1 Gd1 Hdl gd-sft		£61,897
	12/16	Fair	2m4f Gd1 Hdl gd-yld		£43,382
	4/16	Punc	2m Gd1 Hdl 4yo yield		£43,382
	4/16	Aint	2m1f Cls1 Gd1 Hdl 4yo soft		£56,437
	12/15	Leop	2m Gd2 Hdl 3yo heavy		£21,415
	5/15	Vich	2m1¹/₂f Hdl 3yo soft		£7,814

Outstanding mare who has won ten Grade 1 races, including a hat-trick in the Hatton's Grace Hurdle; probably best at that 2m4f trip but also effective over 2m and 3m; even sent off favourite for last season's Champion Hurdle only to disappoint in the spring for the second year in a row.

Apple's Shakira (Fr)

5 b m Saddler Maker - Apple's For Ever (Nikos)

Nicky Henderson   John P McManus

PLACINGS: 111143/P6-   RPR **142**h

Starts	1st	2nd	3rd	4th	Win & Pl
8	4	-		1	£74,989
	1/18	Chel	2m1f Cls2 Gd2 Hdl 4yo soft		£18,224
	12/17	Chel	2m1f Cls2 Hdl 3yo soft		£12,512
	11/17	Chel	2m1½f Hdl 3yo soft		£17,085
	5/17	Vich	2m¹/₂f Hdl 3yo v soft		£8,615

Won first four races as a juvenile hurdler two seasons ago, going off 6-5 for the Triumph Hurdle, but managed only fourth that day and was third at Aintree; ran just twice in handicap company last season, doing best when a close sixth in the Coral Cup.

Aramon (Ger)

6 b g Monsun - Aramina (In The Wings)

Willie Mullins (Ir)

Supreme Horse Racing Club & Michael Songer

PLACINGS: 12131262-6   RPR **148**h

Starts	1st	2nd	3rd	4th	Win & Pl
9	3	3	1	-	£132,106
	12/18	Leop	2m Nov Gd1 Hdl gd-yld		£52,212
	11/18	Navn	2m Nov Gd3 Hdl good		£17,688
	8/18	Kbgn	2m4f Mdn Hdl good		£6,269

Highly tried as a novice hurdler last season, running in six Grade 1 races and winning one at Leopardstown by ten lengths; pushed Klassical Dream to a head next time but well beaten twice subsequently by that rival; given plenty to do when second to Felix Desjy at Aintree.

Articulum (Ire)

9 b g Definite Article - Lugante (Luso)

Terence O'Brien (Ir)

Martin McDonagh, Paul G Murphy & M J Nixon

PLACINGS: /3211/0/1P4247/213-P   RPR **149**c

Starts	1st	2nd	3rd	4th	Win & Pl
15	4	3	2	2	£60,085
	1/19	Naas	2m Nov Ch gd-yld		£11,429
	11/17	Cork	2m Mdn Hdl sft-hvy		£7,897
	3/16	Limk	2m3f NHF 5-7yo heavy		£4,748
	1/16	Naas	2m3f NHF 5-7yo sft-hvy		£4,566

Useful 2m novice chaser last season, outrunning 25-1 odds when third in the Racing Post Arkle at Cheltenham behind Duc Des Genievres; stepped up to 3m on final run at Punchestown (had bumper form at 2m3f on heavy ground) but looked a non-stayer, albeit when losing a shoe.

Ask For Glory (Ire)

5 b g Fame And Glory - Ask Helen (Pistolet Bleu)

Paul Nicholls   Colm Donlon & Mr & Mrs P K Barber

PLACINGS: 119-   RPR **125**+b

Starts	1st	2nd	3rd	4th	Win & Pl
2	1	-	-	-	£3,898
	12/18	Chep	2m Cls4 NHF 4-6yo soft		£3,899

Shortest-priced British-trained runner in last

season's Champion Bumper at Cheltenham but looked one-paced in ninth; had won a point-to-point and bumper debut by wide margins and could still prove a force in staying novice hurdles.

Aso (Fr)

9 b/br g Goldneyev - Odyssee Du Cellier (Dear Doctor)

Venetia Williams   The Bellamy Partnership

PLACINGS: 3561/4218434/5/1162-   RPR **172**c

Starts	1st	2nd	3rd	4th	Win & Pl
29	9	6	4	3	£325,209
158	1/19	Chel	2m4½f Cls1 Gd3 133-158 Ch Hcap gd-sft	£42,285
150	11/18	Newb	2m4f Cls2 130-152 Ch Hcap gd-sft	£31,396
145	12/16	Chep	2m3½f Cls2 127-149 Ch Hcap soft	£25,320
	4/16	NAbb	2m5f Cls3 Nov Ch soft	£7,280
	1/16	MRas	2m5¹/₂f Cls2 Ch soft	£12,777
	1/15	Hayd	2m Cls1 Nov Gd2 Hdl heavy	£15,661
	12/14	Tntn	2m3f Cls4 Nov Hdl soft	£3,574
	11/14	Wwck	2m Cls4 Nov Hdl soft	£3,899
	7/13	Gran	1m4f NHF 3yo gd-sft	£4,065

Better than ever when returning from more than a year out last season; won two good handicaps before stepping up to Grade 1 level and bounced back from a poor run at Ascot to finish a fine second to Frodon in the Ryanair Chase (also third in that race in 2017).

Atlanta Ablaze

8 b m Kayf Tara - Rocheflamme (Snurge)

Henry Daly   The Last Man Standing

PLACINGS: 13458/F/2531131U1FP-   RPR **148**+c

Starts	1st	2nd	3rd	4th	Win & Pl
21	5	1	4	1	£60,275
	2/19	Winc	3m1f Cls1 List Ch good	£15,575
	12/18	Wwck	2m4f Cls1 Nov List Ch gd-sft	£14,238
119	10/18	Hrfd	2m5f Cls3 117-127 Ch Hcap gd-fm	£12,762
110	8/18	Bang	3m Cls4 108-123 Ch Hcap good	£4,614
	10/16	Ludl	2m5f Cls4 Nov Hdl gd-fm	£5,198

Transformed by wind surgery last summer and won four of her next six races over fences, including Listed mares' chases at Warwick and Wincanton; running a massive race when falling two out in the National Hunt Chase and that may have left its mark when pulled up at Perth.

Azzuri

7 b g Azamour - Folly Lodge (Grand Lodge)

Dan Skelton   The Blind Squirrels

PLACINGS: 22/121136431/18401-0   RPR **151**+c

Starts	1st	2nd	3rd	4th	Win & Pl
22	7	5	3	2	£102,279
132	4/19	Ayr	2m¹/₂f Cls1 List 130-156 Ch Hcap good	£22,780
131	7/18	Klny	2m1f 129-149 Ch Hcap good	£26,106
123	4/18	Ayr	2m Cls3 Nov 123-132 Ch Hcap good	£10,007
	8/17	Sthl	1m7¹/₂f Cls4 Nov Ch good	£3,899
	7/17	Sthl	1m7¹/₂f Cls4 Nov Ch good	£3,899
	5/17	Ludl	2m Cls4 Nov Hdl good	£3,899
	3/17	Hntg	2m Cls4 Mdn Hdl soft	£3,574

Landed a big gamble when winning a good 2m handicap chase at Ayr in April having also been well backed at Aintree the previous week only to be withdrawn due to soft ground; had been given wind surgery since losing his way earlier in the season and clearly well ahead of mark.

Bacardys (Fr)
8 b g Coastal Path - Oasice (Robin Des Champs)

Willie Mullins (Ir) Shanakiel Racing Syndicate

PLACINGS: 31/3F11P1/3FF0/7F6-2 RPR **152+**h

Starts	1st	2nd	3rd	4th	Win & Pl
17	5	1	3	-	£200,908
	4/17 Punc	2m4f Nov Gd1 Hdl gd-yld			£50,427
	2/17 Leop	2m2f Nov Gd1 Hdl soft			£45,385
	12/16 Leop	2m Mdn Hdl yield			£6,331
	4/16 Aint	2m1f Cls1 Gd2 NHF 4-6yo soft			£22,508
	12/15 Leop	2m NHF 4yo heavy			£5,349

Has run to a similar pattern during the last two seasons, both times starting off over fences only to switch back to hurdles after falls; without a win since landing two Grade 1 novice hurdles in 2017 but ran arguably best race back in that sphere when second to Unowhatimeanharry at Punchestown.

Bachasson (Fr)
8 gr g Voix Du Nord - Belledonne (Shafoun)

Willie Mullins (Ir) Edward O'Connell

PLACINGS: /111128U/F21/11F/14- RPR **149**h

Starts	1st	2nd	3rd	4th	Win & Pl
18	10	2	-	1	£115,482
	12/18 Punc	2m4f Hdl good			£10,903
	1/18 Tram	2m5f List Ch heavy			£16,327
	11/17 Thur	2m6f List Ch sft-hvy			£14,981
	2/17 Gowr	2m4f Ch heavy			£7,371
	10/15 Tipp	2m Nov Gd3 Hdl good			£15,116
	9/15 Gway	2m2f Nov Hdl good			£9,093
	7/15 Gway	2m Nov Hdl 4yo yield			£10,078
	7/15 Slig	2m Mdn Hdl 4yo yield			£5,616
	9/14 Stra	1m4f NHF 3yo v soft			£5,000
	7/14 Vitt	1m4f NHF 3yo gd-sft			£4,583

Very lightly raced in recent seasons but has shown very smart form over hurdles and fences; easily won two Listed chases two seasons ago before falling at the second fence in the Cheltenham Gold Cup; won back over hurdles last term before a disappointing fourth in the Boyne Hurdle.

Bags Groove (Ire)
8 b g Oscar - Golden Moment (Roselier)

Harry Fry Michael Pescod

PLACINGS: /22151/8110/2111514- RPR **157+**c

Starts	1st	2nd	3rd	4th	Win & Pl
19	9	5	-	1	£120,072
	2/19 Kemp	2m4¹/₂f Cls1 Nov Gd2 Ch good			£18,224
	12/18 Hntg	2m7¹/₂f Cls3 Nov Ch gd-sft			£9,747
	11/18 Winc	2m4f Cls1 Nov Gd2 Ch good			£18,438
	10/18 Ffos	2m5f Cls3 Nov Ch gd-sft			£9,357
140	11/17 Kemp	2m5f Cls2 128-154 Hdl Hcap good			£11,886
132	10/17 Aint	2m4f Cls2 117-142 Hdl Hcap gd-sft			£17,204
	3/17 Tntn	2m3f Cls4 Nov Hdl good			£3,899
	1/17 Tntn	2m3f Cls4 Nov Hdl good			£4,224
	1/16 Hntg	1m5¹/₂f Cls6 NHF 4-6yo gd-sft			£1,560

Very smart novice chaser last season, winning four times including small-field Grade 2 contests at Wincanton and Kempton; well beaten in two toughest Grade 1 tests, albeit with excuses both times (trainer felt race came too soon over Christmas and unsuited by soft ground at Aintree).

Balko Des Flos (Fr)
8 ch g Balko - Royale Marie (Garde Royale)

Henry de Bromhead (Ir) Gigginstown House Stud

PLACINGS: 2133F3/123214/43973- RPR **169+**c

Starts	1st	2nd	3rd	4th	Win & Pl
24	6	3	6	3	£460,938
	3/18 Chel	2m5f Cls1 Gd1 Ch good			£200,263
146	8/17 Gway	2m6¹/₂f 137-160 Ch Hcap good			£126,068
	1/17 Fair	2m5¹/₂f Ch soft			£5,879
	1/16 Punc	2m4f Mdn Hdl sft-hvy			£6,088
	5/15 Slig	2m2f NHF 4yo yield			£5,349
	1/15 Leop	2m NHF 4yo soft			£4,279

Without a win since an impressive victory in the 2018 Ryanair Chase; largely out of sorts last season but showed much more when third behind Kemboy in the Betway Bowl (would have been second but for mistake at last); perhaps best over that 3m trip on balance of form.

Ballyandy
8 b g Kayf Tara - Megalex (Karinga Bay)

Nigel Twiston-Davies Options O Syndicate

PLACINGS: 14/23214/14P/3P4133- RPR **152**h

Starts	1st	2nd	3rd	4th	Win & Pl
20	7	3	4	4	£214,149
142	1/19 Uttx	2m4f Cls2 116-142 Hdl Hcap soft			£9,384
	9/17 Prth	2m4f Cls3 Nov Ch heavy			£7,507
135	2/17 Newb	2m¹/₂f Cls3 Gd3 126-146 Hdl Hcap soft			£88,273
	3/16 Chel	2m¹/₂f Cls1 Gd1 NHF 4-6yo good			£39,865
	11/15 Newb	2m¹/₂f Cls1 List NHF 4-6yo heavy			£11,390
	11/15 Chel	2m¹/₂f Cls1 List NHF 4-6yo gd-sft			£11,390
	10/15 Worc	2m Cls6 NHF 3-5yo gd-sft			£1,560

Former Betfair Hurdle winner who did well back over timber last season having failed to build on a promising start over fences two seasons ago; won at Uttoxeter and twice finished third in stronger handicaps, notably when beaten half a length in the Coral Cup.

Ballyhill (Fr)
8 b/br g Al Namix - Laly Light (Start Fast)

Nigel Twiston-Davies S Such & CG Paletta

PLACINGS: 00/235F109P/8213330- RPR **151**c

Starts	1st	2nd	3rd	4th	Win & Pl
27	4	3	5	3	£99,074
134	12/18 Aint	2m4f Cls3 122-135 Ch Hcap good			£11,696
133	1/18 Chel	2m5f Cls1 Gd3 133-154 Ch Hcap heavy			£42,713
	11/16 Ludl	2m5f Cls3 Hdl good			£6,498
	10/16 Hrfd	2m Cls4 Nov Hdl good			£3,249

Has won good handicap chases at Cheltenham and Aintree in last two seasons; raised 10lb

for latest win but continued to run well when twice third back at Cheltenham, notably behind subsequent Cheltenham Festival one-two Siruh Du Lac and Janika in January.

Ballymoy (Ire)

6 b g Flemensfirth - John's Eliza (Dr Massini)

Nigel Twiston-Davies | Simon Munir & Isaac Souede

PLACINGS: 4/335111/141176- | RPR **153**h

Starts	1st	2nd	3rd	4th	Win & Pl
11	6	-	1	1	£128,696
147	1/19	Asct	2m3¹/₂f Cls1 Gd3 121-147 Hdl Hcap gd-sft.......£28,475
142	12/18	Hayd	2m3f Cls2 127-147 Hdl Hcap heavy..............£12,512
139	10/18	Chep	2m 122-139 Hdl Hcap gd-sft..............£12,996
132	4/18	Sand	2m Cls2 Nov 118-137 Hdl Hcap gd-sft.......£61,900
	3/18	Bang	2m¹/₂f Cls4 Nov Hdl soft..............£4,094
	2/18	Uttx	2m Cls4 Mdn Hdl heavy..............£4,094

Progressive hurdler who was making it six wins out of seven when landing a valuable handicap at Ascot in January; found higher mark beyond him next time and well below par when stepped up to Grade 2 level; expected by connections to come into his own as a staying novice chaser.

Ballyoisin (Ire)

8 b g Presenting - Regal Force (King's Ride)

Enda Bolger (Ir) | John P McManus

PLACINGS: F1FF/31212F8/11115-1 | RPR **168+**c

Starts	1st	2nd	3rd	4th	Win & Pl
19	9	2	2	-	£216,103
162	8/19	Klny	2m5f 131-162 Ch Hcap good.............£26,577
	11/18	Navn	2m Gd2 Ch good.............£23,496
131	9/18	List	2m 117-144 Hdl Hcap soft.............£52,212
	6/18	Punc	2m5f Ch good.............£11,429
	5/18	Klny	2m4¹/₂f Gd3 Ch good.............£20,885
150	10/17	Cork	2m1f 122-150 Ch Hcap yld-sft.............£25,214
144	7/17	Klny	2m1f 129-157 Ch Hcap good.............£25,214
	1/17	Fair	2m1f Ch soft.............£8,410
	9/15	Navn	2m Mdn Hdl good.............£6,419

Much improved last summer and resumed progress after a layoff when hacking up in a handicap chase at Killarney in August off 162; won for fifth time in six races that day, with sole defeat in a 2m Grade 1 at Leopardstown last Christmas, and could try again at the top level.

Ballyoptic (Ire)

9 b g Old Vic - Lambourne Lace (Un Desperado)

Nigel Twiston-Davies | Mills & Mason Partnership

PLACINGS: F2F4P5/5124142/F6PF- | RPR **140**c

Starts	1st	2nd	3rd	4th	Win & Pl
22	6	3		3	£214,452
	2/18	Weth	3m Cls1 Nov Gd2 Ch heavy.............£20,284
	11/17	Extr	3m Cls2 Nov Ch soft.............£14,206
148	10/16	Chep	2m3¹/₂f Cls1 Gd3 131-148 Hdl Hcap good.....£28,475
	4/16	Aint	3m¹/₂f Cls1 Nov Gd1 Hdl soft.............£56,270
	3/16	Uttx	2m4f Cls4 Nov Hdl soft.............£5,064
	2/16	Ffos	2m4f Cls4 Nov Hdl 4-7yo heavy.............£4,549

Smart stayer who came within a nose of winning the Scottish National in 2018; sixth in last season's Welsh National but failed to complete in all three other runs, falling four out having run well in the Grand National (second fall over those fences).

Ballywood (Fr)

5 b g Ballingarry - Miss Hollywood (True Brave)

Alan King | Highclere Thoroughbred Racing

PLACINGS: 3/31120/4411214- | RPR **153+**c

Starts	1st	2nd	3rd	4th	Win & Pl
13	5	2	2	3	£80,237
140	3/19	Ludl	2m Cls2 114-140 Ch Hcap good.............£13,971
133	12/18	Donc	2m¹/₂f Cls3 Nov 133-135 Ch Hcap good......£7,343
127	12/18	Tntn	2m2f Cls3 111-134 Ch Hcap good.............£9,357
	6/17	Claf	2m1f Hdl 3yo v soft.............£19,692
	6/17	Diep	2m1f Hdl 3yo v soft.............£9,026

Went chasing as a four-year-old last season and soon rewarded connections' boldness, winning three times including a good handicap at Ludlow; pulled too hard to get longer 2m4f trip on final run at Ayr.

Band Of Outlaws (Ire)

4 b g Fast Company - Band Of Colour (Spectrum)

Joseph Patrick O'Brien (Ir) | John P McManus

PLACINGS: 31115-23 | RPR **147**h

Starts	1st	2nd	3rd	4th	Win & Pl
7	3	1	2		£103,526
139	3/19	Chel	2m¹/₂f Cls1 Gd3 129-141 Hdl 4yo Hcap soft......£45,016
	2/19	Naas	2m Nov Hdl 4yo good.............£10,267
	12/18	Limk	2m Mdn Hdl 3yo sft-hvy.............£7,359

Took well to hurdles last season and won the Fred Winter at Cheltenham impressively; disappointing when sent off favourite at Grade 1 level at Aintree next time but came close to landing another big handicap when third in the Galway Hurdle.

Bapaume (Fr)

6 b g Turtle Bowl - Brouhaha (American Post)

Willie Mullins (Ir) | Mrs S Ricci

PLACINGS: 31/2383P5/214324-342 | RPR **160**h

Starts	1st	2nd	3rd	4th	Win & Pl
22	4	6	4	3	£434,892
	6/18	Autl	2m3¹/₂f Gd2 Hdl v soft.............£69,690
	4/17	Punc	2m Gd1 Hdl 4yo gd-yld.............£50,427
	12/16	Leop	2m Gd2 Hdl 3yo yield.............£19,522
	4/16	Fntb	1m7f Hdl 3yo v soft.............£7,059

Grade 1 winner as a juvenile hurdler who has developed into a high-class staying hurdler despite sole win coming in the 2018 Prix la Barka; second in that race this summer to extend run of near misses, including when fourth in the Stayers' Hurdle at Cheltenham.

Baron Alco (Fr)

8 ch g Dom Alco - Paula (Network)

Gary Moore | John Stone

PLACINGS: 86/11120/312122/214- | RPR **157**c

Starts	1st	2nd	3rd	4th	Win & Pl
21	7	6	2	2	£204,450
146	11/18	Chel	2m4f Cls1 Gd3 135-161 Ch Hcap good......£90,299
	1/17	Plum	2m1f Cls3 Nov Ch soft.............£7,988
	11/16	Plum	2m3¹/₂f Cls3 Nov Ch good.............£6,657
127	12/15	Kemp	2m5f Cls3 118-135 Hdl Hcap good.............£9,747
123	11/15	Font	2m1¹/₂f Cls3 110-124 Hdl Hcap soft.............£6,330
116	10/15	Strf	2m2¹/₂f Cls3 107-129 Hdl Hcap good......£6,330
	11/14	Sand	2m Cls3 Hdl 3yo soft.............£6,498

Has been plagued by injuries but returned from

18 months out in tremendous form last season, winning the BetVictor Gold Cup from Frodon; returned sore after finishing only fourth behind that rival in the Caspian Caviar Gold Cup but ready to return from another subsequent layoff.

Battleoverdoyen (Ire)
6 b g Doyen - Battle Over (Sillery)

Gordon Elliott (Ir)   Gigginstown House Stud

PLACINGS: 1/111P-   RPR **144+**h

Starts	1st	2nd	3rd	4th	Win & Pl
4	3	-	-	-	£60,619
	1/19	Naas	2m4f Nov Gd1 Hdl good		£46,991
	12/18	Navn	2m Mdn Hdl yield		£8,177
	11/18	Punc	2m NHF 4-7yo good		£5,451

Won first three starts under rules last season, progressing rapidly to win a Grade 1 novice hurdle at Naas in January; sent off favourite for the Ballymore at Cheltenham but unable to land a blow and pulled up; point-to-point winner and likely to go novice chasing.

Beakstown (Ire)
6 b g Stowaway - Midnight Reel (Accordion)

Dan Skelton   Bryan Drew

PLACINGS: 12/121P-   RPR **141+**h

Starts	1st	2nd	3rd	4th	Win & Pl
5	2	2	-	-	£26,663
	1/19	Wwck	2m5f Cls1 Nov Gd2 Hdl good		£19,933
	11/18	Uttx	2m4f Cls5 Mdn Hdl good		£3,119

Useful novice hurdler last season, staying on strongly when winning a Grade 2 at Warwick in January, but pulled up in the Ballymore at the Cheltenham Festival; should stay further; point-to-point winner and expected to make a mark as a staying chaser.

Beer Goggles (Ire)
8 br g Oscar - Tynelucy (Good Thyne)

Nicky Martin   Bradley Partnership

PLACINGS: 70711/3VPF311/21315/   RPR **157**h

Starts	1st	2nd	3rd	4th	Win & Pl
23	6	3	3	2	£70,459
	12/17	Newb	3m Cls1 Gd2 Hdl soft		£28,475
	10/17	NAbb	3m2¹/₂f Cls2 131-157 Hdl Hcap good		£15,358
	4/17	Ayr	3m¹/₂f Cls3 97-127 Hdl Hcap gd-sft		£7,798
	3/17	Newb	3m Cls4 105-116 Hdl Hcap gd-sft		£4,549
	3/16	Hexm	2m7¹/₂f Cls5 77-104 Hdl Hcap heavy		£2,601
	3/16	Sedg	3m3f Cls4 94-110 Hdl Hcap heavy		£4,159

Shock winner of the Long Distance Hurdle at Newbury two seasons ago; may well have been flattered by that win and only fifth in the Cleeve next time but had been progressive prior to that, winning three of his last five handicaps; missed last season through injury.

Bellshill (Ire)
9 b g King's Theatre - Fairy Native (Be My Native)

Willie Mullins (Ir)   Andrea & Graham Wylie

PLACINGS: 1302/111F3/14d1/41P-4   RPR **169**c

Starts	1st	2nd	3rd	4th	Win & Pl
23	11	3	2	2	£546,939
	2/19	Leop	3m Gd1 Ch good		£114,527
	4/18	Punc	3m¹/₂f Gd1 Ch yield		£143,584
	2/18	Fair	3m1f Gd3 Ch soft		£23,496
	12/16	Limk	2m3¹/₂f Nov Gd2 Ch heavy		£19,305
	11/16	Gowr	2m4f Ch yld-sft		£7,235
	4/16	Punc	3m Nov Gd1 Hdl gd-yld		£43,382
	1/16	Naas	2m4f Nov Gd1 Hdl heavy		£39,706
	12/15	Navn	2m4f Nov Gd2 Hdl heavy		£20,155
	11/15	Cork	2m Mdn Hdl heavy		£7,488
	4/15	Punc	2m Gd1 NHF 4-7yo gd-yld		£44,186
	11/14	Thur	2m NHF 4-7yo soft		£4,313

Talented but fragile staying chaser; progressed well two seasons ago (signed off with Grade 1 win at Punchestown) and looked to be coming to the boil again last season after narrow Irish Gold Cup victory only for jumping to fall apart in two subsequent runs.

Benatar (Ire)
7 b g Beneficial - Carrigeen Lily (Supreme Leader)

Gary Moore   Ashley Head

PLACINGS: 11424/1113/4437-   RPR **151**c

Starts	1st	2nd	3rd	4th	Win & Pl
12	4	1	2	4	£79,033
	12/17	Asct	2m5f Cls1 Nov Gd2 Ch gd-sft		£19,933
	11/17	Plum	2m3¹/₂f Cls3 Nov Ch gd-sft		£6,975
	11/17	Asct	2m3f Cls3 Nov 126-142 Ch Hcap good		£9,747
142	11/17	Font	2m3f Cls5 Mdn Hdl soft		£2,274

Not far off the best novice chasers two seasons ago, winning three times and finishing third in the JLT at Cheltenham; unable to build on that last term, though shaped well when third in the Silver Cup at Ascot and sent off favourite when disappointing back there next time.

Benie Des Dieux (Fr)
8 b m Great Pretender - Cana (Robin Des Champs)

Willie Mullins (Ir)   Mrs S Ricci

PLACINGS: 141/633/1/1111/F-11   RPR **156+**h

Starts	1st	2nd	3rd	4th	Win & Pl
14	9	-	2	1	£424,703
	5/19	Autl	3m1¹/₂f Gd1 Hdl v soft		£141,892
	5/19	Punc	2m4f Gd1 Hdl gd-yld		£53,153
	4/18	Punc	2m4f Gd1 Hdl yld-sft		£52,212
	3/18	Chel	2m4f Cls1 Gd1 Hdl heavy		£67,582
	2/18	Naas	2m List Ch heavy		£17,688
	12/17	Carl	2m4f Cls1 List Ch soft		£17,286
	12/16	Limk	2m3¹/₂f Ch sft-hvy		£6,105
	4/15	Autl	2m2f Hdl 4-5yo v soft		£22,326
	10/14	Autl	2m2f Hdl 3yo heavy		£22,000

Outstanding mare who would have won all eight races for Willie Mullins but for falling at the last when set to win a second Mares' Hurdle at Cheltenham last season; went on to retain

mares' crown at Punchestown before storming home in the French Champion Hurdle at Auteuil.

Beware The Bear (Ire)

9 b g Shantou - Native Bid (Be My Native)

| Nicky Henderson | | | | | G B Barlow |

PLACINGS: 431/11174/1P4P/411P-   RPR **161**+c

Starts		1st	2nd	3rd	4th	Win & Pl
17		7	1	1	4	£160,911
151	3/19	Chel	3m1f Cls1 Gd3 140-155 Ch Hcap soft			£61,897
146	1/19	Chel	3m2½f Cls2 121-146 Ch Hcap gd-sft			£15,475
145	12/17	Newc	2m7½f Cls1 List 126-150 Ch Hcap soft			£40,053
136	12/16	Newb	2m7½f Cls3 Nov 116-136 Ch Hcap gd-sft			£6,498
130	11/16	Asct	3m Cls3 Nov 123-135 Ch Hcap gd-sft			£7,148
	5/16	Sthl	3m Cls4 Nov Hdl good			£3,899
	4/16	Bang	2m7f Cls5 Mdn Hdl heavy			£3,139

Much improved last season when helped by a wind operation and sharpened up by headgear; won two good handicaps at Cheltenham, most notably the Ultima in March; 9lb higher in the weights when pulled up in the bet365 Gold Cup at Sandown on his final run.

Bigmartre (Fr)

8 b g Montmartre - Oh La Miss (Le Balafre)

| Harry Whittington | | | | | P J Dixon |

PLACINGS: /1860/11271/6P43001-   RPR **155**+c

Starts		1st	2nd	3rd	4th	Win & Pl
27		7	3	3	2	£118,707
140	4/19	Prth	2m4f Cls2 126-140 Ch Hcap good			£18,768
	4/18	Ayr	2m4½f Cls1 Nov Gd2 Ch good			£30,247
137	12/17	Newb	2m1½f Cls3 Nov 130-139 Ch Hcap gd-sft			£12,974
132	10/17	Ludl	2m Cls3 Nov 123-134 Ch Hcap gd-fm			£9,082
133	12/16	Kemp	2m Cls3 124-139 Hdl Hcap good			£12,512
	12/15	Hayd	1m7½f Cls4 Nov Hdl 4-6yo heavy			£3,899
	10/15	Font	2m1½f Cls4 Nov Hdl good			£5,198

Smart chaser on his day, winning a Grade 2 novice chase at Ayr and running away with a handicap at Perth last spring; had struggled in

more competitive handicaps, finishing no better than 11th in three runs over fences when faced with fields of ten or more runners.

Birchdale (Ire)

5 b g Jeremy - Onewayortheother (Presenting)

| Nicky Henderson | | | | | John P McManus |

PLACINGS: 1/11P-   RPR **147**+h

Starts		1st	2nd	3rd	4th	Win & Pl
3		2				£22,767
	1/19	Chel	2m4½f Cls1 Nov Gd2 Hdl gd-sft			£18,219
	12/18	Wwck	2m5f Cls4 Mdn Hdl gd-sft			£4,549

Raw chasing type who won twice during a light campaign last season, most notably when taking advantage of Brewin'upastorm's final-flight fall in a Grade 2 at Cheltenham (would have been close); weakened quickly and pulled up at the last when up in trip for the Albert Bartlett.

Black Corton (Fr)

8 br g Laverock - Pour Le Meilleur (Video Rock)

| Paul Nicholls | | | | | The Brooks Family & J Kyle |

PLACINGS: 21111121154/2P2221-2   RPR **165**+c

Starts		1st	2nd	3rd	4th	Win & Pl
31		14	9	4	2	£340,014
	4/19	Sand	2m6½f Cls1 Gd2 Ch good			£31,323
	2/18	Asct	3m Cls1 Nov Gd2 Ch soft			£22,780
	12/17	Kemp	3m Cls1 Nov Gd1 Ch soft			£43,466
	11/17	Chel	3m1½f Cls2 Nov Ch soft			£15,640
	10/17	Chel	3m1½f Cls2 Nov Ch good			£16,218
	10/17	NAbb	2m5f Cls2 Ch good			£18,705
	8/17	Font	2m5½f Cls4 Nov Ch gd-fm			£3,899
	7/17	Worc	2m7f Cls4 Nov Ch good			£3,899
	6/17	Font	2m1½f Cls4 Nov Ch gd-sft			£3,899
135	4/17	Tntn	2m3f Cls3 124-135 Hdl Hcap good			£7,280
	10/16	Kemp	2m Cls1 Nov List Hdl good			£11,390
	10/16	NAbb	2m2½f Cls4 Nov Hdl 4-6yo good			£4,549
	4/16	Extr	2m1f Cls5 Mdn Hdl good			£2,599
	5/15	Pina	1m7f NHF 4yo gd-sft			£5,426

Managed first win outside novice company over

fences when running away with a Grade 2 chase at Sandown on final run last season and followed up with a fine second in the Galway Plate; had run well in other good races from 2m4f to 3m previously, finishing second in the Charlie Hall Chase among others.

Black Op (Ire)

8 br g Sandmason - Afar Story (Desert Story)

Tom George					R S Brookhouse
PLACINGS: 1/19/41221/33304-					RPR **156**h

Starts	1st	2nd	3rd	4th	Win & Pl
12	3	2	3	2	£110,633
4/18	Aint	2m4f Cls1 Nov Gd1 Hdl soft			£56,141
1/18	Donc	2m5f Cls5 Mdn Hdl soft			£3,119
2/17	Donc	2m¹/₂f Cls6 NHF 4-6yo good			£1,949

Won a Grade 1 at Aintree and finished second behind Samcro at Cheltenham as a novice hurdler two seasons ago but struggled when switched back to hurdles last term after an aborted chase campaign; had been let down by his jumping over fences but retains novice status.

Blackbow (Ire)

6 b g Stowaway - Rinnce Moll (Accordion)

Willie Mullins (Ir)					Roaringwater Syndicate
PLACINGS: 1/11152/					RPR **142**b

Starts	1st	2nd	3rd	4th	Win & Pl
4	2	1	-	-	£63,511
2/18	Leop	2m Gd2 NHF 4-7yo soft			£39,159
12/17	Leop	2m NHF 4yo yield			£5,528

Top of the pecking order among his trainer's bumper performers two seasons ago according to market moves (shortest price among Cheltenham team when fifth and favourite at Punchestown when second); missed last season through injury but remains a top prospect for novice hurdles.

Blue Flight (Fr)

6 b g Blue Bresil - Lover Flight (Saint Cyrien)

Nigel Twiston-Davies					J Fyffe
PLACINGS: 25/123431/P311124-					RPR **154**c

Starts	1st	2nd	3rd	4th	Win & Pl
12	4	2	3	2	£80,139
	3/19	Kels	2m7¹/₂f List Ch gd-sft		£34,170
128	2/19	Kels	2m7¹/₂f Cls3 Nov 117-130 Ch Hcap good		£8,187
122	1/19	Asct	2m3f Cls3 120-130 Am Ch Hcap gd-sft		£9,608
	4/18	Prth	2m4f Cls4 Mdn Hdl soft		£4,431

Shot up 30lb in the handicap last season, getting off the mark over fences off 122 at Ascot in January and ending up rated 151 after finishing fourth in the Scottish Grand National; youngest horse in that race and surely open to further improvement.

Blue Sari (Fr)

4 b g Saddex - Blue Aster (Astarabad)

Willie Mullins (Ir)					John P McManus
PLACINGS: 12-					RPR **126**+b

Starts	1st	2nd	3rd	4th	Win & Pl
2	1	1	-	-	£21,727
1/19	Gowr	2m NHF 4yo soft			£5,827

Top-class bumper performer who won by 11 lengths on debut at Gowran Park before running the unbeaten Envoi Allen to three-quarters of a length in the Champion Bumper at Cheltenham; should be a leading novice hurdler.

Beware The Bear takes the final fence in front of Vintage Clouds before striking at last season's Cheltenham Festival

Bob Mahler (Ire)

7 b g Mahler - Cooladurragh (Topanoora)

Warren Greatrex   Bolingbroke, Bunch, Howard & Sutton

PLACINGS: 33UF/532212/823811-P   RPR **143**+c

Starts	1st	2nd	3rd	4th	Win & Pl
18	3	4	5	-	£35,967

132	4/19	Chel	3m1¹/₂f Cls3 Nov 114-133 Ch Hcap good..........£10,840
128	3/19	Newb	2m7¹/₂f Cls3 Nov 114-136 Ch Hcap gd-sft £7,343
	3/18	Weth	3m Cls4 Nov Hdl soft.....................................£4,484

Patchy record when sent chasing last season but hit form in the spring, winning novice handicaps at Sandown (beat good subsequent winner Larry) and Cheltenham (by seven lengths); pulled up at Uttoxeter in May; trainer sees him as a Ladbrokes Trophy type.

Borice (Fr)

8 b g Network - Judice (Agent Bleu)

Gordon Elliott (Ir)   Simon Munir & Isaac Souede

PLACINGS: 8/2122424P3/7509-111   RPR **144**+c

Starts	1st	2nd	3rd	4th	Win & Pl
29	6	8	2	2	£421,688

136	7/19	Gway	2m6¹/₂f 135-158 Ch Hcap good..........................£159,459
	7/19	Prth	2m4f Cls4 Nov Hdl gd-sft...............................£4,431
	6/19	Uttx	2m7¹/₂f Cls4 Nov Hdl gd-sft...........................£4,194
	6/17	Autl	2m4f Ch 5-6yo v soft....................................£30,769
	10/16	Autl	2m5¹/₂f Ch 5yo v soft...................................£19,412
	7/16	Lign	2m2f Ch 4-5yo good.....................................£4,235

Bought to join Gordon Elliott last year and got things right in his third crack at a major staying handicap when winning the Galway Plate this summer; also still a novice over hurdles and had looked adept in that discipline with two wide-margin victories prior to Galway.

Born Survivor (Ire)

8 b g King's Theatre - Bob's Flame (Bob Back)

Dan Skelton   Mrs G Widdowson & Mrs R Kelvin-Hughes

PLACINGS: /243F60/13380/17141-   RPR **153**+c

Starts	1st	2nd	3rd	4th	Win & Pl
19	6	1	3	3	£89,322

142	4/19	Ayr	2m4¹/₂f Cls1 List 130-152 Ch Hcap good...........£28,475
139	11/18	Weth	2m3¹/₂f Cls1 List 129-151 Ch Hcap good.............£17,085
137	5/18	Sthl	2m4¹/₂f Cls3 111-137 Ch Hcap good.................£10,007
	11/17	Weth	1m7f Cls3 Nov Ch soft...................................£6,657
	2/16	Weth	2m3¹/₂f Cls4 Nov Hdl good............................£3,249
	12/15	Wwck	2m5f Cls4 Nov Hdl soft.................................£3,249

Long held in high regard (sent off 6-4 for a Grade 2 novice hurdle at Warwick in January 2016) but had been largely disappointing until progressing well over fences last season; won his second Listed handicap of the campaign at Ayr in April but raised 10lb for that.

Boyhood (Ire)

8 b g Oscar - Glen Dubh (Supreme Leader)

Tom George   H Stephen Smith & The Gabbertas Family

PLACINGS: 613/2214/141/230-1   RPR **144**h

Starts	1st	2nd	3rd	4th	Win & Pl
13	5	3	2	2	£53,773

	5/19	NAbb	3m2f Cls3 Ch gd-sft.....................................£9,357
130	1/18	Chel	3m Cls2 123-142 Hdl Hcap heavy....................£15,640
123	11/17	Ling	2m3¹/₂f Cls3 112-125 Hdl Hcap soft..................£6,963
116	11/16	Donc	2m3¹/₂f Cls4 Nov 105-118 Hdl Hcap gd-sft.........£4,549
	2/16	Muss	1m7¹/₂f Cls6 NHF 4-6yo soft...........................£1,949

Lightly raced in recent seasons but has run well in good staying handicap hurdles; missed nearly a year with a splint problem after winning at Cheltenham in January 2018 but returned to be second there again last term; made a winning chase debut in May.

Braid Blue (Ire)

6 b g Gold Well - Outo'Theblue (Grand Lodge)

Gordon Elliott (Ir)   P J McBurney

PLACINGS: 115561-111   RPR **145**+h

Starts	1st	2nd	3rd	4th	Win & Pl
9	6	-	-	-	£26,239

	7/19	Prth	3m Cls4 Nov Hdl good...................................£4,431
	7/19	Ffos	3m Cls4 Nov Hdl good...................................£4,029
	6/19	Prth	2m4f Cls4 Nov Hdl good................................£4,549
	4/19	Prth	2m4f Cls4 Mdn Hdl good...............................£4,431
	8/18	Prth	2m Cls4 NHF 4-6yo good...............................£3,165
	7/18	Kbgn	2m4f NHF 5-7yo good....................................£5,451

Outstanding novice hurdler of the summer and won for the third time at Perth (completing a four-timer in total) at the end of July; looked even better when stepped up to 3m; loses novice status at the end of November.

Brain Power (Ire)

8 b g Kalanisi - Blonde Ambition (Old Vic)

Nicky Henderson   Michael Buckley

PLACINGS: 1/381185/1UF2F/41PP-   RPR **157**+

Starts	1st	2nd	3rd	4th	Win & Pl
20	7	2	1	1	£267,914

	12/18	Chel	2m1f Cls1 Gd2 Hdl gd-sft..............................£78,846
	11/17	Kemp	2m2f Cls4 Nov Ch gd-sft................................£4,660
149	12/16	Asct	1m7¹/₂f Cls1 Gd3 125-150 Hdl Hcap gd-sft.........£85,425
142	12/16	Sand	2m Cls1 List 120-144 Hdl Hcap gd-sft...............£33,762
	3/16	Kemp	2m Cls4 Nov Hdl good..................................£3,249
	11/15	Kemp	2m Cls4 Nov Hdl 4-6yo gd-sft.........................£3,899
	2/15	Newc	2m1¹/₂f Cls6 NHF 4-6yo gd-sft........................£1,560

Has an increasingly patchy record but managed to win last season's International Hurdle before twice flopping in the spring; had finished second in the Racing Post Arkle in 2018 but was soon switched back to hurdles last term after a disappointing reappearance over fences.

Brandon Castle

7 b g Dylan Thomas - Chelsey Jayne (Galileo)

Neil King   I A Low & J S English

PLACINGS: 111P8-   RPR **142+**h

Starts	1st	2nd	3rd	4th	Win & Pl
5	3				£15,725

130	2/19	Plum	2m Cls3 112-132 Hdl Hcap good	£6,238
	1/19	Plum	2m Cls4 Nov Hdl gd-sft	£5,393
	12/18	Plum	2m Cls4 Nov Hdl soft	£4,094

Useful and progressive Flat stayer who won first three races when switched to hurdles last season, including by nine lengths on handicap debut at Plumpton; disappointing when favourite back there for the Sussex Champion Hurdle after being pulled up in the Supreme.

Brave Eagle (Ire)

7 b g Yeats - Sinful Pleasure (Sinndar)

Nicky Henderson   Robert Kirkland

PLACINGS: 33/11/210U/112113-11   RPR **162+**c

Starts	1st	2nd	3rd	4th	Win & Pl
14	9	2	1	-	£107,308

152	6/19	Uttx	3m2f Cls1 List 126-152 Ch Hcap good	£39,389
144	5/19	Hayd	2m4¹/₂f Cls2 127-144 Ch Hcap good	£18,768
	8/18	Font	2m5¹/₂f Cls4 Nov Ch good	£4,614
	7/18	Worc	2m7f Cls4 Ch good	£4,614
139	6/18	Sthl	3m Cls3 114-139 Hdl Hcap good	£6,238
134	5/18	Plum	2m4¹/₂f Cls3 109-134 Cond Hdl Hcap good	£6,238
131	12/17	Newb	2m4¹/₂f Cls2 131-141 Hdl Hcap heavy	£11,303
	3/17	Font	2m3f Cls4 Nov Hdl good	£3,639
	1/17	Ludl	2m Cls4 Mdn Hdl soft	£3,249

Took record over fences to four out of five when winning the valuable Summer Cup at Uttoxeter

in June off a mark of 152; has run only on good ground since disappointing on soft in the 2018 Martin Pipe Hurdle but had won on heavy at Newbury prior to that.

Brelan D'As (Fr)

8 b g Crillon - Las De La Croix (Grand Tresor)

Paul Nicholls   John P McManus

PLACINGS: 41P/1/33500/2215135-   RPR **142**c

Starts	1st	2nd	3rd	4th	Win & Pl
17	5	2	3	1	£68,496

	2/19	Fknm	2m¹/₂f Cls3 Nov Ch good	£8,058
	12/18	Hayd	1m7¹/₂f Cls3 Nov Ch heavy	£9,615
130	11/16	Winc	2m4f Cls3 115-135 Hdl Hcap good	£5,848
	10/15	Sabl	2m1f Hdl 4yo gd-sft	£8,558
	8/15	Gran	1m7f NHF 4-5yo gd-sft	£3,876

Slow learner over fences (initial novice chase campaign aborted two seasons ago) but won at Haydock and Fakenham last term before a third in the Grand Annual on handicap debut; won at 2m4f over hurdles in 2016 but 0-7 beyond 2m since.

Brewin'upastorm (Ire)

6 b g Milan - Daraheen Diamond (Husyan)

Olly Murphy   Mrs Barbara Hester

PLACINGS: 1/14/14F42-   RPR **149**h

Starts	1st	2nd	3rd	4th	Win & Pl
7	2	1	-	3	£39,322

	12/18	Hntg	2m Cls4 Nov Hdl gd-sft	£5,523
	1/18	Hrfd	2m Cls5 Am NHF 4-6yo soft	£2,599

Ran consistently well in top 2m4f-2m5f novice

Born Survivor puts in a huge leap before scoring at Ayr in April

hurdles last season and might well have beaten Birchdale in a Grade 2 at Cheltenham but for falling at the last; fourth in the Ballymore at Cheltenham next time before chasing home Reserve Tank at Punchestown.

Bright Forecast (Ire)

5 b g Arcadio - Check The Forecast (Shernazar)

Ben Pauling   The Aldaniti Partnership

PLACINGS: 3/1123-   RPR **150**h

Starts	1st	2nd	3rd	4th	Win & Pl
4	2	1	1	-	£33,189
12/18	Leic	1m7¹/₂f Cls3 Nov Hdl good			£6,758
11/18	Newb	2m¹/₂f Cls3 Mdn Hdl soft			£6,758

Ran a huge race when third in the Ballymore Novices' Hurdle at Cheltenham behind City Island and Champ, staying on from the rear; had shown smart form over 2m prior to that but saw out longer 2m5f trip well and looked likely to get further; could go novice chasing.

Brio Conti (Fr)

8 gr g Dom Alco - Cadoulie Wood (Cadoudal)

Paul Nicholls   The Gi Gi Syndicate

PLACINGS: 3/1F28115/1/P14P-   RPR **149**h

Starts	1st	2nd	3rd	4th	Win & Pl
13	5	1	1	1	£70,627
141	2/19	Asct	2m3¹/₂f Cls2 122-148 Hdl Hcap gd-sft		£28,152
	11/17	Carl	2m4f Cls3 Nov Ch soft		£6,498
134	3/17	Kemp	2m5f Cls5 125-137 Hdl Hcap good		£20,645
	1/17	Donc	2m3¹/₂f Cls5 Mdn Hdl good		£3,249
	5/16	Strf	2m¹/₂f Cls5 Mdn Hdl 4-6yo gd-sft		£2,274

Useful novice hurdler three seasons ago and returned from more than a year off by running well in top handicaps last season, winning at Ascot and finishing a close fourth in the Coral Cup; had won sole start over fences in late 2017 before long absence.

Bristol De Mai (Fr)

8 gr g Saddler Maker - La Bole Night (April Night)

Nigel Twiston-Davies   Simon Munir & Isaac Souede

PLACINGS: 2/221375/11632/1F34-   RPR **176+**c

Starts	1st	2nd	3rd	4th	Win & Pl
30	10	8	5	2	£643,788
	11/18	Hayd	3m1¹/₂f Cls1 Gd1 Ch good		£112,540
	11/17	Hayd	3m1¹/₂f Cls1 Gd1 Ch heavy		£113,072
	11/17	Weth	3m Cls1 Gd2 Ch soft		£57,218
154	1/17	Hayd	3m Cls1 Gd2 142-162 Ch Hcap soft		£28,475
	2/16	Sand	2m4f Cls1 Nov Gd1 Ch gd-sft		£25,628
	1/16	Hayd	2m4f Cls1 Nov Ch heavy		£18,438
	12/15	Leic	2m4f Cls3 Nov Ch soft		£6,330
	11/15	Wwck	2m Cls3 Nov Ch 4-5yo gd-sft		£9,384
	12/14	Chep	2m Cls1 Gd1 Hdl 3yo heavy		£19,933
	9/14	Autl	2m2f Hdl 3yo v soft		£19,200

Has won the Betfair Chase for the last two seasons with fine front-running performances, but also proved himself much more than a Haydock specialist last term with a fine third in the Cheltenham Gold Cup last March; hard to keep right according to his trainer but has been more consistent since wind surgery in 2018.

Bun Doran (Ire)

8 b g Shantou - Village Queen (King's Theatre)

Tom George   Crossed Fingers Partnership

PLACINGS: 153/31P63/2335/122-5   RPR **155**c

Starts	1st	2nd	3rd	4th	Win & Pl
18	4	3	5	1	£99,607
138	11/18	Chel	2m Cls2 122-140 Ch Hcap good		£27,855
134	12/16	Newc	2m4f Cls3 109-135 Ch Hcap soft		£9,747
	1/16	Hayd	2m3f Cls4 Nov Hdl 4-7yo heavy		£3,899
	11/15	Chep	2m Cls6 NHF 4-6yo soft		£1,560

Has a poor strike-rate but has consistently run well in top 2m handicap chases over the last two seasons; finally won a good race at Cheltenham last term and improved again when second twice more at the track, including in the Grand Annual in March.

Burrows Saint (Fr)

6 b g Saint Des Saints - La Bombonera (Mansonnien)

Willie Mullins (Ir)   Mrs S Ricci

PLACINGS: 62/2742/1203/4111-5   RPR **155+**c

Starts	1st	2nd	3rd	4th	Win & Pl
15	4	4	1	2	£350,401
144	4/19	Fair	3m5f 135-157 Ch Hcap gd-yld		£243,243
	3/19	Limk	3m1¹/₂f Nov Gd3 Ch good		£22,590
	3/19	Gowr	2m4f Ch soft		£8,047
	11/17	Punc	2m4f Mdn Hdl 4yo sft-hvy		£7,108

Impressive winner of last season's Irish Grand National on just his fourth start over fences; had won over 2m4f and 3m prior to that and should have no problems dropping back in trip having travelled strongly at Fairyhouse; finished fifth in the Grand Steeple-Chase de Paris during the summer.

Buveur D'Air (Fr)

8 b g Crillon - History (Alesso)

Nicky Henderson   John P McManus

PLACINGS: 1/11111/1111/121F2-1   RPR **173+**h

Starts	1st	2nd	3rd	4th	Win & Pl
23	17	3	1	1	£1,186,775
	5/19	Punc	2m Gd1 Hdl gd-yld		£159,459
	2/19	Sand	2m Cls1 List Hdl soft		£17,286
	12/18	Newc	2m¹/₂f Cls1 Gd1 Hdl soft		£62,629
	3/18	Chel	2m¹/₂f Cls1 Gd1 Hdl heavy		£266,384
	2/18	Sand	2m Cls1 List Hdl soft		£17,085
	12/17	Kemp	2m Cls1 Gd1 Hdl soft		£68,340
	12/17	Newc	2m¹/₂f Cls1 Gd1 Hdl soft		£61,897
	4/17	Aint	2m4f Cls1 Gd1 Hdl good		£112,260
	3/17	Chel	2m¹/₂f Cls1 Gd1 Hdl gd-sft		£227,800
	2/17	Sand	2m Cls1 List Hdl heavy		£14,238
	12/16	Wwck	2m Cls4 Nov Ch soft		£5,198
	12/16	Hayd	1m7¹/₂f Cls2 Nov Ch soft		£11,574
	4/16	Aint	2m¹/₂f Cls1 Nov Gd1 Hdl soft		£42,203
	1/16	Hntg	2m4f Cls4 Nov Hdl gd-sft		£3,249
	11/15	Newb	2m¹/₂f Cls3 Mdn Hdl soft		£6,498
	10/14	Nant	1m4f NHF 3yo gd-sft		£6,650
	8/14	Sjdm	1m5f NHF 3yo soft		£4,167

Won the Champion Hurdle in 2017 and 2018 but lost his air of invincibility last season when twice beaten either side of a fall in his hat-trick bid at Cheltenham; got back on track with a Grade 1 win at the Punchestown festival on his final run, albeit in a modest race for the grade.

Injured Jockeys Fund

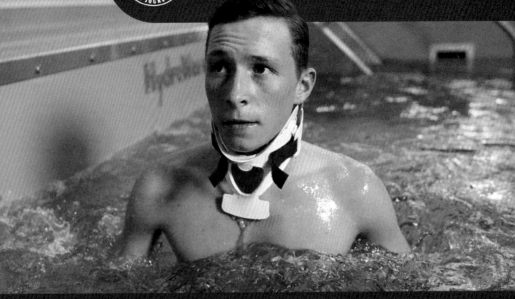

We provide appropriate support in a prompt and sympathetic manner to those jockeys, past or present, who are injured, unable to ride, or generally in need.

As a not-for-profit, self funding organisation we are reliant on the support and generosity of our supporters.

To find out how you can become involved and support the Injured Jockeys Fund or make a donation please visit us at:

www.ijf.org.uk

or call: **01638 662246**

Sir Anthony McCoy OBE
President - Injured Jockeys Fund

Compassion • Care • Support
Injured Jockeys Fund (Registered Charity No. 1107395)

Cadmium (Fr)

7 b g Early March - Mirquille (Passing Sale)

Willie Mullins (Ir)　　　Supreme Horse Racing Club & Kenneth Sharp

PLACINGS: 4/1/3141/1521344121-　　　RPR **165**+c

Starts		1st	2nd	3rd	4th	Win & Pl
17		2	7	2	4	£206,285
152	4/19	Aint	2m5f Cls1 Gd3 136-162 Ch Hcap soft			£78,582
	2/19	Naas	2m Gd3 Ch good			£24,716
	10/18	Punc	2m2¹/₂f Nov Gd3 Ch good			£17,688
	6/18	Rosc	2m Nov Ch good			£7,632
133	4/18	Punc	2m 122-150 Ch Hcap yld-sft			£33,938
	2/18	Fair	2m1¹/₂f Ch soft			£9,267
	12/16	Limk	2m3f Mdn Hdl yield			£4,522

Took a long time to build on promise of runaway win at Punchestown in April 2018 but seems to relish bigger fields than has often been the case and flourished in another big handicap when landing the Topham at Aintree in April.

Caid Du Lin (Fr)

7 gr g Della Francesca - Asia Du Lin (Agent Bleu)

Dr Richard Newland　　　　　Foxtrot Racing

PLACINGS: /2317220P2/12P21027-　　　RPR **150**c

Starts		1st	2nd	3rd	4th	Win & Pl
25		4	8	3	-	£139,450
139	11/18	Asct	2m1f Cls2 135-154 Ch Hcap gd-sft			£78,200
	9/18	Worc	2m1/2f Cls4 Nov Ch good			£4,614
127	10/17	Font	2m1¹/₂f Cls3 105-127 Hdl Hcap good			£5,848
	10/16	Nior	2m3f Hdl 4yo gd-sft			£7,059

Took well to fences last autumn and won a valuable 2m1f handicap chase at Ascot; mixed form when back from a break in the spring (doesn't appreciate soft ground according to his trainer) but ran another good race at Ascot when beaten a head in a novice handicap.

Calett Mad (Fr)

7 b/br g Axxos - Ornelia (April Night)

Nigel Twiston-Davies　　　Simon Munir & Isaac Souede

PLACINGS: 12952/11541P1/94522-　　　RPR **152**c

Starts		1st	2nd	3rd	4th	Win & Pl
22		6	5	2	3	£129,153
138	4/18	Prth	3m Cls1 Nov List Hdl soft			£15,575
	2/18	Muss	3m2f Cls2 117-142 Hdl Hcap soft			£12,996
	10/17	Chel	3m Cls3 Nov Hdl good			£6,343
	9/17	Prth	3m Cls4 Nov Hdl heavy			£3,399
138	1/17	Tntn	2m7f Cls3 128-138 Ch Hcap good			£8,229
130	11/16	Newc	2m7¹/₂f Cls3 Nov 124-135 Ch Hcap soft			£9,986

Has long shaped like an out-and-out stayer and improved when stepped up to marathon distances last season, finishing a half-length second in the Borders National at Kelso and filling the same spot in the Classic Chase at Warwick.

Calipto (Fr)

9 b g Califet - Peutiot (Valanour)

Venetia Williams　　　　　Lady Bolton

PLACINGS: 338/6F/5551/U5U131P-　　　RPR **152**+c

Starts		1st	2nd	3rd	4th	Win & Pl
26		6	2	4	2	£148,902
143	2/19	Asct	3m Cls1 List 140-159 Ch Hcap gd-sft			£42,713
138	1/19	Winc	2m4f Cls2 129-149 Ch Hcap good			£12,996
129	3/18	Carl	2m4f Cls3 109-130 Ch Hcap gd-sft			£8,447
	10/15	Font	2m3f Cls4 Ch gd-sft			£6,498
	2/14	Newb	2m1¹/₂f Cls3 Nov Hdl heavy			£6,498
	11/13	Newb	2m1¹/₂f Cls3 Hdl 3yo gd-sft			£6,498

Lost his way having once looked a promising

Calipto (right) scored twice last season after a lengthy spell below his best

youngster for Paul Nicholls but coaxed back to form by Venetia Williams last season, winning handicaps at Wincanton and Ascot; still not very fluent with his jumping and let down by mistakes in top handicaps.

Call Me Lord (Fr)

6 b/br g Slickly - Sosa (Cape Cross)

Nicky Henderson   Simon Munir & Isaac Souede

PLACINGS: 5111/31321/73-   RPR **161**h

Starts	1st	2nd	3rd	4th	Win & Pl
11	5	1	3	-	£143,102
	4/18	Sand	2m5¹/₂f Cls1 Gd2 Hdl gd-sft.......................£31,323		
143	1/18	Sand	2m Cls2 117-143 Hdl Hcap heavy......................£15,640		
135	4/17	Sand	2m Cls2 109-135 Hdl 4yo Hcap good.............£31,280		
	3/17	Comp	2m2f Hdl 4yo heavy..£19,692		
	12/16	Cagn	2m¹/₂f Hdl 3yo soft..£11,294		

Lightly raced since moving from France as a juvenile and has had five out of eight runs at Sandown due to reported need for a right-handed track, winning three times and being placed in the last two runnings of the Imperial Cup; didn't stay 3m when favourite for the Long Walk.

Capeland (Fr)

7 b g Poliglote - Neiland (Cyborg)

Paul Nicholls   Mrs Kathy Stuart

PLACINGS: 162/242/22211212284-   RPR **150+**c

Starts	1st	2nd	3rd	4th	Win & Pl
20	6	10	-	2	£91,281
133	12/18	Ludl	2m Cls2 120-147 Ch Hcap soft.........................£16,458		
130	11/18	Winc	1m7¹/₂f Cls3 Nov 112-130 Ch Hcap gd-fm.......£10,397		
127	11/18	Winc	2m4f Cls3 105-127 Cond Ch Hcap good.........£10,072		
	10/16	NAbb	2m2¹/₂f Cls4 Nov Hdl good.................................£4,549		
	1/16	Chel	1m6f Cls1 List NHF 4yo heavy.........................£11,888		
	5/15	Le L	1m3¹/₂f NHF 3yo heavy.......................................£5,814		

Consistent and progressive novice chaser last season, finishing first or second in all ten races before taking a big step up in class for the JLT at Cheltenham (creeping into contention when making a bad blunder four out); pulled too hard off a slow gallop on final run at Ascot.

Captain Cattistock

6 b g Black Sam Bellamy - Pearl Buttons (Alflora)

Paul Nicholls   Peter Hart

PLACINGS: 1/411414/6F3131-   RPR **147**c

Starts	1st	2nd	3rd	4th	Win & Pl
12	5	-	2	3	£40,081
	4/19	Font	3m2f Cls4 Nov Ch good....................................£4,614		
137	2/19	Extr	3m Cls3 Nov 118-137 Ch Hcap gd-sft.............£10,397		
	3/18	Winc	2m5¹/₂f Cls4 Nov Hdl heavy...............................£4,224		
130	2/18	Winc	2m4f Cls3 115-130 Hdl Hcap heavy...................£8,814		
	11/17	Winc	2m5¹/₂f Cls4 Nov Hdl soft...................................£4,224		

Described in glowing terms by his trainer before going chasing last season and progressed fairly

Carefully Selected (Ire)

7 b g Well Chosen - Knockamullen Girl (Alderbrook)

Willie Mullins (Ir)   Miss M A Masterson

PLACINGS: 21/1123/1-3   RPR **147**h

Starts	1st	2nd	3rd	4th	Win & Pl
6	3	1	2	-	£52,719
	3/19	Limk	2m6f Mdn Hdl heavy...£7,214		
	2/18	Naas	2m NHF 4-7yo soft...£7,087		
	12/17	Leop	2m4f NHF 4-7yo soft...£6,318		

Missed nearly all of last season but made a winning start over hurdles at Limerick in March before coming third to Minella Indo in a 3m Grade 1 at Punchestown; had been a top-class bumper performer, finishing second in the 2018 Champion Bumper at Cheltenham.

Casablanca Mix (Fr)

7 ch m Shirocco - Latitude (Kadalko)

Nicky Henderson   Evan-Robert Hanbury

PLACINGS: 4513P4/321F/22930-11   RPR **154+**c

Starts	1st	2nd	3rd	4th	Win & Pl
23	8	3	4	3	£144,275
143	7/19	MRas	2m5¹/₂f Cls1 List 125-149 Ch Hcap gd-sft.......£28,475		
138	5/19	Aint	2m4f Cls3 132-141 Ch Hcap good....................£9,097		
	11/17	Hntg	2m4f Cls4 Nov Ch gd-sft....................................£5,198		
	9/16	Autl	2m2f Hdl 4yo v soft..£18,353		
	5/16	Autl	2m2f Hdl 4yo heavy...£16,941		
	4/16	Mlns	2m4f 4-5yo gd-sft..£6,353		
	11/15	Pari	1m4f NHF 3yo heavy..£11,628		
	10/15	Fntb	1m5f NHF 3yo v soft...£5,814		

Largely disappointing last season but came good this summer, easily winning the Summer Plate at Market Rasen; said to love fast ground by her trainer but ran well on only run on soft since arriving from France (set to win a novice chase easily until falling at the last).

Cash Back (Fr)

7 b g Linda's Lad - Holding (Useful)

Willie Mullins (Ir)   Watch This Space Syndicate

PLACINGS: 82677/22/12-5   RPR **140**h

Starts	1st	2nd	3rd	4th	Win & Pl
10	1	4	-	-	£37,599
	3/19	Thur	2m Mdn Hdl gd-yld..£6,105		

Late starter over hurdles last season having missed more than a year after move from France but soon made an impression, easily winning a maiden hurdle at Thurles and finishing second in a Grade 2 at Fairyhouse; looks a fine chasing type.

Castlegrace Paddy (Ire)

8 b g Flemensfirth - Thunder Road (Mtoto)

Pat Fahy (Ir)　　　　　　　　Clipper Logistics Group

PLACINGS: 2/42415/115/14F6-3　　　　RPR **159**c

Starts	1st	2nd	3rd	4th	Win & Pl
13	4	1	1	3	£100,762

	12/18	Cork	2m¹/₂f Gd2 Ch soft	£31,327
	3/18	Thur	2m2f Nov List Ch soft	£16,327
	12/17	Fair	2m Ch heavy	£7,897
	3/17	Gowr	2m Mdn Hdl sft-hvy	£6,844

Made it three wins out of four over fences with winning reappearance in a Grade 2 last season and acquitted himself well in the face of some stiff tasks subsequently; not beaten far in a Grade 1 at Leopardstown over Christmas and a fair sixth in the Champion Chase at Cheltenham.

Cepage (Fr)

7 b g Saddler Maker - Sience Fiction (Dom Alco)

Venetia Williams　　　　　　The Bellamy Partnership

PLACINGS: 531/4141F33/23414/2-　　　RPR **152**c

Starts	1st	2nd	3rd	4th	Win & Pl
18	4	3	4	5	£108,948

136	3/18	Kemp	2m4¹/₂f Cls2 127-139 Ch Hcap soft	£25,024
119	12/16	Newb	2m¹/₂f Cls4 99-119 Ch Hcap gd-sft	£4,549
	5/16	Lign	2m5¹/₂f Ch 4yo v soft	£4,588
	4/16	Pari	2m3f Hdl 4yo v soft	£7,412

Progressive handicap chaser who ran a huge race on sole outing last season when second to Frodon in the Caspian Caviar Gold Cup, pulling 15 lengths clear of the third; missed the rest of the season but now back in training.

Ch'tibello (Fr)

8 b g Sageburg - Neicha (Neverneyev)

Dan Skelton　　　　　The Can't Say No Partnership

PLACINGS: /35132/42280/569213-　　　RPR **158**+h

Starts	1st	2nd	3rd	4th	Win & Pl
21	4	6	4	1	£294,023

146	3/19	Chel	2m1f Cls1 Gd3 127-153 Hdl Hcap gd-sft	£56,270
	11/16	Hayd	2m Cls2 Hdl heavy	£61,900
135	4/16	Ayr	2m Cls1 Gd2 133-147 Hdl Hcap gd-sft	£57,520
	4/15	Comp	2m1f Hdl 4yo v soft	£8,186

Back on track after wind surgery last season and made the most of a lenient handicap mark to win last season's County Hurdle at Cheltenham having dropped 11lb from his peak; close third in the Aintree Hurdle next time when placed in a Grade 1 or Grade 2 for the fifth time.

Chacun Pour Soi (Fr)

7 b g Policy Maker - Kruscyna (Ultimately Lucky)

Willie Mullins (Ir)　　　　　　　　Mrs S Ricci

PLACINGS: 1253/1-1　　　　RPR **165**+c

Starts	1st	2nd	3rd	4th	Win & Pl
6	3	1	1	-	£94,733

	5/19	Punc	2m Nov Gd1 Ch yield	£61,126
	3/19	Naas	2m Ch yld-sft	£8,047
	8/15	Diep	2m1f Hdl 3yo v soft	£8,558

Hadn't run for nearly two and a half years before winning at Naas in March but quickly proved arguably the best 2m novice chaser of last season, beating Cheltenham Festival winners Defi Du Seuil and Duc Des Genievres at Punchestown; trainer expects him to get further.

Champ (Ire)

7 b g King's Theatre - China Sky (Definite Article)

Nicky Henderson　　　　　　　　John P McManus

PLACINGS: 12/2/111121-　　　　RPR **153**+h

Starts	1st	2nd	3rd	4th	Win & Pl
9	6	3	-	-	£147,822

	4/19	Aint	3m¹/₂f Cls1 Nov Gd1 Hdl soft	£56,130
	12/18	Newb	2m4¹/₂f Cls1 Nov Gd1 Hdl gd-sft	£25,628
139	12/18	Newb	2m4¹/₂f Cls2 120-145 Hdl Hcap soft	£25,992
	5/18	Wwck	2m5¹/₂f Cls4 Nov Hdl gd-sft	£4,549
	5/18	Prth	2m4f Cls4 Mdn Hdl good	£4,224
	1/17	Sthl	1m7¹/₂f Cls6 Mdn NHF 4-6yo soft	£2,053

Top-class novice hurdler last season, winning five out of six with sole defeat coming when second to City Island in the Ballymore Novices' Hurdle; smooth winner of the Sefton at Aintree when stepped up to 3m; set to go novice chasing.

Champagne Classic (Ire)

8 b g Stowaway - Classical Rachel (Shahanndeh)

Gordon Elliott (Ir)　　　　　Gigginstown House Stud

PLACINGS: 1/212321311/32-　　　RPR **145**+c

Starts	1st	2nd	3rd	4th	Win & Pl
11	4	4	3	-	£121,290

	4/17	Punc	3m Nov Gd1 Hdl gd-yld	£50,427
138	3/17	Chel	2m4¹/₂f Cls1 Nov 125-145 Cond Hdl Hcap good	£40,664
	2/17	Thur	2m6¹/₂f Mdn Hdl soft	£5,791
	11/16	Fair	2m4f NHF 4-7yo soft	£4,070

Top-class novice hurdler three seasons ago (won the Martin Pipe at Cheltenham and followed up in a 3m Grade 1 at Punchestown) but missed the following campaign and ran just twice last term; placed in two good novice chases, including a half-length second to Chris's Dream.

Champagne Platinum (Ire)

5 gr g Stowaway - Saffron Holly (Roselier)

Nicky Henderson　　　　　　　　John P McManus

PLACINGS: 1/11-5　　　　RPR **134**+h

Starts	1st	2nd	3rd	4th	Win & Pl
3	2	-	-	-	£10,704

	12/18	Newb	2m¹/₂f Cls4 Hdl gd-sft	£4,809
	12/18	Newc	2m¹/₂f Cls4 Mdn Hdl 4-6yo soft	£4,094

Won first two novice hurdles impressively last season but missed the Cheltenham Festival with a

foot problem and only fifth of six when returning in a Grade 1 at Punchestown; described by his trainer as a fantastic novice chase prospect.

Charbel (Ire)

8 b g Iffraaj - Eoz (Sadler's Wells)

Kim Bailey				Mrs Julie Martin & David R Martin

PLACINGS: /512F3/44F/312135P6-				RPR **163+**c

Starts	1st	2nd	3rd	4th	Win & Pl
24	7	4	3	3	£183,735
	12/18	Hntg	2m4f Cls1 Gd2 Ch gd-sft		£37,018
154	10/18	Chep	2m3¹/₂f Cls2 128-154 Ch Hcap gd-sft		£25,024
	10/16	Uttx	2m Cls3 Ch good		£9,384
	2/16	Muss	1m7¹/₂f Cls2 Nov Hdl gd-sft		£14,389
	10/15	Strf	2m¹/₂f Cls3 Nov Hdl 4-6yo good		£6,498
	3/15	Limk	2m List NHF 4yo heavy		£12,597
	2/15	Leop	2m NHF 4yo soft		£5,349

Plagued by jumping issues and lost his way again towards the end of last season but had underlined his talent with some big performances earlier in the campaign; ran Politologue to half a length at Ascot before hacking up by eight lengths in the Peterborough Chase.

Charmant (Fr)

7 b g Balko - Ravissante (Mad Tax)

James Ewart				A Phillips & Mr & Mrs Sperling

PLACINGS: 3365324/11424/1141F-				RPR **144+**c

Starts	1st	2nd	3rd	4th	Win & Pl
18	5	2	4	4	£35,276
133	3/19	Ayr	2m¹/₂f Cls3 123-135 Ch Hcap soft		£9,357
125	12/18	Kels	2m1f Cls3 113-132 Ch Hcap good		£8,187
117	11/18	Sedg	2m¹/₂f Cls4 Nov 105-118 Ch Hcap good		£4,614
110	12/17	Ayr	2m Cls4 84-110 Hdl Hcap heavy		£3,899
102	12/17	Sedg	2m1f Cls5 Nov 79-102 Hdl Hcap soft		£2,599

Took to fences brilliantly last season, showing much-improved form as he won three times at around 2m; stepped up to 2m4f at Carlisle on final run but stamina yet to be tested when fell five out (still going well); had otherwise looked an assured jumper.

Chesterfield (Ire)

9 ch g Pivotal - Antique (Dubai Millennium)

Seamus Mullins				The Rumble Racing Club

PLACINGS: 1F/80211/00443/2231-				RPR **145+**c

Starts	1st	2nd	3rd	4th	Win & Pl
19	6	4	2	2	£166,233
	11/18	Kemp	2m2f Cls4 Ch good		£4,938
	3/18	Kemp	2m Cls4 NHF std-slw		£4,874
143	4/17	Ayr	2m Cls1 Gd2 135-155 Hdl Hcap good		£59,798
132	4/17	Aint	2m¹/₂f Cls2 120-143 Am Hdl Hcap good		£30,950
123	11/14	Chel	2m¹/₂f Cls3 Nov 100-130 Hdl Hcap soft		£7,507
	10/14	Hntg	2m Cls4 Nov Hdl good		£3,899
	7/14	Worc	2m Cls4 Nov Hdl good		£3,249

Smart 2m handicap hurdler (first and third in successive Scottish Champion Hurdles) before belatedly being sent over fences last season; twice ran well in defeat before getting off the mark at Kempton; had been seen by trainer as a live Arkle outsider before being ruled out by injury.

Chief Justice

4 b g Acclamation - Freedom Pass (Gulch)

Gordon Elliott (Ir)				Irvin S Naylor

PLACINGS: 2111212501-4				RPR **138+**h

Starts	1st	2nd	3rd	4th	Win & Pl
11	5	3		1	£93,276
137	4/19	Aint	2m¹/₂f Cls2 115-141 Am Hdl Hcap good		£30,950
	12/18	Fair	2m Gd3 Hdl 3yo good		£17,688
	10/18	Gowr	2m Hdl 3yo good		£8,177
	9/18	List	2m Hdl 3yo good		£10,903
	8/18	Worc	2m Cls4 Nov Hdl 3yo gd-sft		£4,094

Very useful juvenile hurdler last season and won for the fifth time at Aintree's Grand National meeting in an open handicap; had been well beaten in the Fred Winter Hurdle but reportedly didn't have a good preparation (given wind surgery since previous run).

Chosen Mate (Ire)

6 br g Well Chosen - Norwich Star (Norwich)

Gordon Elliott (Ir)				The Northern Four Racing Partnership

PLACINGS: P/11215-P				RPR **144**h

Starts	1st	2nd	3rd	4th	Win & Pl
5	2	1	-	-	£40,143
	2/19	Naas	2m Nov Gd2 Hdl good		£24,716
	1/19	Fair	2m Mdn Hdl yield		£7,214

Bought at Cheltenham sales last November after winning a point-to-point and went on to win two novice hurdles, including a 2m Grade 2 at Naas in February; fair effort when fifth at Grade 1 level at Aintree, seemingly just failing to see out longer 2m4f trip; badly hampered when pulled up in Galway Hurdle.

Chris's Dream (Ire)

7 b g Mahler - Janebailey (Silver Patriarch)

Henry de Bromhead (Ir)				Robcour

PLACINGS: 010/62119/1215-P				RPR **146+**c

Starts	1st	2nd	3rd	4th	Win & Pl
12	4	2	-	-	£70,926
	2/19	Navn	3m Nov Gd2 Ch yield		£23,919
	12/18	Navn	2m4f Ch yield		£7,904
	2/18	Clon	3m Nov Gd3 Hdl heavy		£20,409
	12/17	Limk	2m3f Mdn Hdl soft		£5,771

Has looked good in winning two novice chases and two novice hurdles in the last two seasons, most notably a 3m Grade 2 chase against Champagne Classic in February; disappointing in all three runs at Grade 1 level, doing best when a moderate fifth at Aintree in April.

Christopher Wood (Ire)

4 b g Fast Company - Surf The Web (Ela-Mana-Mou)

Paul Nicholls				Ms Sharon Kinsella

PLACINGS: 113-0				RPR **140**h

Starts	1st	2nd	3rd	4th	Win & Pl
4	2		1		£18,372
	3/19	Newb	2m¹/₂f Cls4 Hdl 4yo gd-sft		£4,549
	2/19	Font	2m1¹/₂f Cls4 Hdl 4yo soft		£3,249

Mile winner on the Flat (rated 85) who took well

to hurdles last season, winning his first two races and not beaten far when third behind Triumph winner Pentland Hills in a Grade 1 at Aintree; disappointing when taking on older horses for the first time in the Swinton.

Cilaos Emery (Fr)

7 b g Califet - Queissa (Saint Preuil)

Willie Mullins (Ir)   Luke McMahon

PLACINGS: 11251/42/1-   RPR **142**+c

Starts	1st	2nd	3rd	4th	Win & Pl
8	4	2	-	1	£98,517

1/19	Gowr	2m Ch soft	£8,047
4/17	Punc	2m1½f Nov Gd1 Hdl gd-yld	£50,427
12/16	Navn	2m Mdn Hdl sft-hvy	£6,331
4/16	Punc	2m NHF 4yo gd-yld	£5,426

Talented but fragile two-miler who has run just three times since beating Melon in a Grade 1 novice hurdle at Punchestown in April 2017; hugely impressive when winning a beginners' chase at Gowran Park last season but missed big spring targets through injury.

City Island (Ire)

6 b g Court Cave - Victorine (Un Desperado)

Martin Brassil (Ir)   Sean & Bernardine Mulryan

PLACINGS: 2/11d111-6   RPR **155**+h

Starts	1st	2nd	3rd	4th	Win & Pl
7	4	1	-	-	£98,501

3/19	Chel	2m5f Cls1 Nov Gd1 Hdl soft	£70,338
2/19	Naas	2m3f Nov Hdl good	£11,099
12/18	Leop	2m Mdn Hdl gd-yld	£8,177
5/18	Punc	2m NHF 5-7yo good	£5,451

Easily won a couple of ordinary novice hurdles before stepping up in class with aplomb when too strong for dual Grade 1 winner Champ in the Ballymore Novices' Hurdle at Cheltenham; well below par when only sixth on only subsequent run at Punchestown.

Claimantakinforgan (Fr)

7 b g Great Pretender - Taquine D'Estrees (Take Risks)

Nicky Henderson   Grech & Parkin

PLACINGS: S1/16235/11352/13-   RPR **150**c

Starts	1st	2nd	3rd	4th	Win & Pl
12	4	2	3	-	£76,744

11/18	Uttx	2m Cls3 Ch good	£7,408
12/17	Asct	1m7½f Cls1 Nov Gd2 Hdl soft	£19,933
11/17	Newb	2m1½f Cls4 Nov Hdl gd-sft	£4,549
11/16	Hayd	1m7½f Cls4 NHF 4-6yo heavy	£3,249

High-class bumper performer and novice hurdler who produced an eyecatching chase debut at Uttoxeter last season before a distant third at Cheltenham; missed the rest of last season but subsequently bought by Highflyer Bloodstock for £100,000 to stay with Nicky Henderson.

Clan Des Obeaux (Fr)

7 b g Kapgarde - Nausicaa Des Obeaux (April Night)

Paul Nicholls

Mr & Mrs P K Barber, G Mason & Sir A Ferguson

PLACINGS: 6/412514/2123/41152-   RPR **176**+c

Starts	1st	2nd	3rd	4th	Win & Pl
19	7	5	4	3	£376,840

2/19	Asct	3m Cls1 Gd2 Ch gd-sft	£28,475
12/18	Kemp	3m Cls1 Gd1 Ch gd-sft	£142,375
11/17	Hayd	2m5½f Cls2 Ch heavy	£32,490
3/17	Extr	2m3f Cls3 Nov Ch gd-sft	£7,148
11/16	Newb	2m4f Cls1 Nov Gd2 Ch gd-sft	£19,933
12/15	Newb	2m1½f Cls4 Hdl 3yo soft	£3,249
4/15	Lrsy	1m4f NHF 3yo gd-sft	£3,876

Progressed into a top-class staying chaser last season and gained his most notable victory in the King George at Kempton; only fifth when well fancied for the Gold Cup, taking Cheltenham record to 0-5, and no match for Kemboy when second in the Betway Bowl at Aintree.

Class Conti (Fr)

7 b g Poliglote - Gazelle Lulu (Altayan)

Willie Mullins (Ir)   Patrick Joubert

PLACINGS: 113/4114/462UP/1-P   RPR **152**c

Starts	1st	2nd	3rd	4th	Win & Pl
14	5	1		3	£110,661

4/19	Tram	2m5f Ch heavy	£11,099
8/16	Lign	2m¹/₂f NHF 4-5yo good	£4,044
6/16	Autl	2m1¹/₂f Ch 4yo v soft	£19,412
11/15	Autl	2m1¹/₂f Hdl 3yo heavy	£17,860
10/15	Autl	2m2f Hdl 3yo v soft	£20,465

Half-brother to Silviniaco Conti; has spent much of his career in France but made a spectacular debut for Willie Mullins last season when winning by 23 lengths at Thurles (only two finishers in gruelling contest); scoped dirty when a pulled-up favourite on next run at Punchestown.

Clondaw Castle (Ire)

7 b g Oscar - Lohort Castle (Presenting)

Tom George   J French, D McDermott, S Nelson & T Syder

PLACINGS: F/118/1317/521144-   RPR **147+**c

Starts	1st	2nd	3rd	4th	Win & Pl
134	5	1	1	2	£47,012

2/19	Hntg	2m¹/₂f Cls3 Nov 119-134 Ch Hcap good	£9,653
1/19	Leic	2m Cls3 Nov Ch gd-fm	£8,058
1/18	Kels	2m Cls4 Nov Hdl soft	£4,159
11/17	Hntg	2m Cls4 Mdn Hdl gd-sft	£3,249
3/17	Strf	2m¹/₂f Cls4 Mdn NHF 4-6yo soft	£3,249

Progressive novice chaser last season; won twice before a huge run when stepped sharply up in class for the Racing Post Arkle, finishing fourth having been closest to Duc Des Genievres for much of the closing stages; disappointing when fourth again at Aintree.

Last season's King George winner Clan Des Obeaux makes light of the opposition to win the Denman Chase at Ascot

131

Cloth Cap (Ire)

7 b g Beneficial - Cloth Fair (Old Vic)

Jonjo O'Neill   Trevor Hemmings

PLACINGS: 74/54716F/3113-   RPR **142+**c

Starts	1st	2nd	3rd	4th	Win & Pl
12	3	-		2	£45,497
125	11/18	Catt	3m1f Cls3 122-135 Ch Hcap good		£10,007
118	11/18	Strf	2m6½f Cls4 104-122 Ch Hcap good		£5,588
111	12/17	Hntg	2m4½f Cls4 86-112 Ch Hcap gd-sft		£5,198

Took well to fences last season, winning handicaps at Stratford and Catterick in November before returning from a break to finish a fine third in the Scottish Grand National; kept away from soft ground since a bad run over hurdles.

Cloudy Dream (Ire)

9 gr g Cloudings - Run Away Dream (Acceglio)

Donald McCain   Trevor Hemmings

PLACINGS: 12/1122221/222235/3-   RPR **162+**c

Starts	1st	2nd	3rd	4th	Win & Pl
21	7	9	4	-	£258,344
	4/17	Ayr	2m4½f Cls1 Nov Gd2 Ch good		£26,283
	11/16	Hayd	2m1½f Cls2 Ch soft		£12,996
	10/16	Carl	2m Cls4 Ch soft		£3,899
122	3/16	MRas	2m2½f Cls3 115-129 Hdl Hcap soft		£9,384
	11/15	Donc	2m3½f Cls4 Nov Hdl 4-6yo good		£3,899
	10/15	Carl	2m1f Cls6 NHF 4-6yo good		£1,560
	4/15	Hexm	2m Cls6 NHF 4-5yo good		£1,711

Smart novice chaser three seasons ago (second behind Altior in the Arkle) for Malcolm Jefferson but became something of a bridesmaid in open company; switched to Donald McCain last season and finished a good third in the Old Roan at Aintree on his only start.

Cobra De Mai (Fr)

7 b g Great Pretender - Miria Galanda (Chef De Clan)

Dan Skelton   Norman Lake & Susan Carsberg

PLACINGS: 1P154122/4914P71514-   RPR **152+**c

Starts	1st	2nd	3rd	4th	Win & Pl
32	10	5	1	8	£116,871
142	4/19	Chel	3m2f Cls2 128-147 Ch Hcap good		£15,511
139	3/19	Leic	2m4f Cls3 133-139 Ch Hcap good		£6,498
138	11/18	Strf	2m3½f Cls3 119-141 Ch Hcap good		£10,007
133	2/18	Wwck	2m4f Cls2 131-144 Ch Hcap gd-sft		£18,768
	10/17	Sedg	2m½f Cls4 Nov Ch good		£3,899
	5/17	Hntg	2m½f Cls4 Nov Ch good		£4,534
116	5/17	Worc	2m Cls4 97-117 Ch Hcap good		£3,379
116	5/17	Wwck	2m Cls4 Nov 99-119 Ch Hcap good		£4,549
	2/16	Weth	2m Cls5 Mdn Hdl 4yo heavy		£2,599
	6/15	Nanc	1m4f NHF 3yo good		£4,264

Won three handicap chases last season, with by

far the most notable success at Cheltenham in April having twice dominated inferior rivals off top weight in Class 3 company prior to that; relished step up to 3m2f that day having not shown any form beyond 2m5f previously.

Coeur Sublime (Ire)

4 b g Elusive Pimpernel - Love Knot (Lomitas)

Gordon Elliott (Ir)   C Jones

PLACINGS: 12F423-   RPR **143**h

Starts	1st	2nd	3rd	4th	Win & Pl
6	1	2	1	1	£46,357
	11/18	DRoy	2m1½f Hdl 3yo gd-yld		£8,177

Failed to add to victory on hurdling debut last season but might well have won at Leopardstown but for falling at the last and ran a huge race when second behind Pentland Hills in the Triumph Hurdle; travelled strongly but cut out quickly when favourite at Fairyhouse next time.

Colreevy (Ire)

6 b m Flemensfirth - Poetics Girl (Saddlers' Hall)

Willie Mullins (Ir)   Mrs N Flynn

PLACINGS: F/1371/3-1   RPR **126**b

Starts	1st	2nd	3rd	4th	Win & Pl
6	3	-	2	-	£94,388
	5/19	Punc	2m1½f Gd1 NHF 4-7yo yield		£53,153
	4/18	Punc	2m1½f Gd3 NHF 4-7yo yield		£26,106
	12/17	Fair	2m NHF 4yo heavy		£6,318

Missed most of last season but returned as an improved horse in the spring; left form of comeback run behind when winning a Grade 1 bumper against geldings at Punchestown having won a Grade 3 mares' bumper on the same card 12 months earlier.

Come To Me (Fr)

7 b g Spanish Moon - Hasta Manana (Useful)

Willie Mullins (Ir)   Miss M A Masterson

PLACINGS: 1/617P-8   RPR **142+**h

Starts	1st	2nd	3rd	4th	Win & Pl
6	2	-	-	-	£11,382
	12/18	Cork	2m Mdn Hdl sft-hvy		£7,087
	12/16	Punc	2m NHF 4yo yld-sft		£4,296

Hugely impressive 17-length winner of a maiden hurdle at Cork last season; sent off just 4-1 for a Grade 1 at Naas next time but found to be coughing after a poor run that day and failed to recover his form in further Grade 1 novice hurdles at Leopardstown and Punchestown.

Concertista (Fr)

5 ch m Nathaniel - Zagzig (Selkirk)

Willie Mullins (Ir)   Simon Munir & Isaac Souede

PLACINGS: 2-   RPR **138+**h

Starts	1st	2nd	3rd	4th	Win & Pl
1	-	1	-	-	£19,080

Bought off the Flat in France and ran a

remarkable race on stable and hurdling debut when a close second in the mares' novice hurdle at the Cheltenham Festival at 66-1, just getting outstayed having cruised to the front; fascinating prospect for mares' hurdles.

Coney Island (Ire)

8 b g Flemensfirth - Millys Gesture (Milan)

Edward Harty (Ir)   John P McManus

PLACINGS: **32151/2212/1PP/376-8**   RPR **162**c

Starts	1st	2nd	3rd	4th	Win & Pl
16	4	4	2	-	£123,346
	12/17	Asct	2m5f Cls2 Ch gd-sft		£16,245
	12/16	Fair	2m4f Nov Gd1 Ch gd-yld		£36,875
130	3/16	Fair	3m Nov 109-131 Hdl Hcap yield		£23,860
	12/15	Leop	2m Mdn Hdl 4yo heavy		£6,953

Looked a potential star as a novice (won one

Grade 1 and ran Our Duke to half a length in another) but largely disappointing in just seven runs since; showed bits of promise last season, notably when staying on into sixth in the Ryanair after being given plenty to do.

Count Meribel

7 ch g Three Valleys - Bakhtawar (Lomitas)

Nigel Twiston-Davies   Charles C Walker

PLACINGS: **233222/111265P/1147-**   RPR **150+**c

Starts	1st	2nd	3rd	4th	Win & Pl
19	5	5	2	1	£61,329
	11/18	Chel	2m4f Cls2 Nov Ch good		£15,562
137	11/18	Carl	2m4f Cls3 Nov 115-137 Ch Hcap good		£8,123
	11/17	Asct	2m5½f Cls2 Nov Hdl gd-sft		£12,996
	11/17	Carl	2m4f Cls4 Nov Hdl soft		£4,224
	10/17	Carl	2m3½f Cls4 Nov Hdl soft		£4,224

Struggles to maintain his form through a

Colreevy was high-class in bumpers last season and looks interesting for novice hurdles

campaign but has shown smart form early in the last two seasons and won his first two chases last season; given a break before returning for the RSA at Cheltenham and ran well for a long way before finishing seventh.

Cracking Smart (Fr)

7 b g Great Pretender - Maya Du Frene (Le Pommier D'Or)

Gordon Elliott (Ir)   Gigginstown House Stud

PLACINGS: F21/1122/630-8   RPR **151**h

Starts	1st	2nd	3rd	4th	Win & Pl
11	3	3	1	-	£61,315
	11/17	Cork	3m Nov List Hdl soft		£20,171
	10/17	Punc	2m4f Mdn Hdl yld-sft		£7,108
	4/17	Fair	2m NHF 4-7yo gd-yld		£5,265

Hugely promising as a novice hurdler two seasons ago (won twice before finishing second to Next Destination twice) but struggled last term; showed a little more when third behind Tiger Roll in the Boyne Hurdle and beaten only ten lengths in the Coral Cup.

Crosspark

9 b g Midnight Legend - Blue Shannon (Be My Native)

Caroline Bailey   C W Booth

PLACINGS: 2U13/4P443/44115312-   RPR **148**c

Starts	1st	2nd	3rd	4th	Win & Pl
24	6	3	4	5	£153,000
135	2/19	Newc	4m¹/₂f Cls2 125-148 Ch Hcap gd-sft	£50,048
129	12/18	Sthl	3m Cls3 117-137 Hdl Hcap gd-sft	£6,238
124	11/18	Uttx	3m2f Cls3 111-129 Ch Hcap gd-sft	£7,408
132	2/17	Leic	2m4f Cls3 132-138 Ch Hcap heavy	£7,596
123	5/16	Sthl	2m4¹/₂f Cls3 Nov 123-134 Ch Hcap soft	£6,389
	11/15	Sthl	3m Cls4 Nov Hdl soft	£3,899

Progressed into a smart staying handicap chaser last season, winning three times including the Eider at Newcastle; relished step up to that marathon trip but just outstayed when second in the Scottish Grand National (in front earlier); has won on good and heavy ground.

Cyrname (Fr)

7 b g Nickname - Narquile (Passing Sale)

Paul Nicholls   Mrs Johnny De La Hey

PLACINGS: 521/56/7121214/3711-   RPR **181**+c

Starts	1st	2nd	3rd	4th	Win & Pl
16	6	3	1	1	£225,773
	2/19	Asct	2m5f Cls1 Gd1 Ch gd-sft	£85,425
150	1/19	Asct	2m5f Cls2 135-152 Ch Hcap gd-sft	£46,920
	2/18	Kemp	2m4¹/₂f Cls1 Nov Gd2 Ch good	£18,224
	12/17	Kemp	2m Cls1 Nov Gd2 Ch	£23,491
130	11/17	Hntg	2m¹/₂f Cls3 Nov 123-131 Ch Hcap good	£7,798
	1/16	Pau	2m1¹/₂f Hdl 4yo v soft	£11,294

Last season's highest-rated chaser on Racing Post Ratings after a 17-length demolition job in the Ascot Chase, his second wide-margin win over that course and distance; beaten in both previous runs at Grade 1 level as a novice but appears to have left that form behind; on track for a clash with Altior in the 1965 Chase back at Ascot in November; seemingly less effective going left-handed.

Daklondike (Ire)

7 b g Gold Well - Strong Irish (Corrouge)

David Pipe   Prof Caroline Tisdall

PLACINGS: 1/43164/41411P/P1UR-   RPR **152**+c

Starts	1st	2nd	3rd	4th	Win & Pl
15	5	-	1	4	£62,747
139	12/18	Hayd	2m7f Cls2 132-142 Ch Hcap heavy	£31,280
133	12/17	Newb	3m2f Cls3 129-135 Ch Hcap heavy	£11,696
126	12/17	Winc	3m1f Cls3 108-126 Ch Hcap soft	£9,583
114	11/17	Weth	3m Cls4 98-122 Ch Hcap soft	£3,899
	11/16	Ling	2m Cls4 Nov Hdl heavy	£4,549

Quirky staying chaser who has failed to complete in four of his last five races (even refused to race in the Eider) but won the Tommy Whittle in between to add to trio of wins as a novice in late 2017; has gained all five victories under rules on soft or heavy ground.

Dallas Des Pictons (Fr)

6 b g Spanish Moon - Nadia Des Pictons (Video Rock)

Gordon Elliott (Ir)   Gigginstown House Stud

PLACINGS: 41/1421120-   RPR **149**h

Starts	1st	2nd	3rd	4th	Win & Pl
9	4	2	-	2	£81,119
130	2/19	Leop	3m 119-139 Hdl Hcap good	£46,509
	1/19	Punc	2m4f Mdn Hdl good	£7,214
	5/18	Pina	1m7¹/₂f NHF 4-5yo good	£5,973
	4/18	Loud	1m6f NHF 4-5yo heavy	£4,204

Smart and progressive novice hurdler last season; made a winning handicap debut in a valuable 3m race at Leopardstown and ran another cracker when second in the Martin Pipe at Cheltenham (7-2 favourite); below best when stepped up to Grade 1 level at Aintree.

Dandy Dan (Ire)

6 b g Midnight Legend - Playing Around (Act One)

Kim Bailey   P J Andrews

PLACINGS: 11253/231112-   RPR **153**+c

Starts	1st	2nd	3rd	4th	Win & Pl
11	5	3	2	-	£61,203
	2/19	Ayr	3m Cls3 Nov Ch gd-sft	£7,343
132	10/18	Kels	3m2f Cls2 130-145 Ch Hcap good	£17,373
	10/18	Bang	3m Cls4 Ch good	£4,809
	11/17	Ludl	2m5f Cls4 Nov Hdl good	£3,249
	5/17	Ludl	2m Cls4 NHF 4-6yo good	£3,899

Developed into a smart staying novice chaser last season, winning three in a row either side of a midwinter break; did particularly well to finish second in a valuable novice handicap at Ayr on his final run having not jumped at his best; should stay further.

Danny Kirwan (Ire)

6 b g Scorpion - Sainte Baronne (Saint Des Saints)

Paul Nicholls   Mrs Johnny De La Hey

PLACINGS: 110/22-   RPR **140**h

Starts	1st	2nd	3rd	4th	Win & Pl
4	1	2	-	-	£11,800
	2/18	Kemp	2m Cls5 NHF 4-6yo good	£3,119

Held in high regard at home and landed a

significant touch when making a winning bumper debut in 2018; yet to build on that and beaten at 1-2 on hurdling debut but did much better to finish second behind Angels Breath in a Grade 2 at Ascot when last seen.

Danny Whizzbang (Ire)

6 b g Getaway - Lakil Princess (Bering)

Paul Nicholls — Mrs Angela Tincknell

PLACINGS: P1/11- — RPR **141+**h

Starts	1st	2nd	3rd	4th	Win & Pl
2	2	-	-	-	£9,032
3/19	Extr	2m7f Cls4 Nov Hdl gd-sft			£4,224
11/18	Hrfd	3m1½f Cls4 Mdn Hdl gd-sft			£4,809

Won both novice hurdles last season, impressively defying a penalty at Market Rasen in March; missed a Grade 2 at Cheltenham earlier in the season but deliberately given a quiet campaign otherwise as trainer feels his future lies as a staying chaser.

Daphne Du Clos (Fr)

6 b m Spanish Moon - Katarina Du Clos (Panoramic)

Nicky Henderson — Sullivan Bloodstock

PLACINGS: 121/5- — RPR **108**h

Starts	1st	2nd	3rd	4th	Win & Pl
4	2	1	-	-	£20,621
2/17	Newb	2m1/2f Cls1 List NHF 4-6yo soft			£11,390
10/16	Sbri	1m4f NHF 3yo gd-sft			£4,779

Among the leading fancies for the 2017 Champion Bumper at Cheltenham before being ruled out by injury and had already beaten eventual fifth Western Ryder in a Listed contest at Newbury; finally due to return from injury and should make a good novice hurdler.

Darasso (Fr)

6 br g Konig Turf - Nassora (Assessor)

Joseph Patrick O'Brien (Ir) — John P McManus

PLACINGS: 32/2121116/2511- — RPR **157+**c

Starts	1st	2nd	3rd	4th	Win & Pl
13	6	4	1	-	£229,998
3/19	Navn	2m Gd2 Ch soft			£23,919
2/19	Gowr	2m Gd3 Hdl yield			£31,892
3/18	Comp	2m3½f Ch 5yo heavy			£20,389
3/18	Comp	2m3½f Ch 5yo heavy			£22,088
0	11/17	Autl	2m3½f List Hdl 4yo Hcap v soft		£40,385
0	10/17	Autl	2m2f List Hdl 4yo Hcap v soft		£40,385

Built on high-class French form (twice beat Janika in Listed hurdles) when dropped back to 2m to win Graded races over hurdles and fences on final two runs last season; had looked a clear

non-stayer when fifth behind Presenting Percy in the Galmoy Hurdle.

Dashel Drasher

6 b g Passing Glance - So Long (Nomadic Way)

Jeremy Scott — Mrs B Tully & R Lock

PLACINGS: 106/3341111- — RPR **145+**h

Starts	1st	2nd	3rd	4th	Win & Pl
10	5	-	2	1	£42,646
4/19	Chel	2m4½f Cls2 Nov Hdl good			£12,380
3/19	Newb	2m4½f Cls3 Nov Hdl gd-sft			£6,238
2/19	Asct	2m3½f Cls2 Nov Hdl gd-sft			£15,857
1/19	Chep	2m3½f Cls4 Nov Hdl gd-sft			£4,094
2/18	Winc	1m7½f Cls5 NHF 4-6yo heavy			£2,274

Exciting front-runner who reeled off a four-timer in novice hurdles at around 2m4f at the end of last season, making all every time and finishing off with an impressive victory at Cheltenham; likely to go novice chasing.

De Rasher Counter

7 b g Yeats - Dedrunknmunky (Rashar)

Emma Lavelle — Makin' Bacon Partnership

PLACINGS: F211/3521F72/3P7121- — RPR **153+**c

Starts	1st	2nd	3rd	4th	Win & Pl
14	4	3	2	-	£51,489
140	3/19	Uttx	3m Cls2 Nov 118-140 Ch Hcap heavy		£25,024
133	12/18	Newb	2m6½f Cls3 Nov 129-148 Ch Hcap gd-sft		£7,343
124	1/18	Font	2m3f Cls3 105-127 Hdl Hcap heavy		£6,238
3/17	Clon	2m NHF 5-7yo sft-hvy			£5,265

Came into his own when gradually stepped up in trip over fences last season and produced a couple of terrific performances in good novice handicaps at Newbury and Uttoxeter; good second at Chepstow under a penalty in between; particularly effective on heavy ground.

Death Duty (Ire)

8 b g Shantou - Midnight Gift (Presenting)

Gordon Elliott (Ir) — Gigginstown House Stud

PLACINGS: 13/112/1111U3/111F/ — RPR **162**c

Starts	1st	2nd	3rd	4th	Win & Pl
14	9	1	2	-	£186,942
12/17	Fair	2m4f Nov Gd1 Ch soft			£42,863
10/17	Punc	2m2f Nov Gd3 Ch soft			£17,083
10/17	Tipp	2m7f Ch soft			£6,318
1/17	Naas	2m4f Nov Gd1 Hdl soft			£45,385
12/16	Navn	2m4f Nov Gd2 Hdl sft-hvy			£18,438
11/16	Navn	2m4f Nov Gd3 Hdl yld-sft			£18,438
10/16	Rosc	2m4f Mdn Hdl heavy			£4,522
12/15	Navn	2m List NHF 4-7yo heavy			£12,597
10/15	DRoy	2m NHF 4-7yo yld-sft			£4,814

Expected to return from nearly two years out; didn't build on rich early promise over hurdles but had won his first three novice chases three seasons ago, including the Drinmore, before damaging ligaments at Leopardstown (fell at the last when well held by Footpad).

Defi Du Seuil (Fr)
6 b g Voix Du Nord - Quarvine Du Seuil (Lavirco)

Philip Hobbs				John P McManus
PLACINGS: /11111111/47/51211-2				RPR **164**+c

Starts	1st	2nd	3rd	4th	Win & Pl
17	11	3	-	1	£382,879
3/19	Chel	2m4f Cls1 Nov Gd1 Ch gd-sft			£88,209
2/19	Sand	2m4f Cls1 Nov Gd1 Ch soft			£31,691
12/18	Extr	2m3f Cls2 Nov Ch soft			£16,245
4/17	Aint	2m1f Cls1 Gd1 Hdl 4yo good			£56,181
3/17	Chel	2m1f Cls1 Gd1 Hdl 4yo good			£71,188
1/17	Chel	2m1f Cls1 Gd2 Hdl 4yo soft			£17,085
12/16	Chep	2m Cls1 Gd1 Hdl 3yo gd-sft			£28,475
12/16	Chel	2m1f Cls2 Hdl 3yo gd-sft			£12,512
11/16	Chel	2m¹/₂f Cls1 Gd2 Hdl 3yo gd-sft			£17,165
10/16	Ffos	2m Cls5 Mdn Hdl 3yo good			£2,599
4/16	Pari	1m4f NHF 3yo v soft			£5,882

Lost his way over hurdles after a brilliant unbeaten juvenile campaign but worked his way back to form last season and gained a second Cheltenham Festival win in the JLT Novices' Chase; good second to Chacun Pour Soi at Punchestown but may be better back up to 2m4f.

Definitly Red (Ire)
10 ch g Definite Article - The Red Wench (Aahsaylad)

Brian Ellison				Phil & Julie Martin
PLACINGS: /131U1P/3116U/112B-5				RPR **169**c

Starts	1st	2nd	3rd	4th	Win & Pl
30	14	5	2	-	£398,029
12/18	Aint	3m1f Cls1 Gd2 Ch soft			£34,822
11/18	Weth	3m Cls1 Gd2 Ch good			£58,727
1/18	Chel	3m1¹/₂f Cls1 Gd2 Ch heavy			£56,950
12/17	Aint	3m Cls1 Gd2 Ch heavy			£28,135
3/17	Donc	3m2f Cls2 137-161 Ch Hcap soft			£34,408
12/16	Weth	3m Cls1 Gd3 131-153 Ch Hcap gd-sft			£22,780
10/16	Carl	2m4f Cls2 122-148 Hdl Hcap gd-sft			£12,512
4/16	Ayr	2m4¹/₂f Cls1 List 132-148 Ch Hcap soft			£25,628
1/16	Catt	3m1f Cls4 Nov Ch soft			£7,148
2/15	Hayd	2m7f Cls1 Nov Gd2 Hdl soft			£15,735
1/15	Catt	2m3¹/₂f Cls4 Nov Hdl gd-sft			£4,874
11/14	Chel	2m¹/₂f Cls1 List NHF 4-6yo soft			£11,390
2/14	Newb	2m¹/₂f Cls1 List NHF 4-6yo heavy			£11,390
12/13	Uttx	2m Cls6 Mdn NHF 4-6yo heavy			£1,949

Has a fine record in staying chases just below the top level, winning a pair of Grade 2 races in each of the last two seasons; unable to build on last season's early successes (even beaten at 1-6 at Kelso) but was still in contention when brought down in the Gold Cup.

Delta Work (Fr)
6 br g Network - Robbe (Video Rock)

Gordon Elliott (Ir)				Gigginstown House Stud
PLACINGS: 213324312/1113-1				RPR **166**+c

Starts	1st	2nd	3rd	4th	Win & Pl
14	6	3	4	1	£279,088
4/19	Punc	3m1¹/₂f Nov Gd1 Ch yld-sft			£53,153
12/18	Leop	3m Nov Gd1 Ch good			£52,212
12/18	Fair	2m4f Nov Gd1 Ch good			£46,991
11/18	DRoy	2m3¹/₂f Ch good			£8,177
3/18	Chel	3m Cls1 Gd3 135-155 Hdl Hcap soft			£56,950
5/17	Punc	2m¹/₂f Mdn Hdl good			£6,844

Former Pertemps Final winner who also won

four out of five over fences last season; ran another cracker when suffering sole defeat in the RSA Chase at Cheltenham (close third behind Topofthegame and Santini) and impressed again when winning by 12 lengths at Punchestown.

Derrinross (Ire)
8 b g Scorpion - Cybele Eria (Johann Quatz)

Philip Dempsey (Ir)				
			Mrs M Furlong, Mrs N Dempsey & J P Dempsey
PLACINGS: 1/23/422/116-				RPR **146**+h

Starts	1st	2nd	3rd	4th	Win & Pl
8	2	3	1	1	£54,134
12/18	Limk	3m Nov Gd2 Hdl soft			£26,106
12/18	Cork	3m Nov Gd3 Hdl sft-hvy			£19,049

Fragile gelding who took his form to a new level last season when returning from a year's absence, winning Graded novice hurdles at Cork and Limerick; ran well when sixth in the Albert Bartlett at Cheltenham; better on softer ground.

Destrier (Fr)
6 b g Voix Du Nord - Razia (Robin Des Champs)

Dan Skelton				Three Celts
PLACINGS: 0/1152/3113-				RPR **156**c

Starts	1st	2nd	3rd	4th	Win & Pl
9	4	1	2		£38,343
1/19	Ayr	2m¹/₂f Cls4 Nov Ch gd-sft			£5,458
12/18	Sthl	1m7¹/₂f Cls3 Nov 111-127 Ch Hcap gd-sft			£7,343
1/18	Weth	2m Cls4 Nov Hdl 4-7yo heavy			£4,809
11/17	Leic	1m7¹/₂f Cls3 Nov Hdl gd-sft			£6,330

Big improver when sent novice chasing, jumping superbly to win first two races over fences and running a cracker for one so inexperienced when a close third behind Ornua in a 2m Grade 1 at Aintree (made a bad early blunder); open to significant improvement.

Diakali (Fr)
10 gr g Sinndar - Diasilixa (Linamix)

Gary Moore				Nick Peacock
PLACINGS: 3/34/10/41/66/111P5-				RPR **148**+c

Starts	1st	2nd	3rd	4th	Win & Pl
24	10	2	3	4	£373,711
10/18	Chel	2m Cls2 Nov Ch good			£15,728
6/18	NAbb	2m¹/₂f Cls3 Nov Ch good			£9,357
6/18	Font	2m2f Cls4 Nov Ch good			£4,614
4/17	Fair	2m Hdl gd-yld			£11,564
7/15	Tipp	2m Gd3 Hdl good			£31,492
11/13	Naas	2m Gd3 Hdl 4yo yld-sft			£14,533
6/13	Autl	2m3¹/₂f Gd1 Hdl 4yo v soft			£98,780
4/13	Punc	2m Gd1 Hdl 4yo heavy			£40,325
1/13	Punc	2m Gd3 Hdl 4yo heavy			£14,533
11/12	Gowr	2m Mdn Hdl 3yo heavy			£5,750

Grade 1 hurdler in his youth (won twice at the top level as a juvenile and just beaten in the 2014 Aintree Hurdle) who emerged from a long period of injuries and poor form with a stellar summer campaign over fences in 2018; subsequently aimed at the Arkle only to fail a veterinary test.

Dickie Diver (Ire)

6 b g Gold Well - Merry Excuse (Flemensfirth)

Nicky Henderson | John P McManus

PLACINGS: 1/214- | RPR **145**h

Starts	1st	2nd	3rd	4th	Win & Pl
3	1	1	-	1	£11,699
2/19	Chep	2m3½f Cls4 Mdn Hdl gd-sft			£3,574

Highly promising in three novice hurdles last season; just pipped by subsequent Grade 2 winner Lisnagar Oscar first time out and followed maiden victory with an eyecatching fourth in the Albert Bartlett at Cheltenham (finished well after not getting a clear run).

Dingo Dollar (Ire)

7 ch g Golden Lariat - Social Society (Moscow Society)

Alan King | M Warren, J Holmes, R Kidner & J Wright

PLACINGS: 1/20171/4F112/4362P- | RPR **151**c

Starts	1st	2nd	3rd	4th	Win & Pl
15	4	3	1	2	£76,814
2/18	Donc	3m Cls4 Nov Ch gd-sft			£4,494
130	12/17	Newb	2m7½f Cls4 Nov 125-137 Ch Hcap soft		£6,498
4/17	Font	3m1½f Cls4 Nov Hdl good			£3,249
1/17	Bang	2m7f Cls4 Mdn Hdl gd-sft			£3,249

Finished a fine third in last season's Ladbrokes Trophy when prominent throughout; well fancied for all three subsequent runs on the back of that but might have found good ground quicker than ideal, with trainer even feeling he wasn't letting himself down when second in the Grimthorpe.

Discorama (Fr)

6 b g Saddler Maker - Quentala (Lone Bid)

Paul Nolan (Ir) | Thomas Friel & Andrew Gemmell

PLACINGS: 2/123725/15F2-2 | RPR **151+**c

Starts	1st	2nd	3rd	4th	Win & Pl
12	2	5	1	-	£78,399
11/18	Naas	2m3f Ch yield			£7,904
12/17	Fair	2m2f Mdn Hdl soft			£7,108

Smart operator who has finished second at the Cheltenham Festival for the last two seasons, going down narrowly to Le Breuil in a gruelling National Hunt Chase last term; followed up with a good second behind Delta Work at Punchestown, staying on after appearing to find drop to 3m too sharp.

MY **FIVE** **TO WATCH**
Keith Melrose

● Delta Work ● Dynamite Dollars
● Kalashnikov ● Kildisart ● McFabulous

Dolos (Fr)

6 b g Kapgarde - Redowa (Trempolino)

Paul Nicholls | Mrs Johnny De La Hey

PLACINGS: 0212/2013272/22315-1 | RPR **162+**c

Starts	1st	2nd	3rd	4th	Win & Pl
22	5	7	6	-	£148,584
154	5/19	Kemp	2m2f Cls2 128-154 Ch Hcap good		£14,389
149	2/19	Sand	1m7½f Cls2 128-154 Ch Hcap soft		£18,768
11/17	Asct	2m3f Cls3 Ch gd-sft			£9,986
4/17	Chep	2m Cls4 Nov Hdl good			£3,899
10/16	Chep	2m Cls4 Hdl 3yo good			£3,899

Classy 2m handicap chaser who won off 154 at Warwick in May; yet to convince over further and only fifth when favourite for the Greatwood Gold Cup; trainer fears his mark flatters him but has time on his side having started chasing as just a four-year-old two seasons ago.

Dommage Pour Toi (Fr)

6 b g Magadan - Phenyl Des Mottes (Bonnet Rouge)

Henry de Bromhead (Ir) | Gigginstown House Stud

PLACINGS: P321-5 | RPR **140**h

Starts	1st	2nd	3rd	4th	Win & Pl
4	1	1	1	-	£27,616
4/19	Fair	2m4f Nov Gd2 Hdl gd-yld			£22,590

Progressive novice hurdler last season; took a big leap forward when getting off the mark at 33-1 in a Grade 2 at Fairyhouse and backed that up with a solid fifth behind Reserve Tank in a Grade 1 at Punchestown; likely to go novice chasing.

Dortmund Park (Fr)

6 b g Great Pretender - Qena (Le Balafre)

Gordon Elliott (Ir) | Gigginstown House Stud

PLACINGS: 1/1611481/59-7 | RPR **141**h

Starts	1st	2nd	3rd	4th	Win & Pl
11	5			1	£87,307
4/18	Punc	2m4f Nov Gd1 Hdl soft			£52,212
1/18	Thur	2m6½f Nov Hdl heavy			£7,904
1/18	Fair	2m4f Mdn Hdl heavy			£7,087
6/17	Nant	1m4f NHF 4-5yo good			£10,684
4/17	Le L	1m3½f NHF 4yo soft			£5,128

Grade 1 winner as a novice hurdler two seasons ago, albeit when slightly fortunate at Punchestown after three rivals departed two out (had been only eighth in the Albert Bartlett); failed to make an impression in three runs in top company last season.

Double Shuffle (Ire)

9 b g Milan - Fiddlers Bar (Un Desperado)

Tom George | Crossed Fingers Partnership

PLACINGS: 2P512P/22274/F252P0- | RPR **162**c

Starts	1st	2nd	3rd	4th	Win & Pl
26	4	8	1	2	£202,336
143	12/16	Kemp	3m Cls2 126-143 Ch Hcap good		£25,024
134	12/15	Ludl	2m4f Cls3 Nov 120-134 Ch Hcap soft		£11,372
3/15	Newb	2m4f Cls4 Nov Hdl gd-sft			£3,422
2/15	Donc	2m1½f Cls4 Nov Hdl 4-7yo good			£3,574

Has largely struggled since finishing a length second to Might Bite in the 2017 King George

Douvan missed last season through injury but is still only nine and could have more to offer if making it back to the track this term

but got some leeway off the handicapper last term and underlined his love of Kempton with another second in a valuable handicap chase in February; also gained his last win there in 2016.

Dounikos (Fr)

8 b g Smadoun - Baby Sitter (Nikos)

Gordon Elliott (Ir)   Gigginstown House Stud

PLACINGS: 11249/114PPP/07F1PP-   RPR **156**+c

Starts	1st	2nd	3rd	4th	Win & Pl
20	5	2	-	2	£100,499
147	2/19	Punc	3m4½f 129-152 Ch Hcap gd-yld	£53,153
	12/17	Limk	2m3½f Nov Gd2 Ch heavy	£22,440
	11/17	Gowr	2m4f Ch heavy	£8,950
	11/16	Thur	2m7f Mdn Hdl good	£4,522
	10/16	Dpat	2m2f NHF 4-7yo yld-sft	£4,070

Won last season's Grand National Trial at Punchestown, finally fulfilling early promise over fences (had won first two chases and finished a close fourth in a red-hot Grade 1 at Leopardstown); pulled up in the Grand National and Irish National.

Douvan (Fr)

9 b g Walk In The Park - Star Face (Saint Des Saints)

Willie Mullins (Ir)   Mrs S Ricci

PLACINGS: 111/111111/11117/F2/   RPR **178**c

Starts	1st	2nd	3rd	4th	Win & Pl
18	14	2	-	-	£569,969
	2/17	Punc	2m Gd2 Ch soft	£22,692
	12/16	Leop	2m1f Gd1 Ch yield	£43,382
	12/16	Cork	2m1f Gd2 Ch sft-hvy	£21,691
	4/16	Punc	2m Nov Gd1 Ch yield	£49,890
	4/16	Aint	2m Cls1 Nov Gd1 Ch gd-sft	£56,270
	3/16	Chel	2m Cls1 Gd1 Ch gd-sft	£85,827
	1/16	Leop	2m1f Nov Gd1 Ch soft	£39,706
	12/15	Leop	2m1f Nov Gd1 Ch heavy	£42,558
	11/15	Navn	2m1f Ch soft	£8,558
	4/15	Punc	2m Nov Gd1 Hdl gd-yld	£44,186
	3/15	Chel	2m1½f Cls1 Nov Gd1 Hdl gd-sft	£68,340
	1/15	Punc	2m Nov Gd2 Hdl soft	£20,155
	11/14	Gowr	2m Nov Hdl 4yo heavy	£7,475
	6/14	Comp	2m1f Hdl 4yo v soft	£8,800

Once looked invincible, winning his first 13 starts for Willie Mullins including two Cheltenham Festival triumphs, but has been beset by physical problems since; enjoyed a short-lived return in early 2018 (fell when going well in the Champion Chase) but missed last season through injury.

139

Downtown Getaway (Ire)

6 b g Getaway - Shang A Lang (Commander Collins)

Nicky Henderson   TFP

PLACINGS: 1/217-   RPR **132**+h

Starts	1st	2nd	3rd	4th	Win & Pl
4	2	1	-	-	£14,114

1/19	Asct	2m5¹/₂f Cls3 Nov Hdl 4-7yo gd-sft	£6,758
12/17	Fair	2m NHF 4yo soft	£5,265

Bought for £350,000 after beating a dual subsequent winner by 12 lengths on bumper debut in Ireland; didn't quite hit the heights expected over hurdles last season but won at Ascot and thrown in at the deep end when eighth in a Grade 1 at Aintree on final run.

Drovers Lane (Ire)

7 b g Oscar - Minnie Turbo (General View)

Rebecca Curtis   Hyde Hill, Moran Outhart & Trembath

PLACINGS: 3/1/85/411217116-4   RPR **154**+c

Starts	1st	2nd	3rd	4th	Win & Pl
12	5	1	-	2	£47,733

	12/18	Chel	2m4¹/₂f Cls2 Nov Ch good	£15,475
135	11/18	MRas	2m5¹/₂f Cls3 Nov 122-135 Ch Hcap gd-sft	£7,798
127	10/18	Hrfd	3m1f Cls3 Nov 118-132 Ch Hcap gd-fm	£8,058
	7/18	Worc	2m Cls4 Nov Hdl good	£4,094
	7/18	Uttx	2m4f Cls4 Mdn Hdl good	£4,159

Won three of first four races over fences last season, most notably at Cheltenham in December; came up short when stepped up to Grade 1 company in the spring but travelled well for a long way when sixth in the RSA and again when fourth behind Delta Work at Punchestown.

Duc Des Genievres (Fr)

6 gr g Buck's Boum - Lobelie (Round Sovereign)

Willie Mullins (Ir)				Sullivan Bloodstock

PLACINGS: 132556/2311-3   RPR **166**+c

Starts	1st	2nd	3rd	4th	Win & Pl
11	3	2	3	-	£160,269
3/19	Chel	2m Cls1 Nov Gd1 Ch soft			£102,772
2/19	Gowr	2m4f Ch yld-sft			£8,047
5/17	Mlns	2m2f Hdl 4yo v soft			£7,385

Wide-margin winner of last season's Racing Post Arkle at Cheltenham, though race looked weak beforehand and fell apart after early casualties; failed to back that up when third behind Chacun Pour Soi at Punchestown; has done most of his racing at around 2m4f.

Duc Des Genievres takes the final fence at Cheltenham before winning last season's Racing Post Arkle

Dynamite Dollars missed last season but is expected to be back in action this term

Duca De Thaix (Fr)

6 b g Voix Du Nord - Nouca De Thaix (Subotica)

Gordon Elliott (Ir)   Gigginstown House Stud

PLACINGS: 1/416090/232211433-5   RPR **153**+c

Starts	1st	2nd	3rd	4th	Win & Pl
20	5	4	3	3	£148,626
143	1/19	Fair	2m1f 131-152 Ch Hcap good		£53,153
133	12/18	Fair	2m¹/₂f 116-136 Ch Hcap good		£26,106
	12/17	Limk	2m Gd3 Hdl 4yo heavy		£17,872
	10/16	Autl	2m2f Hdl 3yo v soft		£16,941
	10/16	Fntb	1m5f NHF 3yo gd-sft		£6,618

Took well to fences last season and won back-to-back handicaps at Fairyhouse, including a valuable contest in January; form tailed off when stepped up to Graded races later in the season; showed best form on good ground but had won a Grade 3 hurdle on heavy.

MY FIVE TO WATCH
Justin O'Hanlon

●Andy Dufresne ●Chacun Pour Soi ●Delta Work ●Honeysuckle ●Sixshooter

Dynamite Dollars (Fr)

6 b/br g Buck's Boum - Macadoun (Cardoun)

Paul Nicholls   Michael Geoghegan

PLACINGS: 336/113554/12111-   RPR **162**+c

Starts	1st	2nd	3rd	4th	Win & Pl
14	6	1	3	1	£106,207
	1/19	Donc	2m¹/₂f Cls1 Nov Gd2 Ch good		£19,933
	12/18	Kemp	2m Cls1 Nov Gd2 Ch gd-sft		£23,048
	12/18	Sand	1m7¹/₂f Cls1 Nov Gd1 Ch soft		£31,095
	10/18	MRas	2m1f Cls3 Nov Ch good		£7,798
	11/17	Extr	2m1f Cls3 Nov Hdl soft		£5,523
	10/17	Chep	2m Cls4 Nov Hdl gd-sft		£3,899

Had looked modest over hurdles but proved a different proposition when switched to fences last season, winning four out of five including a Grade 1 at Sandown when reeling in Ornua; looked a leading contender for the Racing Post Arkle until ruled out through injury.

Early Doors (Fr)

6 b g Soldier Of Fortune - Ymlaen (Desert Prince)

Joseph Patrick O'Brien (Ir)   John P McManus

PLACINGS: 13/112930/521-2   RPR **156**+h

Starts	1st	2nd	3rd	4th	Win & Pl
12	4	3	2	-	£121,648
145	3/19	Chel	2m4¹/₂f Cls2 126-145 Cond Hdl Hcap gd-sft		£43,330
	11/17	Naas	2m Gd3 Hdl 4yo sft-hvy		£17,083
	10/17	Wxfd	2m Mdn Hdl 4yo soft		£6,055
	2/17	Punc	2m¹/₂f NHF 4yo heavy		£5,265

Produced a high-class performance to win last

season's Martin Pipe Hurdle at Cheltenham under topweight, stepping up on his third in the same race as a novice 12 months earlier; had both other runs last season at Grade 1 level, including a distant second to Apple's Jade.

Easy Game (Fr)
5 b g Barastraight - Rule Of The Game (Lavirco)

Willie Mullins (Ir)   Wicklow Bloodstock

PLACINGS: 4/11231183-7   RPR **145**+h

Starts	1st	2nd	3rd	4th	Win & Pl
10	4	1	2	1	£73,333
	12/18	Navn	2m4f Nov Gd2 Hdl yield		£22,190
	11/18	Navn	2m4f Nov Gd3 Hdl good		£22,190
	7/18	Gway	2m¹/₂f Nov Hdl 4yo good		£10,903
	7/18	Klny	2m4¹/₂f Mdn Hdl good		£6,269

Began hurdling last summer and progressed to win four times before the turn of the year, including a Grade 2 at Navan; well backed for the Ballymore after a break but well beaten in eighth and did only slightly better at Fairyhouse and Punchestown.

Ecco
4 b g Maxios - Enjoy The Life (Medicean)

Paul Nicholls   Colm Donlon

PLACINGS: 66-   RPR **135**h

Starts	1st	2nd	3rd	4th	Win & Pl
2	-	-	-	-	£2,064

Useful Flat horse in Germany (well beaten in the German Derby on last run) who was highly tried when belatedly getting started over hurdles last season and ran a cracker to finish sixth in the Triumph Hurdle; will set a good standard in novice hurdles.

Eclair De Beaufeu (Fr)
5 b g Monitor Closely - Tenebreuse Gemm (Visionary)

Gordon Elliott (Ir)   Gigginstown House Stud

PLACINGS: 1/3233114U6-   RPR **138**h

Starts	1st	2nd	3rd	4th	Win & Pl
10	3		3	1	£32,220
	1/19	Fair	2m Hdl good		£9,989
	12/18	Limk	2m Mdn Hdl 4yo soft		£7,359
	3/18	Porn	1m4f NHF 4yo stand		£5,310
	12/17	Seic	1m5¹/₂f NHF 3yo soft		£4,701

Progressive novice hurdler last season who was running a huge race in the County Hurdle at Cheltenham when unseating at the last (had just been headed); had needed five runs to get off

the mark but soon followed up and came fourth in another big handicap at Leopardstown.

Eglantine Du Seuil (Fr)
5 b m Saddler Maker - Rixia Du Seuil (Ultimately Lucky)

Willie Mullins (Ir)   Sullivan Bloodstock

PLACINGS: 1/1313-3   RPR **140**h

Starts	1st	2nd	3rd	4th	Win & Pl
6	3		3	-	£82,572
	3/19	Chel	2m1f Cls1 Nov Gd2 Hdl gd-sft		£50,643
	8/18	Slig	2m Mdn Hdl good		£6,269
	10/17	Fntb	1m5f NHF 3yo soft		£7,692

Shock winner of last season's mares' novice hurdle at the Cheltenham Festival, getting up on the line to strike at 50-1; stepped up to 2m4f subsequently and ran a fine race when a close third behind Reserve Tank at Punchestown; looks likely to stay even further.

Elegant Escape (Ire)
7 b g Dubai Destination - Graineuaile (Orchestra)

Colin Tizzard   J P Romans

PLACINGS: 4577/2212133/121266-   RPR **167**c

Starts	1st	2nd	3rd	4th	Win & Pl
19	6	5	2	1	£296,879
151	12/18	Chep	3m5¹/₂f Cls1 Gd3 133-155 Ch Hcap good		£85,425
	11/18	Sand	3m Cls1 List Ch soft		£17,085
	2/18	Extr	3m Cls2 Ch heavy		£12,512
	12/17	Newb	2m7¹/₂f Cls1 Nov Gd2 Ch gd-sft		£23,048
	11/16	Asct	2m5¹/₂f Cls2 Nov Hdl gd-sft		£12,512
	10/16	Chep	2m3¹/₂f Cls4 Mdn Hdl gd-sft		£3,899

Proved himself a thorough stayer when winning last season's Welsh Grand National; forced into top company after 8lb rise for that win and just came up short, getting outpaced before staying on into second in the Cotswold Chase and coming sixth in the Gold Cup and Betway Bowl.

Elfile (Fr)
5 b m Saint Des Saints - Rapide (Assessor)

Willie Mullins (Ir)   Kenneth Alexander

PLACINGS: 22121/162-1   RPR **137**+h

Starts	1st	2nd	3rd	4th	Win & Pl
9	4	4	-	-	£69,193
	5/19	Punc	2m Nov List Hdl gd-yld		£19,392
	1/19	Punc	2m4f Mdn Hdl good		£7,214
	11/17	Ange	1m7f NHF 3yo soft		£9,402
	9/17	Angl	1m5f NHF 3yo good		£4,274

Dual French bumper winner who also made a winning hurdles debut last season and continued to progress through the spring; stepped up on

her Cheltenham Festival sixth when second behind Honeysuckle at Fairyhouse and won a Listed mares' novice at Punchestown.

Elgin

7 b g Duke Of Marmalade - China Tea (High Chaparral)

Alan King   Elite Racing Club

PLACINGS: 51/211227/411615/   RPR **155**h

Starts 14	1st 6	2nd 3	3rd -	4th 1	Win & Pl £172,810
	2/18	Winc	1m7¹/₂f Cls1 Gd2 Hdl soft		£34,331
145	11/17	Chel	2m¹/₂f Cls1 Gd3 137-163 Hdl Hcap soft		£56,950
140	11/17	Asct	1m7¹/₂f Cls1 List 121-141 Hdl Hcap good		£34,170
	12/16	Kemp	2m Cls2 Nov Hdl good		£11,261
	11/16	Newc	2m¹/₂f Cls4 Mdn Hdl 4-6yo soft		£4,549
	3/16	Hayd	1m7¹/₂f Cls5 NHF 4-6yo good		£2,274

Massive improver two seasons ago, winning two valuable handicaps and stepping up to Graded level; came up short against the top hurdlers in the Champion Hurdle but ran a decent race in fifth and Kingwell Hurdle victory puts him up there with the best over 2m in Britain; missed last season through injury.

Elimay (Fr)

5 gr m Montmartre - Hyde (Poliglote)

Willie Mullins (Ir)   John P McManus

PLACINGS: 4/13222/26-11   RPR **142**+h

Starts 10	1st 3	2nd 4	3rd 1	4th 1	Win & Pl £137,725
	5/19	Klny	2m1f List Hdl good		£16,622
	5/19	Punc	2m4f Hdl yield		£13,851
	5/17	Autl	2m1¹/₂f Hdl 3yo v soft		£19,692

Bought to go chasing having shown good form in France (runner-up in Grade 3 and Listed races) but has continued to thrive over hurdles; only sixth in the Mares' Hurdle at Cheltenham last season but improved to win at Punchestown and Killarney.

Elixir De Nutz (Fr)

5 gr g Al Namix - Nutz (Turgeon)

Colin Tizzard   Terry Warner

PLACINGS: 16/F2111-   RPR **148**+h

Starts 7	1st 4	2nd 1	3rd -	4th -	Win & Pl £65,789
	1/19	Sand	2m Cls1 Nov Gd1 Hdl soft		£28,475
	12/18	Chel	2m1f Cls3 Nov Hdl 4-6yo good		£9,285
	11/18	Chel	2m¹/₂f Cls1 Nov Gd2 Hdl good		£18,006
	10/17	Agtn	1m6f NHF 3yo gd-sft		£6,838

Leading contender for last season's Supreme Novices' Hurdle at Cheltenham until ruled out through injury; had won his last three, including a Grade 2 at Cheltenham against Supreme third

Itchy Feet and the Tolworth at Sandown against Kingwell winner Grand Sancy; being aimed at the Champion Hurdle.

Emitom (Ire)

5 b g Gold Well - Avenging Angel (Heron Island)

Warren Greatrex   The Spero Partnership

PLACINGS: 1/11112-   RPR **149**+h

Starts 6	1st 5	2nd 1	3rd -	4th -	Win & Pl £41,123
	3/19	Newb	2m4¹/₂f Cls4 Nov Hdl gd-sft		£4,549
	1/19	Ling	2m Cls4 Nov Hdl gd-sft		£4,159
	11/18	Ffos	2m4f Cls4 Mdn Hdl soft		£4,159
	11/18	Asct	2m Cls4 NHF 4-6yo good		£4,549
	4/18	Wwck	2m Cls5 NHF 4-6yo gd-sft		£2,599

Won first five races under rules in bumpers and novice hurdles before suffering sole defeat when a fine second behind Champ in the Sefton at Aintree; saw out trip well on first run at 3m (albeit in slowly run race) and expected to prove a top stayer by connections.

Envoi Allen (Fr)

5 b g Muhtathir - Reaction (Saint Des Saints)

Gordon Elliott (Ir)   Cheveley Park Stud

PLACINGS: 1/1111-   RPR **137**b

Starts 4	1st 4	2nd -	3rd -	4th -	Win & Pl £109,129
	3/19	Chel	2m¹/₂f Cls1 Gd1 NHF 4-6yo soft		£42,203
	2/19	Leop	2m Gd2 NHF 4-7yo gd-yld		£46,509
	12/18	Navn	2m List NHF 4-7yo yield		£14,967
	12/18	Fair	2m NHF 4yo good		£5,451

Unbeaten in four bumpers last season, crowning a brilliant campaign with victory in the Champion Bumper at Cheltenham; did really well to win off a slow pace that day given he is expected to prove best over at least 2m4f; has the scope to make a top jumper.

Epatante (Fr)

5 b m No Risk At All - Kadjara (Silver Rainbow)

Nicky Henderson   John P McManus

PLACINGS: 211/119-   RPR **132**+h

Starts 6	1st 4	2nd 1	3rd -	4th -	Win & Pl £40,437
	2/19	Extr	2m1f Cls4 Nov Hdl gd-sft		£4,549
	11/18	Kemp	2m Cls4 Nov Hdl good		£4,094
	11/17	StCl	1m4¹/₂f Cls1 Gd1 NHF 3yo heavy		£21,368
	9/17	Le L	1m4f NHF 3yo v soft		£7,692

Grade 1 bumper winner in France who impressed in winning first two starts over hurdles last season following move to Nicky Henderson; favourite for the mares' novice hurdle at Cheltenham only to disappoint in ninth.

Makers of fine and functional property maps
ruralmaps.co.uk
01962 793468

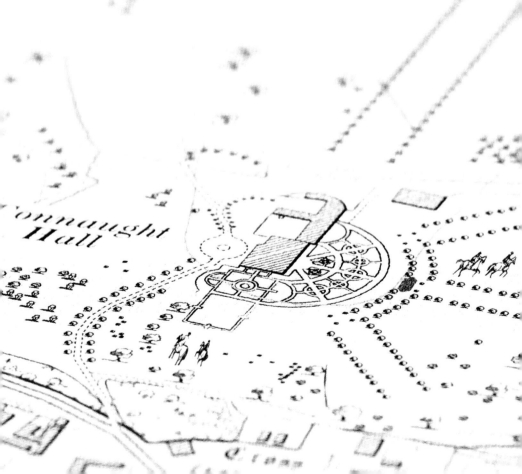

Ex Patriot (Ire)

6 b g Elusive Pimpernel - Carolobrian (Mark Of Esteem)

Ellmarie Holden (Ir)   Paul Holden

PLACINGS: 151d43/331275/5411-   RPR **147**+c

Starts		1st	2nd	3rd	4th	Win & Pl
15		4	3	3	2	£77,796
136	3/19	Gowr	2m2f 120-148 Ch Hcap soft			£26,577
	2/19	Thur	2m¹/₂f Ch good			£6,659
	12/17	Limk	2m4f Hdl heavy			£8,161
	1/17	Fair	2m Mdn Hdl 4yo soft			£6,308

Smart hurdler (fourth in the 2017 Triumph) who gradually improved over fences last season and finished off with a successful handicap debut in a valuable race at Gowran Park; still 9lb lower than hurdles mark after that win and should progress after just four chase runs.

Fakir D'oudairies (Fr)

4 b g Kapgarde - Niagaria Du Bois (Grand Tresor)

Joseph Patrick O'Brien (Ir)   John P McManus

PLACINGS: 4/264B1142-2   RPR **146**h

Starts		1st	2nd	3rd	4th	Win & Pl
10		2	3	-	3	£87,755
	1/19	Chel	2m1f Cls1 Gd2 Hdl 4yo gd-sft			£18,006
	1/19	Cork	2m Mdn Hdl 4-5yo soft			£7,492

Not far off last season's leading juvenile hurdlers, finishing second behind Pentland Hills at Aintree and Fusil Raffles at Punchestown; ridden much more forcefully both times than when staying on into fourth in the Supreme; could improve over further.

Old favourite Faugheen pulled up on his final start last season but had proved himself to still be a force when finishing third in the Stayers' Hurdle

Farclas (Fr)

5 gr g Jukebox Jury - Floriana (Seattle Dancer)

Gordon Elliott (Ir)   Gigginstown House Stud

PLACINGS: 2215/6F55P-111   RPR **149**h

Starts	1st	2nd	3rd	4th	Win & Pl
12	4	2	-	-	£128,502

6/19	Rosc	2m Nov Ch good	£8,324
5/19	Punc	2m Nov Ch good	£11,099
5/19	DRoy	2m3½f Ch good	£6,659
3/18	Chel	2m1f Cls1 Gd1 Hdl 4yo soft	£71,188

Won the Triumph Hurdle in 2018 but failed to make any impression in open company last season, finishing no better than fifth (twice, of six and seven) in five runs; got back to winning ways over fences in the summer and likely to be aimed at top novice chases.

Faugheen (Ire)

11 b g Germany - Miss Pickering (Accordion)

Willie Mullins (Ir)   Mrs S Ricci

PLACINGS: 111/1211/1P261/2F3P-   RPR **162**h

Starts	1st	2nd	3rd	4th	Win & Pl
22	14	3	1	-	£964,890

4/18	Punc	3m Gd1 Hdl yld-sft	£143,584
11/17	Punc	2m Gd1 Hdl sft-hvy	£42,863
1/16	Leop	2m Gd1 Hdl soft	£48,529
12/15	Kemp	2m Cls1 Gd1 Hdl gd-sft	£56,950
5/15	Punc	2m Gd1 Hdl gd-yld	£93,023
3/15	Chel	2m½f Cls1 Gd1 Hdl gd-sft	£227,800
12/14	Kemp	2m Cls1 Gd1 Hdl gd-sft	£57,218
11/14	Asc-	2m3½f Cls1 Hdl soft	£50,643
4/14	Punc	2m Nov Gd1 Hdl gd-yld	£46,500
3/14	Chel	2m5f Cls1 Nov Gd1 Hdl good	£68,340
12/13	Limk	3m Nov Gd3 Hdl heavy	£15,061
12/13	Navn	2m4f Nov Hdl gd-yld	£7,293
11/13	Punc	2m6f Mdn Hdl yield	£7,293
5/13	Punc	2m NHF 5yo yield	£4,488

Outstanding Champion Hurdle winner in 2015 and has become a high-class staying hurdler since

returning from a long layoff in 2017; finished a good third in last season's Stayers' Hurdle but suffered from a fibrillating heart when pulled up at Aintree.

Felix Desjy (Fr)

6 ch g Maresca Sorrento - Lamadaun (Smadoun)

Gordon Elliott (Ir)   Gigginstown House Stud

PLACINGS: 1/1165/1752151-2   RPR **152**h

Starts	1st	2nd	3rd	4th	Win & Pl
12	5	2	-	-	£130,437

4/19	Aint	2m⅛f Cls1 Nov Gd1 Hdl soft	£56,130
1/19	Punc	2m Nov Gd2 Hdl good	£23,653
10/18	Gway	2m½f Mdn Auct Hdl yield	£10,903
11/17	DRoy	2m NHF 4-7yo soft	£7,897
10/17	Punc	2m NHF 4-7yo soft	£5,265

Relished switch to forceful tactics over 2m last season, winning a Grade 2 at Fairyhouse when dropped in trip and later adding a Grade 1 at Aintree over Aramon; unsuited by standing start in the Supreme (couldn't lead) but no excuses when second to Klassical Dream at Punchestown.

First Approach (Ire)

6 b g Robin Des Champs - Manhattan Babe (Definite Article)

Noel Meade (Ir)   Mrs Patricia Hunt

PLACINGS: 1/239/12146140-4   RPR **145**h

Starts	1st	2nd	3rd	4th	Win & Pl
12	3	2	1	3	£37,460

1/19	Thur	2m6½f Nov Hdl good	£8,602
11/18	DRoy	2m6f Mdn Hdl good	£8,197
10/18	Tipp	2m4f NHF 5-7yo good	£5,451

Highly tried last season, running in four Grade 1 races and emerging with huge credit a couple of times, including when a five-length fourth behind Minella Indo at Punchestown; won three out of five (a bumper and two novice hurdles, including a dead heat) below that level.

First Assignment (Ire)

6 b g Vinnie Roe - Rebel Dream (Dushyantor)

Ian Williams — The DTTW Partnership

PLACINGS: 1/2413/113394-   RPR **142**h

Starts	1st	2nd	3rd	4th	Win & Pl
10	3	1	3	2	£61,810

130	11/18	Chel	3m Cls1 List 123-147 Hdl Hcap good	£22,527
125	10/18	Chel	2m5f Cls3 116-141 Hdl Hcap good	£10,007
116	1/18	Hntg	2m4¹/₂f Cls4 110-122 Hdl Hcap soft	£5,198

Won first two handicap hurdles last season, most notably by nine lengths on first run over 3m at Cheltenham; came up short after 12lb rise subsequently, albeit still running well in competitive handicaps (ninth in the Pertemps Final); point-to-point winner who could go novice chasing.

First Flow (Ire)

7 b g Primary - Clonroche Wells (Pierre)

Kim Bailey — A N Solomons

PLACINGS: 4/4111P/5-   RPR **140**h

Starts	1st	2nd	3rd	4th	Win & Pl
7	3	-	-	2	£29,089

	1/18	Hayd	1m7¹/₂f Cls1 Nov Gd2 Hdl heavy	£17,085
	12/17	Newb	2m¹/₂f Cls4 Hdl heavy	£4,549
	11/17	Ling	2m Cls4 Nov Hdl soft	£5,198

Did well as a novice hurdler two seasons ago, winning three times including a Grade 2 at Haydock; chasing plans shelved last term after an early-season setback and restricted to just one run due to preference for soft ground, finishing fifth in the Imperial Cup.

Frodon (right) rounded off a tremendous season by winning the Ryanair Chase

Footpad (Fr)

7 b g Creachadoir - Willamina (Sadler's Wells)

Willie Mullins (Ir) — Simon Munir & Isaac Souede

PLACINGS: F/1124243/11111/F28-   RPR **164**c

Starts	1st	2nd	3rd	4th	Win & Pl
23	10	4	3	2	£605,566

	4/18	Punc	2m Nov Gd1 Ch yld-sft	£60,044
	3/18	Chel	2m Cls1 Nov Gd1 Ch heavy	£99,663
	2/18	Leop	2m1f Nov Gd1 Ch soft	£52,212
	12/17	Leop	2m1f Nov Gd1 Ch yield	£45,385
	11/17	Navn	2m1f Ch sft-hvy	£8,950
	6/16	Autl	2m3¹/₂f Gd1 Hdl 4yo soft	£89,338
	5/16	Autl	2m3¹/₂f Gd3 Hdl 4yo v soft	£44,669
	2/16	Leop	2m Gd1 Hdl 4yo sft-hvy	£36,875
	1/16	Gowr	2m Hdl 4yo heavy	£10,037
	11/15	Gowr	2m Mdn Hdl 3yo soft	£6,419

Went unbeaten as a novice chaser, winning five races including the Racing Post Arkle, but had nothing go right last term; suffered an overreach on his return and looked short of fitness when overhauled by Simply Ned next time; bled when disappointing in the Ryanair.

Fox Norton (Fr)

9 b g Lando - Natt Musik (Kendor)

Colin Tizzard — Ann & Alan Potts Limited

PLACINGS: 33331/112211/12P/23-   RPR **165**c

Starts	1st	2nd	3rd	4th	Win & Pl
27	11	6	6	1	£641,625

	11/17	Chel	2m Cls1 Gd2 Ch soft	£42,713
	4/17	Punc	2m Gd1 Ch gd-yld	£126,068
	4/17	Aint	2m4f Cls1 Gd1 Ch good	£112,310
	11/16	Chel	2m Cls1 Gd2 Ch soft	£42,713
146	10/16	Chel	2m1f Cls3 131-157 Ch Hcap good	£31,280
	4/16	Chel	2m¹/₂f Cls2 Nov Ch good	£12,512
	10/15	MRas	2m1f Cls3 Nov Ch good	£7,798
	5/15	Hntg	2m¹/₂f Cls4 Nov Ch good	£3,769
140	2/15	Tntn	2m¹/₂f Cls2 129-145 Hdl Hcap soft	£11,078
	12/13	Donc	2m¹/₂f Cls1 Gd2 Hdl 3yo good	£15,876
	4/13	Fntb	2m Hdl 3yo good	£8,585

Dual Grade 1 winner from 2m-2m4f in early 2017 but has run only twice since being pulled up later that year when stepped up to 3m in the

King George; twice ran well in comeback runs at Ascot last season only to miss Cheltenham after another setback.

Frodon (Fr)

7 b g Nickname - Miss Country (Country Reel)

Paul Nicholls					P J Vogt
PLACINGS: F115/32321350/12111-					RPR **175**c

Starts		1st	2nd	3rd	4th	Win & Pl
31		13	3	5	1	£702,834
	3/19	Chel	2m4½f Cls1 Gd1 Ch gd-sft			£196,945
	1/19	Chel	3m1½f Cls1 Gd2 Ch gd-sft			£56,536
164	12/18	Chel	2m4½f Cls1 Gd3 138-164 Ch Hcap good			£74,035
158	10/18	Aint	2m4f Cls1 Gd2 138-158 Ch Hcap good			£45,016
154	1/18	Chel	2m5f Cls1 Gd3 131-154 Ch Hcap heavy			£42,713
	2/17	Kemp	2m4½f Cls1 Nov Gd2 Ch good			£18,793
	2/17	Muss	2m4f Cls3 Nov Ch good			£7,798
149	12/16	Chel	2m5f Cls1 Gd3 132-158 Ch Hcap soft			£56,950
	11/16	Winc	2m4f Cls1 Nov Gd2 Ch good			£28,486
	9/16	Font	2m5f Cls4 Nov Ch good			£5,198
	9/16	NAbb	2m1½f Cls3 Nov Ch good			£7,187
	2/16	Hayd	1m7½f Cls2 Hdl 4yo heavy			£9,747
	4/15	Autl	1m7f Hdl 3yo heavy			£20,450

Made the jump from high-class handicapper to genuine Grade 1 performer last season when much improved after wind surgery; crowned a memorable season with victory in the Ryanair Chase at Cheltenham having also stretched suspect stamina to 3m1f in the Cotswold Chase.

Fusil Raffles (Fr)

4 b g Saint Des Saints - Tali Des Obeaux (Panoramic)

Nicky Henderson					Simon Munir & Isaac Souede
PLACINGS: 121-1					RPR **147**+h

Starts		1st	2nd	3rd	4th	Win & Pl
4		3	1	-	-	£80,432
	5/19	Punc	2m Gd1 Hdl 4yo gd-yld			£53,153
	2/19	Kemp	2m Cls1 Gd2 Hdl 4yo good			£17,085
	7/18	Seno	2m2f Hdl 3yo soft			£5,947

Winning hurdler in France before adding victories at Kempton and Punchestown (Grade 1, comfortably beat Fakir D'oudairies) for Nicky Henderson; missed the Triumph Hurdle in between with a nasty injury but still proved himself among last season's top juvenile hurdlers.

Gala Ball (Ire)

9 b g Flemensfirth - Nuit Des Chartreux (Villez)

Philip Hobbs					Robert & Janet Gibbs
PLACINGS: 23/F621112/23122/21-					RPR **153**+c

Starts		1st	2nd	3rd	4th	Win & Pl
18		5	7	3	-	£64,267
144	3/19	Newb	2m4f Cls2 131-144 Ch Hcap gd-sft			£12,660
	2/17	Extr	2m3f Cls3 Nov Ch soft			£7,798
133	3/16	Newb	2m1½f Cls3 119-140 Ch Hcap soft			£12,512
	2/16	Winc	2m4f Cls4 Nov Hdl soft			£3,899
	1/16	Winc	1m7½f Cls4 Nov Hdl soft			£3,249

Missed nearly two years with leg trouble but returned better than ever last spring, finishing second in the Greatwood Gold Cup at Newbury before winning over the same course and distance soon after; open to improvement as thought to need softer ground by his trainer.

Galvin (Ire)

5 b g Gold Well - Burren Moonshine (Moonax)

Gordon Elliott (Ir)					R A Bartlett
PLACINGS: 1111162-					RPR **142**h

Starts		1st	2nd	3rd	4th	Win & Pl
7		5	1	-	-	£33,551
	2/19	Ayr	2m Cls4 Nov Hdl soft			£4,094
	1/19	Navn	2m Nov Hdl yield			£8,879
	8/18	Prth	2m Cls4 Mdn Hdl good			£4,549
	7/18	Limk	2m NHF 4-7yo gd-yld			£5,996
	7/18	Rosc	2m NHF 4-7yo good			£5,451

Won first five races in bumpers and novice hurdles last season; far from disgraced when losing unbeaten record in the Ballymore at Cheltenham, fading into sixth behind City Island after smashing through three out; dropped back to 2m when beaten by Getaway Trump at Ayr.

Gardens Of Babylon (Ire)

4 b g Camelot - Condition (Deploy)

Joseph Patrick O'Brien (Ir)					John P McManus
PLACINGS: 12232-10					RPR **142**+h

Starts		1st	2nd	3rd	4th	Win & Pl
7		2	3	1	-	£67,750
	5/19	Punc	2m Nov Hdl gd-yld			£13,851
	12/18	Punc	2m Mdn Hdl 3yo good			£7,087

Ran consistently well in top juvenile hurdles last season, notably when finishing third behind Pentland Hills in the Triumph Hurdle at Cheltenham; half-length second behind French Made at Fairyhouse next time before beating his elders in a novice at Punchestown; disappointing in the Galway Hurdle.

Geordie B

6 gr g Geordieland - Sari Rose (Vertical Speed)

Venetia Williams					C Boultbee-Brooks
PLACINGS: 1/6211-					RPR **141**+h

Starts		1st	2nd	3rd	4th	Win & Pl
5		3	1	-	-	£11,938
	3/19	Extr	2m7f Cls4 Nov Hdl soft			£4,094
	1/19	Ling	2m7f Cls4 Nov Hdl soft			£4,159
	4/18	Hrfd	2m Cls5 Am NHF 4-6yo heavy			£2,274

Won last two novice hurdles last season, easily defying a penalty when following up at Exeter; described as a chaser through and through by his trainer, who also feels he needs soft ground (all three wins on soft or heavy and was a non-runner on good last season).

Get In The Queue

5 b g Mount Nelson - Amarullah (Daylami)

Harry Fry					Paul & Clare Rooney
PLACINGS: 111-					RPR **137**+b

Starts		1st	2nd	3rd	4th	Win & Pl
3		3	-	-	-	£34,053
	3/19	Newb	2m1½f Cls2 NHF 4-5yo gd-sft			£29,505
	2/19	Extr	2m1f Cls5 NHF 4-6yo gd-sft			£2,274
	12/18	Uttx	2m Cls5 NHF 4-6yo soft			£2,274

Hugely impressive in winning all three bumpers

last season, most notably when hacking up by 16 lengths at Exeter under a penalty; well backed for the Champion Bumper at Cheltenham but instead kept to calmer waters when adding a valuable sales bumper at Newbury.

Getabird (Ire)

7 b g Getaway - Fern Bird (Revoque)

Willie Mullins (Ir)				Mrs S Ricci
PLACINGS: O1/11/11017P/12-P				RPR **156**+c

Starts	1st	2nd	3rd	4th	Win & Pl
11	6	1	-	-	£91,534

12/18	Punc	2m Ch yield	£7,632
4/18	Fair	2m Nov Gd2 Hdl heavy	£26,106
1/18	Punc	2m Nov Gd2 Hdl sft-hvy	£23,235
12/17	Punc	2m4f Mdn Hdl heavy	£6,844
1/17	Gowr	2m NHF 5-7yo soft	£6,833
12/16	Fair	2m NHF 4yo gd-yld	£4,070

Yet to hit the heights once anticipated as a youngster but showed promise in a light campaign over fences last year; would have beaten Hardline in a Grade 1 at Limerick but for a slow jump at the last and didn't stay 3m when stepped up in trip at Punchestown.

Getaway Trump (Ire)

6 b g Getaway - Acinorev (Cape Cross)

Paul Nicholls				Owners Group 023
PLACINGS: 34/146/41124411-				RPR **155**+h

Starts	1st	2nd	3rd	4th	Win & Pl
147	4	1		4	£98,106

4/19	Sand	2m Cls2 Nov 122-147 Hdl Hcap good	£61,900
4/19	Ayr	2m Cls3 Nov Hdl good	£9,942
12/18	Extr	2m1f Cls4 Nov Hdl heavy	£4,874
11/18	Plum	2m4½f Cls4 Nov Hdl good	£4,094

Four-time winner as a novice hurdler last season, finally winning a valuable prize off top weight in a novice handicap at Sandown on his final run; had looked to find 2m4f just too far when second to Champ in the Challow and given plenty to do when fourth in the Betfair Hurdle.

Give Me A Copper (Ire)

9 ch g Presenting - Copper Supreme (Supreme Leader)

Paul Nicholls			Done, Ferguson, Kyle, Mason & Wood
PLACINGS: 11/161/U1/4F4-			RPR **144**c

Starts	1st	2nd	3rd	4th	Win & Pl
9	4			2	£32,817

11/17	Kemp	3m Cls3 Nov Ch good	£8,133
4/17	Ayr	2m4½f Cls3 Nov Hdl gd-sft	£6,498
12/16	Extr	2m7f Cls4 Mdn Hdl soft	£3,249
3/16	Cork	2m3f NHF 5-7yo heavy	£4,296

Grand chasing type but has had progress over fences hampered by injury, missing more than a year after winning at Kempton in 2017; unable to overcome lack of experience in top staying handicaps last season but ran a fair race when fourth in the bet365 Gold Cup.

Glen Forsa (Ire)

7 b g Mahler - Outback Ivy (Bob Back)

Mick Channon				T P Radford
PLACINGS: 15/22111UP-				RPR **155**+c

Starts	1st	2nd	3rd	4th	Win & Pl
9	4	2	-	-	£41,016

	2/19	Sand	1m7½f Cls1 Nov Gd2 Ch soft	£18,224
125	12/18	Kemp	2m4½f Cls3 Nov 121-137 Ch Hcap gd-sft	£14,013
114	11/18	Chep	2m7½f Cls4 Nov 102-122 Ch Hcap soft	£3,834
	11/16	Hntg	1m5½f Cls6 Mdn NHF 4-6yo gd-sft	£1,949

Won first three chases last season, kicking off over 2m7½f but looking best when dropping back in trip to 2m in the Kingmaker at Sandown; suspicion he was flattered that day (just three runners and main rival Kalashnikov flopped) and was pulled up at Aintree after early exit in the Arkle.

Glen Rocco

8 ch g Shirocco - Adees Dancer (Danehill Dancer)

Nick Gifford			Kyle, Mason, Brooks, Ferguson & Stevens
PLACINGS: P/1/653/U13216-			RPR **143**+c

Starts	1st	2nd	3rd	4th	Win & Pl
9	2	1	2		£26,609

124	1/19	Kemp	3m Cls2 124-148 Ch Hcap good	£11,574
109	11/18	Font	2m5½f Cls4 Nov 101-120 Ch Hcap gd-sft	£7,216

Bought as a Grand National horse and improved massively when stepped up to 3m last season, running away with a handicap chase at Kempton by 23 lengths; outpaced in sixth over same course and distance when favourite for a valuable handicap soon after.

Global Citizen (Ire)

7 b g Alkaadhem - Lady Willmurt (Mandalus)

Ben Pauling				The Megsons
PLACINGS: 1/152116/21417-				RPR **158**+h

Starts	1st	2nd	3rd	4th	Win & Pl
11	5	2		1	£119,454

	1/19	Hayd	1m7½f Cls1 Gd2 Hdl gd-sft	£42,713
146	12/18	Newb	2m1½f Cls1 List 126-146 Hdl Hcap soft	£28,475
	2/18	Kemp	2m Cls1 Nov Gd2 Hdl good	£17,085
	2/18	Sthl	1m7½f Cls4 Nov Hdl soft	£4,094
	10/17	Worc	2m Cls6 NHF 4-6yo gd-fm	£1,689

Progressive hurdler last season, thriving under forceful tactics; won a Listed handicap at Newbury and claimed scalp of Champion Hurdle third Silver Streak when adding the Grade 2 trial at Haydock to put himself up there with Britain's leading 2m hurdlers.

Go Conquer cruises home in the Sky Bet Chase

Go Conquer (Ire)

10 b g Arcadio - Ballinamona Wish (Kotashaan)

Nigel Twiston-Davies   Paul & Clare Rooney

PLACINGS: /2F2250/11U58/321PP-   RPR **163+**c

Starts	1st	2nd	3rd	4th	Win & Pl
24	6	5	2	1	£181,609

			Win & Pl
151	1/19	Donc	3m Cls1 List 130-153 Ch Hcap good	£56,950
142	11/17	Asct	3m Cls1 Gd3 128-150 Ch Hcap good	£56,950
135	10/17	Font	2m5¹/₂f Cls2 117-143 Ch Hcap good	£11,711
122	4/16	Winc	2m4f Cls3 118-129 Ch Hcap gd-sft	£6,498
	12/14	Kels	2m Cls4 Nov Hdl soft	£3,249
	4/14	Carl	2m1f Cls6 NHF 4-6yo gd-sft	£1,560

Very smart 3m handicap chaser who ran out an impressive winner of last season's Sky Bet Chase; clear non-stayer in the Grand National (had never previously run beyond 3m1f) and might not have recovered when pulled up again at Sandown soon after.

God's Own (Ire)

11 b g Oscar - Dantes Term (Phardante)

Tom George   Crossed Fingers Partnership

PLACINGS: /1233553/6333/12P53-   RPR **166**c

Starts	1st	2nd	3rd	4th	Win & Pl
38	8	8	11	2	£624,001

			Win & Pl
156	11/18	Extr	2m1¹/₂f Cls1 Gd2 141-157 Ch Hcap good	£39,522
	4/16	Punc	2m Gd1 Ch gd-yld	£86,765
	4/16	Aint	2m4f Cls1 Gd1 Ch gd-sft	£112,788
155	11/14	Extr	2m1¹/₂f Cls1 Gd2 152-172 Ch Hcap gd-sft	£35,594
	5/14	Punc	2m Nov Gd1 Ch yield	£56,833
129	11/13	Kemp	2m5f Cls2 129-155 Hdl Hcap gd-sft	£11,574
	2/13	Muss	2m3¹/₂f Cls4 Nov Hdl good	£3,899
	11/12	Donc	2m1¹/₂f Cls4 Nov Hdl soft	£3,899

Not quite the same force as when winning Grade 1 chases at Aintree and Punchestown in April 2016 but won his first race since then in

last season's Haldon Gold Cup; continued to perform to a high level in top chases and finished third behind Altior at Sandown on his final run.

Gold Present (Ire)

9 br g Presenting - Ouro Preto (Definite Article)

Nicky Henderson   Mr & Mrs J D Cotton

PLACINGS: P60/1522F/11PP/39F2-   RPR **158**c

Starts	1st	2nd	3rd	4th	Win & Pl
20	5	5	1	-	£145,735

			Win & Pl
147	12/17	Asct	3m Cls1 List 130-156 Ch Hcap gd-sft	£56,950
142	12/17	Newb	2m6¹/₂f Cls2 124-144 Ch Hcap gd-sft	£25,024
130	11/16	Donc	2m3f Cls3 Nov 120-134 Ch Hcap gd-sft	£12,512
	4/15	MRas	2m2¹/₂f Cls4 Nov Hdl good	£3,899
	3/15	Strf	2m2¹/₂f Cls4 Mdn Hdl gd-sft	£3,249

Won good handicaps at Newbury and Ascot in late 2017 but hampered since by preference for good ground (twice a late withdrawal from the Grand National); twice placed in Graded races last season and fell when running well when getting good ground in a handicap for only time.

Good Boy Bobby (Ire)

6 b g Flemensfirth - Princess Gaia (King's Theatre)

Nigel Twiston-Davies   Paul & Clare Rooney

PLACINGS: 1131/1311-   RPR **140+**h

Starts	1st	2nd	3rd	4th	Win & Pl
8	6	-	2	-	£21,789

			Win & Pl
	4/19	Ffos	2m4f Cls4 Nov Hdl soft	£4,094
	3/19	Sthl	1m7¹/₂f Cls4 Nov Hdl good	£3,249
	10/18	Carl	2m1f Cls4 Nov Hdl gd-sft	£4,549
	3/18	Weth	2m Cls5 NHF 4-6yo heavy	£2,599
	1/18	Chep	2m Cls5 NHF 5-7yo heavy	£2,599
	11/17	Chep	2m Cls6 NHF 4-6yo soft	£1,949

Prolific in bumpers and novice hurdles, winning

three out of four when sent hurdling last season but never above Class 4 level; coped well with step up to 2m4f when defying 12st 1lb at Ffos Las having previously been regarded as too free; likely to go novice chasing.

Good Man Pat (Ire)

6 b g Gold Well - Basically Supreme (Supreme Leader)

Alan King					David Sewell
PLACINGS: P/1322411P/313P5-					RPR **149**c

Starts	1st	2nd	3rd	4th	Win & Pl
12	3	2	3	1	£26,767
135	2/19	Plum	2m3¹/₂f Cls3 Nov 125-135 Ch Hcap soft		£7,882
	3/18	Sthl	3m Cls4 Nov Hdl soft		£4,094
	2/18	Bang	2m7f Cls3 Nov Hdl heavy		£6,238

Stepped up on useful hurdling form when sent novice chasing last season despite lots of room for improvement with his jumping; not beaten far in a Grade 2 novice at Kempton and competitive handicap at Sandown but pulled up at the Cheltenham Festival.

Grand Sancy (Fr)

5 b g Diamond Boy - La Courtille (Risk Seeker)

Paul Nicholls				Martin Broughton Racing Partners
PLACINGS: 42224P/12114210-				RPR **152**h

Starts	1st	2nd	3rd	4th	Win & Pl
14	4	5	-	3	£95,984
	2/19	Winc	1m7¹/₂f Cls1 Gd2 Hdl good		£34,170
	11/18	Hayd	1m7¹/₂f Cls1 Nov List Hdl good		£14,238
	11/18	Winc	1m7¹/₂f Cls3 Nov Hdl 4-6yo good		£6,498
125	10/18	Chep	2m Cls2 121-132 Hdl 4yo Hcap good		£12,996

Failed to win in first season over hurdles but made the most of that experience when much improved as a second-season novice last term, even going close to winning the Tolworth at Sandown; proved himself in open company when winning the Kingwell at Wincanton.

Prolific hunter chase winner Hazel Hill heads for home in the Foxhunter at Cheltenham

Great Field (Fr)

8 b g Great Pretender - Eaton Lass (Definite Article)

Willie Mullins (Ir)				John P McManus

PLACINGS: 2/11/1P/1111/1/FF-4				RPR **160**c

Starts	1st	2nd	3rd	4th	Win & Pl
13	8	1	-	1	£156,098

	3/18	Navn	2m Gd2 Ch heavy	£23,496
	4/17	Punc	2m Nov Gd1 Ch gd-yld	£57,991
	3/17	Thur	2m2f Nov List Ch yld-sft	£15,769
	3/17	Leop	2m1f Nov Ch sft-hvy	£11,038
	1/17	Gowr	2m Ch soft	£7,096
	2/16	Leop	2m2f Hdl soft	£9,496
	11/14	Pari	2m1f Hdl 3yo gd-sft	£8,400
	9/14	Pari	2m1f Hdl 3yo gd-sft	£8,000

Looked hugely exciting when winning first five chases but had his bubble burst last season; fell in first two races, including when looking beaten in a Grade 1 at Leopardstown, and bitterly disappointing when a distant fourth behind Un De Sceaux at Punchestown.

Hardline (Ire)

7 b g Arcadio - Hidden Reserve (Heron Island)

Gordon Elliott (Ir)				Gigginstown House Stud

PLACINGS: 2/211331138/121137-2				RPR **156+**c

Starts	1st	2nd	3rd	4th	Win & Pl
23	8	5	5	-	£197,133

	12/18	Limk	2m3¹/₂f Nov Gd1 Ch soft	£52,212
	12/18	Navn	2m1f Nov Gd3 Ch yield	£20,409
	10/18	Fair	2m Ch good	£6,542
	2/18	Naas	2m Nov Gd2 Hdl soft	£24,279
	2/18	Punc	2m Nov List Hdl heavy	£17,688
	11/17	Clon	2m¹/₂f Hdl sft-hvy	£6,844
	10/17	Wxfd	2m Mdn Hdl heavy	£5,791
	11/16	Thur	2m NHF 4-7yo good	£4,070

Did well in novice chases last season, winning three times and exploiting Getabird's late error in a Grade 1 at Limerick; hasn't finished first or second in five other attempts at that level, though, and was no match for Real Steel (racing off levels) in a novice handicap at Punchestown.

Hazel Hill (Ire)

11 b g Milan - Resenting (Presenting)

Philip Rowley				Mrs D Williams

PLACINGS: /11/1111/11112/111-1				RPR **154+**c

Starts	1st	2nd	3rd	4th	Win & Pl
5	5	-	-	-	£48,525

	5/19	Chel	3m2¹/₂f Cls2 Am Hunt Ch gd-sft	£14,913
	3/19	Chel	3m2¹/₂f Cls2 Am Hunt Ch gd-sft	£26,685
	1/19	Wwck	3m Cls6 Am Hunt Ch gd-sft	£1,872
	3/18	Towc	3m¹/₂f Cls5 Am Hunt Ch heavy	£2,560
	2/18	Leic	2m6¹/₂f Cls5 Nov Am Hunt Ch soft	£2,496

Last season's dominant hunter chaser; easily justified favouritism when winning the Foxhunter

Hell's Kitchen

8 b g Robin Des Champs - Mille Et Une (Trempolino)

Harry Fry				John P McManus

PLACINGS: 312/3/2U1P/7144-5				RPR **164**c

Starts	1st	2nd	3rd	4th	Win & Pl
13	3	2	2	2	£86,372

143	12/18	Asct	2m3f Cls2 126-145 Ch Hcap soft	£21,896
137	12/17	Chel	2m4¹/₂f Cls3 Nov 118-137 Ch Hcap gd-sft	£13,814
	3/16	Newb	2m4¹/₂f Cls4 Nov Hdl soft	£4,549

Has a very patchy record but has proved high-class on his day, with form of handicap wins over Mister Whitaker and Janika franked subsequently; also ran well when fourth in the Champion Chase last season but flopped at Aintree and Punchestown.

Highway One O One (Ire)

7 br g Stowaway - High Accord (Accordion)

Chris Gordon				Anthony Ward-Thomas

PLACINGS: /311221012/12143203-				RPR **151**c

Starts	1st	2nd	3rd	4th	Win & Pl
16	6	5	2	1	£95,289

	11/18	Carl	2m Cls2 Ch soft	£31,396
	9/18	NAbb	2m¹/₂f Cls3 Nov Ch gd-sft	£9,357
	4/18	Kemp	2m Cls4 Nov Hdl gd-sft	£4,094
	12/17	Font	2m1¹/₂f Cls4 Nov Hdl soft	£3,574
	10/17	Plum	2m Cls5 Mdn Hdl gd-sft	£3,249
	9/17	NAbb	2m1f Cls6 NHF 4-6yo gd-sft	£1,711

Found out in Graded novice chases after two early-season wins last season but ran a couple of fine races in handicaps at Cheltenham, chasing home Kildisart and finishing third behind Mister Whitaker in the Silver Trophy in April; disappointing at the Cheltenham Festival in between.

Honeysuckle

5 b m Sulamani - First Royal (Lando)

Henry de Bromhead (Ir)				Kenneth Alexander

PLACINGS: 1/1111-				RPR **144+**h

Starts	1st	2nd	3rd	4th	Win & Pl
4	4	-	-	-	£96,229

	4/19	Fair	2m4f Nov Gd1 Hdl gd-yld	£53,153
	1/19	Fair	2m2f Nov Gd3 Hdl yield	£19,392
	12/18	Thur	2m Nov List Hdl good	£17,688
	11/18	Fair	2m4f Mdn Hdl good	£5,996

Exciting mare who won all four races under rules

at Cheltenham in March; gamely followed up by a neck at the same course in May, making it five wins out of five under rules (and 16 out of 17 including point-to-points).

Follow us @RacingPost

last season; missed Cheltenham (trainer not happy in build-up) but bounced back by winning a Grade 1 novice hurdle at Fairyhouse; could go chasing having beaten fellow top mare Annie Mc by 15 lengths in a point-to-point; should get 3m.

I Just Know (Ire)

9 b g Robin Des Pres - Desperado Queen (Un Desperado)

Sue Smith				Mrs M B Scholey
PLACINGS: 6P/12211P3/3412F/2F-			RPR **148**c	

Starts	1st	2nd	3rd	4th	Win & Pl
20	4	4	4	1	£44,709
131	1/18	Catt	3m6f Cls3 111-133 Ch Hcap soft		£15,890
125	2/17	Catt	3m1f Cls3 115-133 Ch Hcap soft		£7,798
114	1/17	Donc	3m Cls4 Nov 110-122 Ch Hcap gd-sft		£3,899
105	11/16	Hexm	3m Cls4 Nov 79-105 Ch Hcap soft		£5,064

Missed most of last season through injury but had done enough at Kelso (in front when falling two out) to back up bright impression left by runaway win in North Yorkshire Grand National in January 2018; sent off 14-1 for that season's Grand National on the back of that only to fall at Becher's.

If The Cap Fits (Ire)

7 b g Milan - Derravaragh Sayra (Sayarshan)

Harry Fry				Paul & Clare Rooney
PLACINGS: 114/111/21321-			RPR **164**+h	

Starts	1st	2nd	3rd	4th	Win & Pl
11	7	2	1	1	£228,665
4/19	Aint	3m¹/₂f Cls1 Gd1 Hdl good			£101,034
11/18	Asct	2m3¹/₂f Cls1 Gd2 Hdl gd-sft			£56,950
12/17	Kemp	2m Cls2 Nov Hdl soft			£12,512
11/17	Bang	2m1¹/₂f Cls4 Nov Hdl soft			£3,249
10/17	Extr	2m2¹/₂f Cls4 Nov Hdl good			£3,899
2/17	Tntn	2m1¹/₂f Cls5 Am NHF 4-6yo good			£3,184
11/16	Plum	2m1¹/₂f Cls6 NHF 4-5yo gd-sft			£1,625

Began last season being trained as a Champion Hurdle horse but only really flourished when stepped up to 3m to win at Aintree on his final run, beating Roksana and Apple's Jade; very much unexposed as a stayer and should have plenty more to offer.

Indefatigable (Ire)

6 b m Schiaparelli - Spin The Wheel (Kalanisi)

Paul Webber				Philip Rocher & John B O'Connor
PLACINGS: 31/712251-			RPR **137**+h	

Starts	1st	2nd	3rd	4th	Win & Pl
8	3	2	1	-	£37,959
4/19	Chel	2m4¹/₂f Cls1 Nov List Hdl good			£14,068
11/18	Uttx	2m Cls4 Nov Hdl gd-sft			£4,094
4/18	Sthl	1m7¹/₂f Cls5 NHF 4-6yo good			£1,471

Best of the British-trained runners when finishing fifth in the mares' novice hurdle at the Cheltenham Festival, reversing previous form with Posh Trish and building on a neck second to Lady Buttons in a Grade 2 at Doncaster; progressed again to win a Listed race at Cheltenham by ten lengths.

Interconnected

5 br g Network - R De Rien Sivola (Robin Des Champs)

Dan Skelton				Grech & Parkin
PLACINGS: F1/2-			RPR **133**+h	

Starts	1st	2nd	3rd	4th	Win & Pl
1	-	1	-	-	£1,335

Bought for a record £620,000 in May, with new owner hoping he will prove a Gold Cup horse; had won a point-to-point by 20 lengths in February 2018 and ran subsequent Grade 1 runner-up Emitom close on debut under rules last season when trained by Nicky Henderson.

Itchy Feet (Fr)

5 b g Cima De Triomphe - Maeva Candas (Brier Creek)

Olly Murphy				Kate & Andrew Brooks
PLACINGS: 2/111234-			RPR **153**h	

Starts	1st	2nd	3rd	4th	Win & Pl
7	3	2	1	1	£44,067
10/18	Kemp	2m Cls1 Nov List Hdl good			£11,390
10/18	Sthl	1m7¹/₂f Cls4 Nov Hdl good			£4,094
9/18	Strf	2m1¹/₂f Cls5 NHF 4-6yo good			£2,599

Won first two races over hurdles last season to add to bumper success and went on to twice show smart form in defeat at Cheltenham, chasing home Elixir De Nutz before finishing third in the Supreme; well below his best when fourth in a Grade 1 at Aintree next time.

Janika (Fr)

6 b g Saddler Maker - Majaka (Kapgarde)

Nicky Henderson				Simon Munir & Isaac Souede
PLACINGS: 3/3325218211/2224-			RPR **165**+c	

Starts	1st	2nd	3rd	4th	Win & Pl
16	4	6	3	1	£198,763
4/18	Autl	2m6f Ch heavy			£24,637
3/18	Autl	2m2¹/₂f Ch 5yo heavy			£22,088
2/18	Pau	2m3¹/₂f Ch 5yo heavy			£14,442
0	11/17	Autl	2m2f Hdl 4yo Hcap heavy		£22,564

Won his last three chases in France before joining Nicky Henderson last season and desperately unlucky not to add to his haul; finished second in three handicaps under big weights, twice bumping into the progressive Siruh Du Lac; not far off Grade 1 level.

Jarveys Plate (Ire)

6 ch g Getaway - She's Got To Go (Glacial Storm)

Fergal O'Brien				The Yes No Wait Sorries
PLACINGS: 231/32139-			RPR **143**+h	

Starts	1st	2nd	3rd	4th	Win & Pl
6	2	1	2		£24,398
1/19	Chel	2m4¹/₂f Cls1 Nov List Hdl gd-sft			£14,068
4/18	Prth	2m Cls4 NHF 4-6yo soft			£3,165

Progressive novice hurdler last season, running away with a Listed novice at Cheltenham by 13 lengths on New Year's Day; just found out at a higher level subsequently, including when ninth

Moorcroft
Racehorse Welfare Centre

PROVIDING THE
VERY BEST
OF CARE
FOR OUR WONDERFUL
HORSES AWAITING A NEW
HOME AND A NEW LIFE

This centre in the south of England was set up to ensure that retired racehorses whatever age, can be re-trained to find another career in life. Much care and attention is given to each individual horse and when fully retrained new homes are found. The centre retains ownership for life and visits these horses every year to ensure that all is well.

This charity depends on generous donations from horse lovers. Many horses need a time for rehabilitation due to injury etc and start to enjoy an easier life after their racing careers. Visits by appointment are welcomed. Please ring Mary Frances, Manager, on 07929 666408 for more information or to arrange a visit.

Huntingrove Stud, Slinfold, West Sussex RH13 0RB
Tel: 07929 666408 | moorcroftracehorse@gmail.com | www.moorcroftracehorse.org.uk

in the Ballymore; expected by connections to prove better over fences.

Jerrysback (Ire)

7 b g Jeremy - Get A Few Bob Back (Bob Back)

Philip Hobbs					John P McManus

PLACINGS: 42/F111/51223-					RPR **152**c

Starts	1st	2nd	3rd	4th	Win & Pl
7	3	2	1	-	£40,914

12/18	Bang	2m4¹/₂f Cls4 Ch soft		£6,108
2/17	Weth	2m3¹/₂f Cls4 Nov Hdl gd-sft		£3,574
1/17	Plum	2m4¹/₂f Cls4 Nov Hdl heavy		£3,249

Missed more than 18 months after winning both starts over hurdles but returned better than ever last term, perhaps surprising even connections with 50-1 win at Bangor; twice second at Grade 2 level (2m4f-2m5f) and ran well for a long way when third in a gruelling National Hunt Chase.

Joe Farrell (Ire)

10 b g Presenting - Luck Of The Deise (Old Vic)

Rebecca Curtis			M Sherwood, N Morris & J Turner		

PLACINGS: 1/17620/424311/62PP-					RPR **151**+c

Starts	1st	2nd	3rd	4th	Win & Pl
19	5	4	1	2	£147,232

135	4/18	Ayr	4m Cls1 Gd3 129-155 Ch Hcap good	£122,443
124	3/18	Newb	2m7¹/₂f Cls3 Nov 117-131 Ch Hcap soft	£7,343
	11/16	Ffos	2m4f Cls5 Nov Hdl good	£2,274
	7/15	Worc	2m Cls6 NHF 4-6yo gd-fm	£1,754
	11/14	Hntg	1m5¹/₂f Cls6 Mdn NHF soft	£1,625

Won the Scottish National in 2018, capping a sharply progressive novice campaign; trained for the Grand National last season and well backed after a hugely promising prep run at Newbury only to never figure; pulled up again in the bet365 Gold Cup.

Jury Duty (Ire)

8 b g Well Chosen - Swan Heart (Broken Hearted)

Gordon Elliott (Ir)			Sideways Syndicate		

PLACINGS: 236/12122U3/37211UP-					RPR **160**+c

Starts	1st	2nd	3rd	4th	Win & Pl
25	6	6	6	2	£359,253

	3/19	DRoy	3m2f Ch soft	£11,099
	10/18	Fars	2m5f Gd1 Hdl yield	£200,000
	11/17	Punc	2m6¹/₂f Nov Gd2 Ch sft-hvy	£22,440
	10/17	Limk	2m6f Ch soft	£8,161
126	11/16	Navn	2m6¹/₂f 118-146 Hdl Hcap yld-sft	£21,691
111	2/16	Navn	2m4f 88-116 Hdl Hcap sft-hvy	£5,426

Smart staying chaser who thrived under an

enterprising campaign last season; won the Grand National Hurdle in the US before returning to conventional fences with an impressive victory at Down Royal; going well in the Grand National at Aintree when unseating his rider at the 18th.

Kalashnikov (Ire)

6 br g Kalanisi - Fairy Lane (Old Vic)

Amy Murphy					Paul Murphy

PLACINGS: 1/11212/1122U1-					RPR **160**+c

Starts	1st	2nd	3rd	4th	Win & Pl
12	7	4	-	-	£226,577

	4/19	Aint	2m4f Cls1 Nov Gd1 Ch gd-sft	£56,394
	12/18	Plum	2m1f Cls3 Nov Ch soft	£7,343
	11/18	Wwck	2m Cls3 Nov Ch good	£9,495
141	2/18	Newb	2m¹/₂f Cls1 Gd3 129-148 Hdl Hcap soft	£88,273
	12/17	Donc	2m¹/₂f Cls4 Nov Hdl 4-6yo gd-sft	£3,899
	11/17	Weth	2m Cls3 Nov Hdl soft	£5,523
	3/17	Weth	2m Cls5 NHF 4-6yo gd-sft	£2,599

High-class performer who belatedly matched hurdles form (2018 Betfair Hurdle winner and Supreme runner-up the following month) over fences last season when winning a 2m4f Grade 1 at Aintree after a stop-start campaign; looked unlucky in the Racing Post Arkle when badly hampered and unseating his rider at the sixth fence.

Kapcorse (Fr)

6 br g Kapgarde - Angesse (Indian River)

Paul Nicholls					John P McManus

PLACINGS: 4/6761/7117-					RPR **146**+c

Starts	1st	2nd	3rd	4th	Win & Pl
9	3	-	-	1	£39,052

	1/19	Winc	2m5¹/₂f Cls4 Nov Hdl good	£4,874
128	12/18	Newb	2m6¹/₂f Cls2 124-144 Ch Hcap soft	£25,024
116	4/18	Bang	2m4f Cls4 Nov 105-119 Ch Hcap gd-sft	£4,614

Has won two out of three over fences, including a handicap at Newbury last season by ten lengths; described as weak and backward following that victory by his trainer and given a light campaign back over hurdles subsequently; expected to get better with age.

Kateson

6 gr g Black Sam Bellamy - Silver Kate (Insan)

Tom Lacey					
		D M Richards, Roberts, Church, Ward W-Williams			

PLACINGS: 12722/11377-					RPR **141**h

Starts	1st	2nd	3rd	4th	Win & Pl
10	3	3	1	-	£29,697

	11/18	Newb	2m4¹/₂f Cls3 Nov Hdl soft	£6,758
	11/18	Chep	2m3¹/₂f Cls5 Mdn Hdl soft	£3,119
	10/17	Chep	2m Cls4 NHF 4-6yo good	£3,249

Smart performer in bumpers and novice hurdles over the last two seasons, winning his first two races over hurdles last season and twice placed in Graded company; unsuited by good ground twice subsequently; trainer expects him to be even better over fences.

Keeper Hill (Ire)
8 b g Westerner - You Take Care (Definite Article)

Warren Greatrex   McNeill Family

PLACINGS: 11176/121FFP/521003-   RPR **145**+h

Starts	1st	2nd	3rd	4th		Win & Pl
20	7	3	2	-		£84,373
139	1/19	Wwck	3m1f Cls2 126-152 Hdl Hcap good			£15,640
	12/17	Donc	3m Cls1 Nov Gd2 Ch good			£20,554
	11/17	Strf	2m6¹/₂f Cls4 Nov Ch good			£4,431
	2/17	Hntg	2m3¹/₂f Cls1 Nov List Hdl gd-sft			£17,085
	1/17	Hrfd	2m3¹/₂f Cls4 Nov Hdl soft			£3,379
	11/16	Bang	2m3¹/₂f Cls4 Nov Hdl soft			£3,899
	11/15	MRas	2m¹/₂f Cls6 NHF 4-6yo gd-sft			£1,643

Hugely promising as a novice chaser two seasons ago (Grade 2 winner) only to fall twice and lose confidence; put back over hurdles last term and did well in good staying handicaps, winning at Warwick and finishing third behind Aux Ptits Soins at Aintree.

Kemboy (Fr)
7 b g Voix Du Nord - Vitora (Victory Note)

Willie Mullins (Ir)
Supreme Horse Racing Club, Brett T Graham & K Sha

PLACINGS: 1257/214F11/11U1-1   RPR **178**+c

Starts	1st	2nd	3rd	4th		Win & Pl
15	8	2	-	1		£496,772
	5/19	Punc	3m¹/₂f Gd1 Ch yld-sft			£159,459
	4/19	Aint	3m1f Cls1 Gd1 Ch gd-sft			£112,260
	12/18	Leop	3m Gd1 Ch good			£91,372
	11/18	Clon	2m4f Gd2 Ch good			£26,106
147	4/18	Punc	2m5f Nov 126-147 Ch Hcap soft			£52,212
	4/18	Limk	3m Nov Gd3 Ch heavy			£22,190
	1/18	Fair	2m5¹/₂f Ch heavy			£7,632
	12/16	Limk	2m3f Mdn Hdl yield			£4,522

Hugely progressive staying chaser last season and claimed the notable scalp of Cheltenham Gold Cup hero Al Boum Photo in thrilling fashion at Punchestown; was completing a Grade 1 treble after wins at Leopardstown and Aintree but unseated his rider at the first at Cheltenham.

Kilbricken Storm (Ire)
8 b g Oscar - Kilbricken Leader (Supreme Leader)

Colin Tizzard   A Selway & P Wavish

PLACINGS: 45/1311313/1600-   RPR **143**+c

Starts	1st	2nd	3rd	4th		Win & Pl
10	4		3	-		£121,712
	11/18	Ffos	3m Cls3 Nov Ch heavy			£7,069
	3/18	Chel	3m Cls1 Nov Gd1 Hdl soft			£77,600
	12/17	Chel	3m Cls1 Nov Gd2 Hdl soft			£17,085
	11/17	Winc	1m7¹/₂f Cls3 Nov Hdl 4-6yo soft			£6,498

Surprise winner of the Albert Bartlett at Cheltenham two seasons ago but backed that up with a half-length third behind Next Destination and Delta Work at Punchestown; didn't jump

well in two runs over fences last season and twice well beaten when sent back over hurdles.

Kildisart (Ire)
7 b g Dubai Destination - Princess Mairead (Blueprint)

Ben Pauling   Simon Munir & Isaac Souede

PLACINGS: 2/2/212519/21141-   RPR **160**+c

Starts	1st	2nd	3rd	4th		Win & Pl
12	5	4	-	1		£136,915
148	4/19	Aint	3m1f Cls1 Gd3 127-148 Ch Hcap good			£42,203
141	1/19	Chel	2m4¹/₂f Cls2 Nov 120-146 Ch Hcap gd-sft			£17,034
	12/18	Asct	2m5f Cls2 Ch soft			£31,280
135	3/18	Kemp	2m5f Cls2 122-135 Hdl Hcap soft			£21,896
	11/17	Asct	2m3¹/₂f Cls3 Mdn Hdl gd-sft			£6,498

Progressive novice chaser last season, winning three times in five races; looked short of pace at around 2m4f when raised in grade for the JLT at Cheltenham but took a big leap forward when stepped up in trip for the first time at Aintree, running away with a competitive handicap.

Kilfilum Cross (Ire)
8 gr g Beneficial - Singh Street (Dolphin Street)

Henry Oliver   Andy Bell & Fergus Lyons

PLACINGS: 421/7211/43124-   RPR **147**c

Starts	1st	2nd	3rd	4th		Win & Pl
9	3	2	1	2		£38,084
132	2/19	Ludl	3m Cls3 106-132 Am Ch Hcap good			£9,109
	4/18	Kemp	3m1¹/₂f Cls4 Nov Hdl soft			£4,094
	3/18	Chep	2m7¹/₂f Cls4 Nov Hdl soft			£4,194

Finished second in last season's Kim Muir at Cheltenham on just his fourth run over fences, running a huge race for one so inexperienced having gained his sole win a month earlier at Ludlow; pulled up in a novice handicap at Ayr next time.

King Of Realms (Ire)
7 b g King's Theatre - Sunny South East (Gothland)

Ian Williams   Chandler, Ferguson, Hanafin & Kelly

PLACINGS: 130/2210/1421-   RPR **146**+c

Starts	1st	2nd	3rd	4th		Win & Pl
11	4	3	1	2		£42,578
137	3/19	Wwck	3m Cls2 131-152 Ch Hcap good			£18,768
132	11/18	Asct	3m Cls3 Nov 124-132 Ch Hcap gd-sft			£8,058
	1/18	Donc	2m3¹/₂f Cls5 Mdn Hdl 4-7yo soft			£3,119
	11/16	Asct	1m7¹/₂f Cls4 NHF 4-6yo gd-sft			£4,549

Relished going chasing last season; didn't quite live up to Cheltenham Festival ambitions outlined after successful debut at Ascot but bounced back to form on his final run when making all in a handicap at Warwick; could be a future Grand National horse according to connections.

Klassical Dream (Fr)

5 b g Dream Well - Klassical Way (Septieme Ciel)

Willie Mullins (Ir)   Mrs Joanne Coleman

PLACINGS: P324P/111-1   RPR **160+**h

Starts	1st	2nd	3rd	4th	Win & Pl
9	4	1	1	1	£234,468

4/19	Punc	2m¹/₂f Nov Gd1 Hdl yield		£53,153
3/19	Chel	2m¹/₂f Cls1 Nov Gd1 Hdl soft		£70,338
2/19	Leop	2m Nov Gd1 Hdl good		£66,441
12/18	Leop	2m Mdn Hdl 4yo gd-yld		£8,177

Won all four novice hurdles last season, three of them at Grade 1 level including the Supreme at Cheltenham; seemed to appreciate soft ground that day but won just as easily when back on a quicker surface at Punchestown, thrashing Aintree winner Felix Desjy.

Knocknanuss (Ire)

9 b g Beneficial - Dato Vic (Old Vic)

Gary Moore   Hail Sargent Evans

PLACINGS: 1/21/1221P4/F112F55-   RPR **158**c

Starts	1st	2nd	3rd	4th	Win & Pl
15	5	4	-	1	£48,576

133	11/18	Newb	2m¹/₂f Cls3 Nov 123-139 Ch Hcap gd-sft	£12,810
	10/18	Fknm	2m¹/₂f Cls3 Nov Ch good	£8,255
124	12/17	Font	2m1¹/₂f Cls3 105-124 Hdl Hcap soft	£5,393
	5/17	Plum	2m Cls5 Mdn Hdl gd-fm	£3,249
	7/15	Klny	2m1f NHF 5-7yo good	£4,814

Bold-jumping front-runner who took really well to fences last season, making all in minor novice chases at Fakenham and Newbury to win by wide margins; just came up short in Grade 1 company in the spring, finishing fifth in the Racing Post Arkle and at Aintree.

Supermare La Bague Au Roi flies the water jump at Newbury en route to one of her four victories last season

L'Ami Serge (Ire)

9 b g King's Theatre - La Zingarella (Phardante)

Nicky Henderson   Simon Munir & Isaac Souede

PLACINGS: 2/2233251/2122381/7-   RPR **162**h

Starts		1st	2nd	3rd	4th	Win & Pl
30		8	11	6	1	£638,559

	4/18	Aint	2m4f Cls1 Gd1 Hdl soft	£140,525
	6/17	Autl	3m1½f Cls1 Gd1 Hdl v soft	£142,308
	4/17	Sand	2m5½f Cls1 Gd2 Hdl good	£28,475
	1/16	Weth	2m3½f Cls4 Nov Ch heavy	£3,899
	1/16	Plum	2m1f Cls3 Nov Ch heavy	£6,498
	1/15	Sand	2m Cls1 Nov Gd1 Hdl soft	£23,491
	12/14	Asct	1m7½f Cls1 Nov Gd2 Hdl soft	£18,690
132	11/14	Newb	2m½f Cls1 List 129-149 Hdl Hcap soft	£22,780

Hard to win with but had developed into a consistent staying hurdler at the top level before missing last season through injury; picked up two Grade 1 victories prior to that, adding the Aintree Hurdle to the French Champion Hurdle.

La Bague Au Roi (Fr)

8 b m Doctor Dino - Alliance Royale (Turgeon)

Warren Greatrex   Mrs Julien Turner & Andrew Merriam

PLACINGS: /111761/11177/11112-   RPR **155+**c

Starts		1st	2nd	3rd	4th	Win & Pl
20		14	1	-	-	£274,106

2/19	Leop	2m5f Nov Gd1 Ch good	£66,441
12/18	Kemp	3m Cls1 Nov Gd1 Ch gd-sft	£56,950
11/18	Newb	2m4f Cls1 Nov Gd2 Ch gd-sft	£22,780
11/18	Newb	2m6½f Cls3 Ch good	£7,343
1/18	Asct	2m7½f Cls1 Gd2 Hdl soft	£28,810
11/17	Kemp	3m½f Cls1 List Hdl gd-sft	£14,238
11/17	Weth	2m Cls1 List Hdl soft	£12,529
4/17	Hntg	2m4½f Cls4 Nov Hdl good	£3,899
11/16	Newb	2m½f Cls1 Nov List Hdl gd-sft	£13,968
11/16	Weth	2m Cls4 Nov Hdl gd-sft	
10/16	Uttx	2m Cls4 Mdn Hdl good	
12/15	Hntg	2m Cls1 List NHF 4-6yo gd-sft	
10/15	Aint	2m1f Cls4 NHF 4-6yo good	
4/15	NAbb	2m1f Cls6 NHF 4-6yo good	

Prolific hurdler who proved even more effective

when sent chasing, winning four races (two at Grade 1 level over 2m5f and 3m), with sole defeat when second behind Kalashnikov at Aintree; skipped Cheltenham having twice disappointed there over hurdles.

Lady Buttons

9 b m Beneficial - Lady Chapp (High Chaparral)

Philip Kirby   Mrs Jayne Sivills

PLACINGS: 3111P/214414/111142-   RPR **158**c

Starts	1st	2nd	3rd	4th	Win & Pl
27	12	3	1	6	£202,041
	1/19	Donc	2m¹/₂f Cls1 Gd2 Hdl good	£28,475
	12/18	Donc	2m4¹/₂f Cls1 List Ch good	£44,193
140	12/18	Newb	2m¹/₂f Cls2 127-150 Ch Hcap soft	£25,024
	11/18	Weth	2m Cls1 List Hdl good	£12,529
	2/18	Newc	2m¹/₂f Cls2 Nov Ch heavy	£11,711
	11/17	Bang	2m1¹/₂f Cls1 Nov List Ch soft	£14,238
125	3/17	Donc	2m¹/₂f Cls3 106-125 Hdl Hcap soft	£5,697
113	1/17	Sthl	2m4¹/₂f Cls4 97-113 Hdl Hcap soft	£3,249
106	1/17	Newc	2m¹/₂f Cls4 84-110 Hdl Hcap soft	£3,249
	10/14	Worc	2m Cls4 Nov Hdl good	£3,249
	2/14	Weth	2m Cls6 NHF 4-6yo heavy	£1,643
	12/13	Weth	1m4¹/₂f Cls6 NHF 3yo gd-sft	£1,711

Prolific mare who won four times last season, twice each over hurdles and fences from 2m to 2m4f; still unexposed as a chaser after just six runs, with only two defeats coming at Aintree (good second when favourite for a fiercely competitive 2m handicap in April).

Lake View Lad (Ire)

9 gr g Oscar - Missy O'Brien (Supreme Leader)

Nick Alexander   Trevor Hemmings

PLACINGS: 141/26/3132123/113P-   RPR **160**c

Starts	1st	2nd	3rd	4th	Win & Pl
21	8	3	5	1	£131,483
147	12/18	Weth	3m Cls1 Gd3 132-149 Ch Hcap gd-sft	£25,628
139	12/18	Newc	2m7¹/₂f Cls1 List 130-152 Ch Hcap soft	£39,865
136	2/18	Hayd	2m4f Cls3 Nov 124-138 Ch Hcap heavy	£10,820
132	12/17	Newc	2m7¹/₂f Cls3 Nov 115-132 Ch Hcap soft	£6,498
	4/16	Newc	2m4¹/₂f Cls4 Nov Hdl soft	£3,899
	2/16	Weth	2m3¹/₂f Cls4 Nov Hdl heavy	£3,249
	1/16	Ayr	2m4¹/₂f Cls5 Mdn Hdl heavy	£2,469
	11/15	Hexm	2m Cls6 Mdn NHF 4-6yo heavy	£1,949

Progressive staying chaser who won two of the top 3m handicaps in the north last season, the Rehearsal and Rowland Meyrick; stayed on strongly when a fine third in the Ultima at Cheltenham but never a factor when pulled up in the Grand National.

Lalor (Ger)

7 b g It's Gino - Laviola (Waky Nao)

Kayley Woollacott   D G Staddon

PLACINGS: 1211/23201/13P6-   RPR **159**+c

Starts	1st	2nd	3rd	4th	Win & Pl
13	5	3	2	-	£117,173
	11/18	Chel	2m Cls1 Nov Ch good	£19,695
	4/18	Aint	2m¹/₂f Cls1 Nov Gd1 Hdl soft	£56,130
	4/17	Aint	2m1f Cls1 Gd2 NHF 4-6yo good	£25,322
	3/17	Winc	1m7¹/₂f Cls6 Mdn NHF 4-6yo heavy	£1,949
	12/16	Winc	1m7¹/₂f Cls6 NHF 4-6yo soft	£1,625

Ended last season on a low ebb after three successive disappointments; still hard to forget

promise of comfortable victory on chasing debut at Cheltenham over Dynamite Dollars, building on Grade 1 novice hurdle win at Aintree, but has plenty to prove now.

Larry

6 b g Midnight Legend - Gaspaisie (Beyssac)

Gary Moore   Galloping On The South Downs Partnership

PLACINGS: 10/6U42311/4F1421-   RPR **147**+c

Starts	1st	2nd	3rd	4th	Win & Pl
15	5	2	1	3	£47,756
139	4/19	Sand	2m4f Cls2 Nov 119-139 Ch Hcap good	£21,896
128	12/18	Sand	2m4f Cls3 116-129 Ch Hcap gd-sft	£9,384
	4/18	Font	2m3f Cls4 Nov Hdl soft	£4,094
	3/18	Plum	2m4¹/₂f Cls4 Nov Hdl heavy	£4,094
	2/17	Font	2m1¹/₂f Cls6 Mdn NHF 4-6yo gd-sft	£1,754

Steadily progressive over fences last season and signed off by winning a competitive novice handicap at Sandown; yet to score beyond 2m4¹/₂f but had run just as well over 2m7¹/₂f when finishing a neck second at Newbury and trainer is confident he has bigger races in him over further.

Laurina (Fr)

6 b m Spanish Moon - Lamboghina (Alkalde)

Willie Mullins (Ir)   Sullivan Bloodstock

PLACINGS: F2/1111/114-   RPR **160**+h

Starts	1st	2nd	3rd	4th	Win & Pl
9	6	1		1	£184,473
	2/19	Punc	2m4f List Hdl gd-yld	£16,622
	1/19	Sand	2m4f Cls1 List Hdl soft	£12,529
	4/18	Fair	2m4f Nov Gd1 Hdl sft-hvy	£52,212
	3/18	Chel	2m1f Cls1 Nov Gd2 Hdl soft	£51,255
	1/18	Fair	2m2f Nov Gd3 Hdl heavy	£17,688
	12/17	Tram	2m Mdn Hdl heavy	£5,791

Exciting mare who landed her first six races for Willie Mullins before seeing her winning run snapped in tame fashion when sent off just 5-2 for the Champion Hurdle at Cheltenham and finishing only fourth; looked short of pace for 2m that day (last three wins over 2m4f) but still full of potential back up in trip.

Le Breuil (Fr)

7 ch g Anzillero - Slew Dancer (Fabulous Dancer)

Ben Pauling   Mrs Emma Palmer

PLACINGS: 1411P/52015/123241-   RPR **151**c

Starts	1st	2nd	3rd	4th	Win & Pl
16	6	3	1	2	£123,770
	3/19	Chel	3m7¹/₂f Cls1 Nov Gd2 Am Ch soft	£75,491
	11/18	Hntg	2m4f Cls3 Nov Ch good	£9,747
139	4/18	Fknm	2m4f Cls3 113-139 Hdl Hcap gd-sft	£7,213
	3/17	Newb	2m4¹/₂f Cls4 Nov Hdl soft	£4,549
	11/16	Sedg	2m4f Cls4 Nov Hdl gd-sft	£3,899
	5/16	Wwck	2m Cls6 NHF 4-6yo soft	£1,625

Gutsy winner of last season's gruelling National Hunt Chase, wearing down Discorama close home; relished the step up in trip at Cheltenham having shown promise over insufficient distances in earlier novice chases; set to be aimed at the Grand National and is open to further improvement.

Le Patriote (Fr)
7 b g Poliglote - Sentosa (Kaldounevees)

Dr Richard Newland				Canard Vert Racing Club

PLACINGS: 3/161/589741P/811-1   RPR **152+**h

Starts		1st	2nd	3rd	4th	Win & Pl
15		6	-	1	1	£172,683
148	5/19	Hayd	1m7¹/₂f Cls1 Gd3 127-148 Hdl Hcap good			£56,950
142	4/19	Chel	2m4¹/₂f Cls2 122-146 Hdl Hcap good			£15,475
135	11/18	Ayr	2m Cls2 116-142 Hdl Hcap good			£25,992
127	2/18	Asct	2m3¹/₂f Cls2 123-149 Hdl Hcap soft			£28,152
	3/17	Comp	2m2f Hdl soft			£19,692
	11/16	Engh	2m2f Hdl 4yo heavy			£16,941

Big improver in second season in Britain last season and completed a hat-trick in the Swinton Hurdle in May either side of a layoff for a stress fracture of the pelvis; had been due to go novice chasing this summer but instead held back for a crack at bigger hurdles races.

Le Prezien (Fr)
8 br g Blue Bresil - Abu Dhabi (Saint Cyrien)

Paul Nicholls				John P McManus

PLACINGS: 2/21138P/2381P/2570-   RPR **152+**h

Starts		1st	2nd	3rd	4th	Win & Pl
23		6	4	3	-	£193,466
150	3/18	Chel	2m1¹/₂f Cls1 Gd3 139-154 Ch Hcap soft			£62,645
	12/16	Extr	2m1¹/₂f Cls2 Ch soft			£12,512
	11/16	Chel	2m Cls1 Nov Gd2 Ch soft			£19,078
	3/16	Kels	2m2f Cls1 Nov Gd2 Hdl soft			£21,356
	1/16	Donc	2m¹/₂f Cls4 Nov Hdl soft			£3,249
	12/15	Ludl	2m Cls4 Mdn Hdl soft			£3,899

Won the Grand Annual in 2018 and ran a big race back over hurdles on return last season when second behind Silver Streak in the Welsh Champion Hurdle; disappointing subsequently, including twice back at Cheltenham, but given a chance by the handicapper.

Le Richebourg (Fr)
6 b g Network - Fee Magic (Phantom Breeze)

Joseph O'Brien (Ir)				John P McManus

PLACINGS: 32/1116280/511211-   RPR **162+**c

Starts		1st	2nd	3rd	4th	Win & Pl
15		7	3	1	-	£205,116
	2/19	Leop	2m1f Nov Gd1 Ch good			£66,441
	12/18	Leop	2m1f Nov Gd1 Ch good			£52,212
	10/18	Tipp	2m4f Nov Gd3 Ch good			£17,688
	9/18	List	2m1f Ch yld-sft			£8,177
	7/17	Gway	2m1¹/₂f Nov Hdl 4yo yield			£10,530
	7/17	Klny	2m1f Nov Hdl good			£6,844
	5/17	Klny	2m1f Mdn Hdl 4yo good			£6,055

Favourite for the Racing Post Arkle for much of last season until ruled out by injury; had won four out of five novice chases, with sole defeat a narrow one by Delta Work in the Drinmore;

looked better at 2m, twice easily beating Arkle runner-up Us And Them.

Lil Rockerfeller (USA)
8 ch g Hard Spun - Layoune (Mt. Livermore)

Neil King				Davies Smith Govier & Brown

PLACINGS: 0/31620P2/111U3530-3   RPR **152+**c

Starts		1st	2nd	3rd	4th	Win & Pl
35		8	7	10	2	£416,670
	11/18	Extr	3m Cls3 Nov Ch gd-sft			£12,021
	10/18	Chel	3m1¹/₂f Cls2 Nov Ch good			£15,475
	10/18	Uttx	2m4f Cls3 Ch good			£7,408
	11/17	Asct	3m1¹/₂f Cls1 Gd2 Hdl gd-sft			£56,950
	2/16	Font	2m3f Cls1 Gd2 Hdl gd-sft			£45,560
146	12/15	Sand	2m Cls1 List 125-147 Hdl Hcap soft			£34,170
133	4/15	Sand	2m Cls2 111-137 Hdl 4yo Hcap gd-sft			£31,280
125	3/15	Asct	1m7¹/₂f Cls2 120-142 Hdl 4yo Hcap gd-sft			£25,992

Hugely popular and versatile stayer who had his finest hour when second in the 2017 Stayers' Hurdle; won three times over fences last season but jumped poorly in stronger company; best effort back over hurdles when third in a Grade 2 at Fontwell on first run after wind surgery.

Lisnagar Oscar (Ire)
6 b g Oscar - Asta Belle (Astarabad)

Rebecca Curtis				Racing For Fun

PLACINGS: 1/3221153-   RPR **146+**h

Starts		1st	2nd	3rd	4th	Win & Pl
7		2	2	2	-	£43,634
	2/19	Hayd	3m1¹/₂f Cls1 Nov Gd2 Hdl good			£16,938
	1/19	Chep	2m3¹/₂f Cls4 Nov Hdl gd-sft			£4,094

Strong chasing type who proved a smart staying novice hurdler last season; most impressive when running away with a Grade 2 at Haydock by ten lengths on good ground; fair fifth in the Albert Bartlett before being outclassed by Champ and Emitom at Aintree.

Livelovelaugh (Ire)
9 b g Beneficial - Another Evening (Saddlers' Hall)

Willie Mullins (Ir)				Mrs S Ricci

PLACINGS: /1431043/313F/P200-2   RPR **148**c

Starts		1st	2nd	3rd	4th	Win & Pl
20		4	3	4	2	£85,256
	1/18	Cork	2m4f Ch heavy			£7,904
	2/17	Thur	2m4f Nov Hdl soft			£9,477
	5/16	Baln	2m5f Mdn Hdl soft			£4,748
	12/14	Punc	2m NHF 4yo gd-yld			£4,888

Yet to add to sole chase win in January 2018 but went close in valuable handicap chases at Leopardstown and Punchestown last season; three other runs beyond 3m but yet to convince

over further and a clear non-stayer in the Grand National after travelling particularly well.

Looksnowtlikebrian (Ire)

8 b g Brian Boru - Sheebadiva (Norwich)

Tim Vaughan				S C Botham & R G Botham

PLACINGS: 465/61168/2116/11P8-   RPR **147**+c

Starts	1st	2nd	3rd	4th	Win & Pl
18	6	1	-	2	£45,480

129	11/18	Carl	3m2f Cls3 106-131 Ch Hcap good	£15,640
125	10/18	Carl	3m¹/₂f Cls3 120-135 Ch Hcap gd-sft	£8,447
	2/18	Ayr	2m4¹/₂f Cls3 Nov Ch heavy	£7,343
116	12/17	Ffos	2m5f Cls4 Nov 99-118 Ch Hcap heavy	£5,198
100	10/16	Chep	2m3¹/₂f Cls5 74-100 Hdl Hcap gd-sft	£3,249
100	10/16	Font	2m3f Cls5 Nov 74-100 Cond Hdl Hcap gd-sft	£2,924

Made it four wins in first six races over fences when winning twice at Carlisle last season, hacking up by ten lengths on second occasion; well fancied for the Welsh National after that only to be pulled up when always behind but being aimed at the same race again.

Lord Napier (Ire)

6 b g Galileo - Jacqueline (King Charlemagne)

Peter Bowen				F Lloyd

PLACINGS: 51161/6463165-   RPR **148**h

Starts	1st	2nd	3rd	4th	Win & Pl
12	4	-	1	1	£84,096

134	2/19	Sand	2m7¹/₂f Cls1 Gd3 127-152 Hdl Hcap soft	£56,270
121	4/18	Prth	2m4f Cls4 Nov 97-121 Hdl Hcap soft	£4,265
	3/18	Sedg	2m4f Cls4 Nov Hdl soft	£4,094
	2/18	Ludl	2m Cls4 Mdn Hdl soft	£4,549

Improving young hurdler who resumed progress when stepped up in trip last season, winning a valuable 2m7½f handicap at Sandown; below par next time (second flop on heavy ground, though has won on soft) before back on track with a fifth at Grade 1 level at Aintree.

Lostintranslation (Ire)

7 b g Flemensfirth - Falika (Hero's Honor)

Colin Tizzard				Taylor & O'Dwyer

PLACINGS: 4/221672/231221-   RPR **165**+c

Starts	1st	2nd	3rd	4th	Win & Pl
12	3	6	1	-	£158,381

	4/19	Aint	3m1f Cls1 Nov Gd1 Ch soft	£56,394
	1/19	Chel	2m4¹/₂f Cls1 Nov Gd2 Ch gd-sft	£19,695
	12/17	Newb	2m¹/₂f Cls3 Mdn Hdl soft	£6,498

Enjoyed a terrific rivalry with Defi Du Seuil last season, beating him in the Dipper at Cheltenham before finishing second to him in the Scilly Isles and the JLT; proved even better when stepped up to 3m at Aintree, beating RSA winner Topofthegame in the Grade 1 Mildmay.

Louis' Vac Pouch (Ire)

7 b g Oscar - Coming Home (Exit To Nowhere)

Henry Oliver				The Vacuum Pouch Company

PLACINGS: 4641F11/6100/011F2-U   RPR **151**c

Starts	1st	2nd	3rd	4th	Win & Pl
19	6	1	1	2	£54,326

	2/19	Catt	2m3f Cls4 Nov Ch good	£6,108
	2/19	Ludl	2m Cls4 Nov Ch gd-sft	£5,588
132	11/17	Aint	3m1/₂f Cls2 126-152 Hdl Hcap soft	£12,512
125	4/17	MRas	2m4¹/₂f Cls3 105-130 Hdl Hcap good	£12,512
	3/17	MRas	2m¹/₂f Cls4 Nov Hdl good	£3,249
	1/17	Sthl	1m7¹/₂f Cls4 Nov Hdl soft	£3,249

One-time useful hurdler who got back on track when switched to fences last season; ran well in all three completed chases, winning twice and finishing a fine second to Secret Investor at Ayr; unlucky when hampered and unseated rider (still going well) at Punchestown.

Magic Of Light (Ire)
8 b m Flemensfirth - Quest Of Passion (Saumarez)

Jessica Harrington (Ir)   Ann & Alan Potts Limited

PLACINGS: /321F220241/3112U72-   RPR **162**c

Starts		1st	2nd	3rd	4th	Win & Pl
26		6	7	4	3	£367,073
	1/19	Asct	2m7½f Cls1 Gd2 Hdl gd-sft			£28,609
	12/18	Newb	2m7½f Cls1 List Ch Hcap soft			£15,846
128	4/18	Punc	2m5f 114-142 Ch Hcap soft			£39,159
	11/17	Fair	2m5f Ch soft			£6,318
107	4/17	Punc	2m5f 105-123 Hdl Hcap gd-yld			£15,769
	11/16	Navn	2m NHF 4-7yo yld-sft			£4,070

Ran a mighty race to finish second behind Tiger Roll in last season's Grand National, staying on really strongly; had been lucky to get away with some serious errors and has been caught out by stiffer fences, with biggest win last season coming in a Grade 2 mares' hurdle.

Magic Saint (Fr)
5 b g Saint Des Saints - Magic Poline (Trempolino)

Paul Nicholls   Mr & Mrs J D Cotton

PLACINGS: 111135/2510F2-   RPR **152+**c

Starts		1st	2nd	3rd	4th	Win & Pl
12		5	2	1	-	£131,951
142	2/19	Winc	1m7½f Cls2 125-152 Ch Hcap good			£15,784
	3/18	Autl	2m2f Ch 4yo v soft			£22,088
	11/17	Autl	2m1½f Ch 3yo v soft			£21,744
	10/17	Autl	2m1½f Hdl 3yo v soft			£19,692
	9/17	Autl	2m2f Hdl 3yo heavy			£26,667

French recruit who made a big impression when dropped in trip last season to win well at Wincanton; sent off favourite for the Grand Annual after that but well held there and beaten at odds-on when second at Chepstow on final run; has time on his side.

Malaya (Fr)
5 b m Martaline - Clarte D'Or (Kendor)

Paul Nicholls   Mrs Johnny De La Hey

PLACINGS: 12/1212218/FF410-   RPR **144+**h

Starts		1st	2nd	3rd	4th	Win & Pl
14		5	4	-	1	£148,290
136	3/19	Sand	2m Cls1 Gd3 134-160 Hdl Hcap soft			£42,203
134	3/18	Asct	1m7½f Cls2 108-134 Hdl 4yo Hcap soft			£25,024
	11/17	Weth	2m Cls1 List Hdl 3yo gd-sft			£11,390
	5/17	Autl	2m1½f List Hdl 3yo v soft			£34,872
	3/17	Pari	1m7f Hdl 3yo good			£8,205

Plagued by jumping issues last season but did well to overcome a serious blunder two out when winning the Imperial Cup at Sandown; might have found good ground against her when well beaten in the Scottish Champion Hurdle (has gained two biggest wins on soft).

Lostintranslation (yellow) enjoyed some memorable tussles with Defi Du Seuil (left) last season

Malone Road (Ire)
5 b g Kalanisi - Zaffarella (Zaffaran)

Gordon Elliott (Ir)   Cheveley Park Stud

PLACINGS: 1/11-   RPR **135**+b

Starts	1st	2nd	3rd	4th	Win & Pl
2	2	-	-	-	£14,446
	11/18 Punc	2m NHF 4yo good			£6,269
	11/18 DRoy	2m¹/₂f NHF 4-7yo gd-yld			£8,177

Early favourite for last season's Champion Bumper but ultimately missed all big spring targets having suffered a knee injury after second win at Punchestown in November; could make a leading novice hurdler.

Maria's Benefit (Ire)
7 b m Beneficial - Youngborogal (Anshan)

Stuart Edmunds   P D Wells

PLACINGS: 1210/2111114/11U-   RPR **147**+c

Starts	1st	2nd	3rd	4th	Win & Pl
13	8	2	-	1	£101,033
	11/18 Bang	2m1¹/₂f Nov List Ch gd-sft			£14,305
	10/18 NAbb	2m¹/₂f Cls3 Nov Ch heavy			£9,115
	1/18 Donc	2m¹/₂f Cls1 Gd2 Hdl soft			£28,475
	12/17 Tntn	2m¹/₂f Cls1 Nov List Hdl soft			£11,390
127	12/17 Ludl	2m Cls2 114-140 Hdl Hcap gd-sft			£12,660
117	11/17 Sand	2m Cls3 114-131 Hdl Hcap gd-sft			£12,512
	10/17 NAbb	2m1f Cls4 Nov Hdl 4-6yo good			£4,549
	3/17 Hntg	2m Cls6 NHF 4-6yo gd-sft			£1,819

Prolific mare who won five in a row up to Grade 2 level over hurdles two seasons ago and started in similar vein over fences last season, winning her first two including a Listed mares' race; missed the rest of the season after a poor run at Kempton but due to return.

McFabulous (Ire)
5 b g Milan - Rossavon (Beneficial)

Paul Nicholls   Giraffa Racing

PLACINGS: 1711-   RPR **129**+b

Starts	1st	2nd	3rd	4th	Win & Pl
4	3	-	-	-	£31,964
	4/19 Aint	2m1f Cls2 Gd2 NHF 4-6yo soft			£25,322
	3/19 Newb	2m¹/₂f Cls5 NHF 4-6yo gd-sft			£2,599
	10/18 Chep	2m Cls4 NHF 4-6yo good			£3,899

Won three out of four bumpers last season, signing off with a Grade 2 win at Aintree; had long been held in high regard and easily forgiven sole defeat at Cheltenham having returned with sore shins; looks a top prospect for novice hurdles.

Melon
7 ch g Medicean - Night Teeny (Platini)

Willie Mullins (Ir)   Mrs J Donnelly

PLACINGS: 122/1352F/442F-70   RPR **157**h

Starts	1st	2nd	3rd	4th	Win & Pl
14	2	4	1	2	£297,871
	11/17 DRoy	2m Gd2 Hdl soft			£25,214
	1/17 Leop	2m Mdn Hdl good			£6,833

Runner-up in the last two runnings of the Champion Hurdle at Cheltenham but only a remote second to Espoir D'Allen last term in the middle of a poor campaign; more promise until falling three out in the Aintree Hurdle but then failed to beat a single rival at Punchestown and Auteuil.

Mengli Khan (Ire)
6 b g Lope De Vega - Danielli (Danehill)

Gordon Elliott (Ir)   Gigginstown House Stud

PLACINGS: 24/1110233/143334-9   RPR **155**c

Starts	1st	2nd	3rd	4th	Win & Pl
16	4	2	5	3	£151,292
	11/18 Punc	2m Ch good			£7,632
	12/17 Fair	2m Nov Gd1 Hdl soft			£42,863
	11/17 Navn	2m Nov Gd3 Hdl sft-hvy			£17,083
	9/17 Navn	2m Mdn Hdl yield			£7,108

Slightly disappointing for much of last season, failing to build on impressive chase debut win, but did better when stepped up in trip, finishing third in 2m4f Grade 1 novices at Cheltenham and Aintree; ninth on handicap debut in the Galway Plate this summer.

Mercian Prince (Ire)
8 b g Midnight Legend - Bongo Fury (Sillery)

Amy Murphy   Paul Murphy

PLACINGS: 11F43/381105/671801-   RPR **155**+c

Starts	1st	2nd	3rd	4th	Win & Pl
28	7	1	7	1	£128,266
143	4/19 Plum	2m3¹/₂f Cls2 139-143 Ch Hcap good			£31,280
139	1/19 Kemp	2m4¹/₂f Cls3 129-142 Ch Hcap good			£8,447
141	2/18 Weth	2m3¹/₂f Cls2 126-145 Ch Hcap heavy			£12,558
134	1/18 Kemp	2m4¹/₂f Cls3 111-137 Ch Hcap gd-sft			£8,447
128	1/17 Sand	2m4f Cls3 113-131 Ch Hcap soft			£9,384
117	11/16 Sthl	2m4f Cls4 108-120 Ch Hcap gd-sft			£5,198
	6/16 Autl	2m5¹/₂f Ch 5yo v soft			£19,412

Progressive handicap chaser who has won twice in each of the last three seasons, most recently at Kempton and Perth last term when dominating small fields from the front; well beaten in the Greatwood Gold Cup at Newbury and the Topham at Aintree in between.

Mick Jazz (Fr)
8 b g Blue Bresil - Mick Maya (Siam)

Gordon Elliott (Ir)   George P Mahoney

PLACINGS: 6232/P/1231/35133/   RPR **160**h

Starts	1st	2nd	3rd	4th	Win & Pl
14	3	3	5	-	£160,404
	12/17 Leop	2m Gd1 Hdl soft			£50,427
	2/17 Punc	2m Nov List Hdl soft			£17,083
	10/16 Clon	2m¹/₂f Mdn Hdl good			£4,522

Much improved two seasons ago and ran a huge

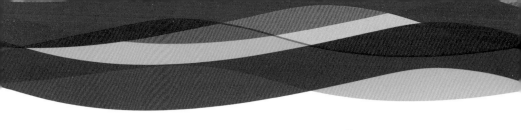

Get your exclusive free bet offers and must-have daily promotions.

racingpost.com/free-bets

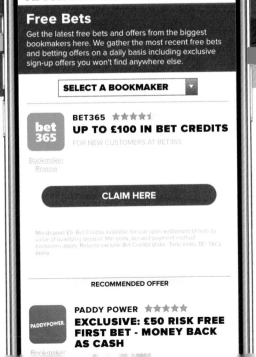

RACING POST

Free Bets

Get the latest free bets and offers from the biggest bookmakers here. We gather the most recent free bets and betting offers on a daily basis including exclusive sign-up offers you won't find anywhere else.

SELECT A BOOKMAKER

bet365 ★★★★✦
UP TO £100 IN BET CREDITS
FOR NEW CUSTOMERS AT BET365

Bookmaker Review

CLAIM HERE

Min deposit £5. Bet Credits available for use upon settlement of bets to value of qualifying deposit. Min odds, bet and payment method exclusions apply. Returns exclude Bet Credits stake. Time limits, 18+ T&Cs apply.

RECOMMENDED OFFER

PADDY POWER ★★★★★
EXCLUSIVE: £50 RISK FREE FIRST BET - MONEY BACK AS CASH

Bookmaker

For The Must-Have
Racing Offers
RACING POST

race to finish third in the Champion Hurdle behind Buveur D'Air, proving earlier Grade 1 win at Leopardstown was no fluke; missed last season through injury.

Midnight Shadow

6 b g Midnight Legend - Holy Smoke (Statoblest)

Sue Smith — Mrs Aafke Clarke

PLACINGS: 127/1222U71/20110-   RPR **155**+h

Starts	1st	2nd	3rd	4th	Win & Pl
15	5	-	-	-	£129,340
	1/19	Chel	2m4¹/₂f Cls1 Gd2 Hdl gd-sft	£28,135
141	12/18	Aint	2m4f Cls2 122-143 Hdl Hcap soft	£18,570
134	11/17	Chel	2m Cls1 Gd2 134-154 Hdl Hcap good	£59,798
	10/17	Uttx	2m Cls4 Nov Hdl 4-6yo soft	£3,899
	12/16	Newc	1m6¹/₂f Cls6 NHF 3yo soft	£1,884

Won the Scottish Champion Hurdle off a low weight in 2018 and proved even better at around 2m4f last term, impressively winning the Relkeel Hurdle at Cheltenham; disappointing when stepped up to 3m in the Cleeve (held in seventh when badly hampered at the last).

Might Bite (Ire)

10 b g Scorpion - Knotted Midge (Presenting)

Nicky Henderson — The Knot Again Partnership

PLACINGS: 517/21F111/1121/57P-   RPR **152**c

Starts	1st	2nd	3rd	4th	Win & Pl
19	10	2	1	-	£599,044
	4/18	Aint	3m1f Cls1 Ch gd-sft	£106,745
	12/17	Kemp	3m Cls1 Gd1 Ch good	£128,138
	11/17	Sand	3m Cls1 List Ch gd-sft	£17,085
	4/17	Aint	3m1f Cls1 Nov Gd1 Ch good	£56,130
	3/17	Chel	3m¹/₂f Cls1 Nov Gd1 Ch gd-sft	£99,663
	2/17	Donc	3m Cls4 Nov Ch gd-sft	£4,758
	12/16	Donc	2m3f Cls4 Nov Ch good	£5,908
138	3/16	Kemp	2m5f Cls2 127-138 Hdl Hcap good	£20,645
	4/15	Chel	2m4¹/₂f Cls2 Nov Hdl good	£10,102
	3/15	Newb	2m4¹/₂f Cls4 Nov Hdl gd-sft	£3,422

Brilliant staying chaser at his peak; won the RSA Chase in memorable circumstances in 2017 before adding the King George and Betway Bowl two seasons ago; nowhere near that level last season and wind surgery no help when pulled up in the Cheltenham Gold Cup.

Min (Fr)

8 b g Walk In The Park - Phemyka (Saint Estephe)

Willie Mullins (Ir) — Mrs S Ricci

PLACINGS: 112/11/11d1224/1151-2   RPR **180**+c

Starts	1st	2nd	3rd	4th	Win & Pl
18	9	5	1	2	£649,865
	4/19	Aint	2m4f Cls1 Gd1 Ch soft	£140,985
	2/19	Leop	2m1f Gd1 Ch good	£66,441
	12/18	Punc	2m4f Gd1 Ch yield	£44,381
	2/18	Leop	2m1f Gd2 Ch soft	£52,212
	11/17	Gowr	2m4f Ch heavy	£10,530
	12/16	Leop	2m1f Nov Gd1 Ch yield	£39,044
	11/16	Navn	2m1f Ch yld-sft	£7,235
	1/16	Punc	2m Nov Gd2 Hdl heavy	£18,529
	12/15	Punc	2m2f Mdn Hdl soft	£5,349

Won three times at Grade 1 level last season, most impressively when making all the running to win the Melling Chase at Aintree by 20 lengths; had disappointed when ridden with more restraint in the Champion Chase (third

successive defeat at Cheltenham, all behind Altior).

Minella Indo (Ire)

6 b g Beat Hollow - Carrigeen Lily (Supreme Leader)

Henry de Bromhead (Ir) — Barry Maloney

PLACINGS: 13/321-1   RPR **156**+h

Starts	1st	2nd	3rd	4th	Win & Pl
5	2	1	2	-	£135,800
	5/19	Punc	3m Nov Gd1 Hdl yield	£53,153
	3/19	Chel	3m Cls1 Nov Gd1 Hdl gd-sft	£73,506

Came from nowhere to emerge as last season's top staying novice hurdler, winning the Albert Bartlett at Cheltenham at 50-1 and following up at Punchestown despite still being fourth best in the market; point-to-point winner and likely to go novice chasing.

Missed Approach (Ire)

9 b g Golan - Polly's Dream (Beau Sher)

Warren Greatrex — Alan & Andrew Turner

PLACINGS: 1P2/413U28/P6321P/6-   RPR **143**+c

Starts	1st	2nd	3rd	4th	Win & Pl
19	5	3	3	1	£110,820
138	3/18	Chel	3m2f Cls2 119-145 Am Ch Hcap soft	£41,972
	1/17	Ling	2m7¹/₂f Cls4 Nov Ch heavy	£3,899
123	11/15	Newb	3m Cls3 120-142 Hdl Hcap soft	£9,384
	11/14	Ffos	2m4f Cls5 Mdn Hdl soft	£1,949
	10/14	Uttx	2m Cls6 NHF 4-6yo good	£1,560

Back from injury after missing last season; had won the 2018 Kim Muir at the Cheltenham Festival, building on a terrific run at the meeting 12 months earlier when second to Tiger Roll in the National Hunt Chase; largely disappointing in between but benefited from wind surgery just prior to Cheltenham.

Mister Blue Sky (Ire)

5 gr g Royal Applause - Mujdeya (Linamix)

Willie Mullins (Ir) — Shanakiel Racing Syndicate

PLACINGS: 121-3   RPR **142**+h

Starts	1st	2nd	3rd	4th	Win & Pl
4	2	1	1	-	£43,003
	4/19	Fair	2m Nov Gd2 Hdl gd-yld	£23,919
	10/18	Wxfd	2m¹/₂f Mdn Hdl 4yo yld-sft	£6,269

Bought off the Flat for 130,000gns as a four-time winner for Sylvester Kirk and made an instant impression over hurdles when winning well at

MY FIVE TO WATCH

Brian Sheerin

● Chacun Pour Soi ● Delta Work ● Envoi Allen ● Fusil Raffles ● Gypsy Island

Wexford; progressed to land a Grade 2 novice hurdle at Fairyhouse before a fair third behind Klassical Dream at Punchestown.

Mister Fisher (Ire)

5 b g Jeremy - That's Amazing (Marignan)

Nicky Henderson				James & Jean Potter
PLACINGS: 10/2118-7				RPR **144**h

Starts	1st	2nd	3rd	4th	Win & Pl
7	3	1	-	-	£34,552
	1/19	Hayd	1m7¹/₂f Cls1 Nov Gd2 Hdl gd-sft		£17,085
	12/18	Kemp	2m Cls2 Nov Hdl gd-sft		£12,512
	3/18	Kemp	2m Cls5 Mdn NHF 4-6yo soft		£3,119

Won novice hurdles at Kempton and Haydock last season, claiming good scalps in Rouge Vif and Bright Forecast (both Grade 1 placed); perhaps unsuited by more undulating track when eighth in the Supreme; only seventh when favourite for the Swinton on handicap debut.

Mister Malarky

6 ch g Malinas - Priscilla (Teenoso)

Colin Tizzard				Wendy & Malcolm Hezel
PLACINGS: 360/3517320/131142-				RPR **154**c

Starts	1st	2nd	3rd	4th	Win & Pl
16	4	2	4	1	£70,601
	2/19	Asct	3m Cls1 Nov Gd2 Ch gd-sft		£22,780
130	1/19	Newb	2m7¹/₂f Cls3 120-130 Ch Hcap good		£7,343
126	11/18	Plum	2m3¹/₂f Cls3 Nov 126-136 Ch Hcap good		£7,522
	11/17	Kemp	2m Cls4 Nov Hdl 4-6yo gd-sft		£3,899

Developed into a smart novice chaser last season; won the Reynoldstown at Ascot and finished best of the rest behind three potential superstars when fourth in the RSA at Cheltenham; looked to progress again when second behind Kildisart in a good handicap at Aintree.

Mister Whitaker (Ire)

7 b g Court Cave - Benbradagh Vard (Le Bavard)

Mick Channon				T P Radford
PLACINGS: 26343/31211/144P1-				RPR **156**+c

Starts	1st	2nd	3rd	4th	Win & Pl
15	5	2	3	3	£134,625
149	4/19	Chel	2m4¹/₂f Cls1 Gd2 130-150 Ch Hcap good		£33,862
	11/18	Carl	2m4f Cls1 List Ch good		£17,085
137	3/18	Chel	2m4¹/₂f Cls1 Nov List 137-145 Ch Hcap soft		£39,865
129	1/18	Chel	2m5f Cls2 Nov 128-147 Ch Hcap soft		£17,204
118	11/17	Carl	2m4f Cls3 Nov 115-134 Ch Hcap gd-sft		£7,798

Sharply progressive novice chaser two seasons ago, winning the novice handicap at

the Cheltenham Festival; didn't quite go on last season but sharpened up by first-time cheekpieces when landing another big win at Cheltenham in the Silver Trophy in April.

Mohaayed

7 b g Intikhab - Reyaada (Daylami)

Dan Skelton				Mrs June Watts
PLACINGS: 24173/10231/471479-				RPR **153**h

Starts	1st	2nd	3rd	4th	Win & Pl
16	4	2	2	3	£191,890
145	12/18	Asct	1m7¹/₂f Cls1 Gd3 121-147 Hdl Hcap soft		£85,425
139	3/18	Chel	2m1f Cls1 Gd3 133-154 Hdl Hcap soft		£56,950
	5/17	MRas	2m¹/₂f Cls4 Hdl good		£4,874
	2/17	Tntn	2m¹/₂f Cls4 Nov Hdl soft		£4,549

Has won big handicap hurdles in each of the last two seasons, adding the Betfair Exchange Trophy at Ascot last term to his 2018 County Hurdle victory; well beaten at Haydock in Grade 2 company and twice struggled off higher marks back in handicaps.

Molly The Dolly (Ire)

8 b m Flemensfirth - Pistol Flash (Pistolet Bleu)

Dan Skelton				Dermot Hanafin
PLACINGS: F1/32/1422/1131-				RPR **152**+c

Starts	1st	2nd	3rd	4th	Win & Pl
10	4	3	2	1	£92,160
139	4/19	Ayr	3m Cls2 Nov 123-142 Ch Hcap good		£62,792
	11/18	Uttx	3m Cls3 Nov Ch gd-sft		£7,408
127	10/18	Aint	3m1f Cls3 Nov 122-135 Ch Hcap good		£9,747
	11/17	Wwck	2m5f Cls4 Nov Hdl gd-sft		£4,549

Progressive novice chaser on a sound surface last season, winning three times; suffered sole defeat on soft in a Listed mares' chase (0-5 under rules on soft or heavy) before returning from a break on good ground to win a valuable novice handicap at Ayr in April.

Momella (Ire)

7 ch m Sholokhov - Missing Link (Elusive Quality)

Harry Fry			Holt, Clark, Macnabb, Nugent & Robinson
PLACINGS: 41/11213/FP9-			RPR **140**+h

Starts	1st	2nd	3rd	4th	Win & Pl
8	3	1	1	-	£47,366
134	12/17	Chel	2m4¹/₂f Cls2 118-139 Hdl Hcap soft		£18,768
	10/17	Fknm	2m4f Cls4 Nov Hdl good		£4,431
	5/17	NAbb	2m5¹/₂f Cls3 Nov Hdl good		£7,115

Very smart novice hurdler two seasons ago for

Follow us @RacingPost

Dan Skelton, winning three times and finishing third in a Grade 1 at Aintree; running a big race when fell first time out last season but below par twice subsequently, including when ninth in the Mares' Hurdle at Cheltenham.

Monalee (Ire)

8 b g Milan - Tempest Belle (Glacial Storm)

Henry de Bromhead (Ir)				Barry Maloney
PLACINGS: /212124/1F12F/3214-P				RPR **168**c

Starts	1st	2nd	3rd	4th	Win & Pl
17	5	6	1	2	£246,343
2/19	Gowr	2m4f Gd2 Ch yld-sft			£31,892
2/18	Leop	2m5f Nov Gd1 Ch soft			£52,212
11/17	Punc	2m4f Ch sft-hvy			£7,371
2/17	Clon	3m Nov Gd3 Hdl heavy			£19,712
11/16	Punc	2m6f Mdn Hdl soft			£6,331

Has shown high-class form in defeat since beating Al Boum Photo in a Grade 1 novice chase in February 2018, taking Grade 1 record to 1-9 and landing only a small-field Grade 2 in that time; yet to win beyond 2m5f over fences but looked short of pace when fourth in the Ryanair Chase.

Monsieur Lecoq (Fr)

5 b g Diamond Boy - Draga (Smadoun)

Jane Williams				Mrs Jane Williams
PLACINGS: P3/3U1120-				RPR **140**h

Starts	1st	2nd	3rd	4th	Win & Pl
8	2	1	2	-	£37,942
122	1/19	Sand	2m Cls2 120-136 Hdl Hcap soft		£15,640
	12/18	Ffos	2m Cls4 Mdn Hdl heavy		£5,133

Sharply progressive novice hurdler last season; won by nine lengths on handicap debut at Sandown in January and nearly followed up in the Imperial Cup there when collared close home at Sandown; below par when tenth just six days later in the County Hurdle.

Monalee jumps to victory at Gowran Park

Mont Des Avaloirs (Fr)
6 b g Blue Bresil - Abu Dhabi (Saint Cyrien)

Paul Nicholls				Mrs Johnny De La Hey

PLACINGS: 2/1F13414/2307P-   RPR **145**h

Starts	1st	2nd	3rd	4th	Win & Pl
13		2		2	£36,121

	4/18	MRas	2m¹/₂f Cls4 Nov Hdl soft	£4,660
	12/17	Aint	2m1f Cls3 Nov Hdl heavy	£7,507
	10/17	Chep	2m Cls4 NHF 4-6yo good	£3,249

Useful novice hurdler two seasons ago and beaten just half a length in last season's Gerry Feilden at Newbury; disappointing when single-figure prices for three other big 2m handicaps, including the Betfair Hurdle; could go back over fences (second on reappearance last term).

Moon Over Germany (Ire)
8 ch g Germany - Elea Moon (Moonax)

Henry de Bromhead (Ir)				Philip J Reynolds

PLACINGS: 6/83123/650/32741-41   RPR **154**+c

Starts	1st	2nd	3rd	4th	Win & Pl
16	3	2	3	2	£85,884

	8/19	Baln	2m1f Ch soft	£10,649
136	4/19	Aint	2m Cls1 Gd3 131-149 Ch Hcap soft	£50,517
	12/15	Navn	2m Mdn Hdl 4yo heavy	£6,419

Proved a revelation when encountering soft ground for the only time last season, running away with a fiercely competitive handicap chase at Aintree by ten lengths; only glimpses of promise in four previous runs over fences and well beaten off 11lb higher mark next time at Punchestown.

Mortal (Ire)
7 b g King's Theatre - Pomme Tiepy (Apple Tree)

Joseph O'Brien (Ir)				Gigginstown House Stud

PLACINGS: 1/4F226/1265-   RPR **152**c

Starts	1st	2nd	3rd	4th	Win & Pl
10	2	2	-	1	£41,259

	12/18	Fair	2m5f Ch good	£7,904
	3/17	Limk	2m NHF 4-7yo soft	£5,265

Failed to win over hurdles but proved a much better chaser last season, running a cracker when second to Delta Work over Christmas (odds-on in running before a mistake at the last); below that level twice subsequently but far from disgraced when fifth in the RSA.

Movewiththetimes (Ire)
8 ch g Presenting - Dare To Venture (Darazari)

Enda Bolger (Ir)				John P McManus

PLACINGS: 1/1512/423P/UF8-F1   RPR **141**c

Starts	1st	2nd	3rd	4th	Win & Pl
14	4	2	1	1	£59,362

	8/19	Klny	2m7f Ch yield	£6,655
	12/16	Winc	1m7¹/₂f Cls4 Nov Hdl gd-sft	£3,249
	10/16	Font	2m1¹/₂f Cls4 Nov Hdl gd-sft	£5,198
	4/16	Winc	1m7¹/₂f Cls6 NHF 4-6yo gd-sft	£1,625

Looked a top-class prospect when finishing second in the Betfair Hurdle as a novice in 2017 but failed to win in two seasons over fences for Paul Nicholls; off the mark as a chaser this summer following switch to Enda Bolger and remains capable of better.

Moyhenna (Ire)
7 b m Westerner - Moskova (Montjeu)

Denis Gerard Hogan (Ir)				Robert Hennelly

PLACINGS: 4/33411245/22FU1-1   RPR **143**c

Starts	1st	2nd	3rd	4th	Win & Pl
15	4	3	2	3	£99,393

	5/19	Punc	2m5f 110-138 Ch Hcap gd-yld	£39,865
132	3/19	Limk	2m6¹/₂f Nov Gd2 Ch heavy	£26,577
	1/18	Punc	2m Mdn Hdl heavy	£7,087
	12/17	Punc	2m2f NHF 4-7yo sft-hvy	£5,791

Progressive chaser in mares' races last season;

hacked up in a Grade 2 novice at Limerick on heavy ground by 25 lengths and followed up in a handicap at Punchestown; drying conditions not considered ideal that day and could have more to come back on softer ground.

Mr Adjudicator

5 b g Camacho - Attlongglast (Groom Dancer)

Willie Mullins (Ir)					David Bobbett
PLACINGS: 1122/28P-171					RPR **156+**h

Starts	1st	2nd	3rd	4th	Win & Pl
10	4	3	-	-	£237,369

	6/19	Autl	2m3½f Gd2 Hdl v soft	£66,892
149	5/19	Punc	2m4f 122-149 Hdl Hcap gd-yld	£53,153
	2/18	Leop	2m Gd1 Hdl 4yo soft	£52,212
	12/17	Leop	2m Mdn Hdl 3yo soft	£7,897

Lightly raced last season but bounced back to form with a golden summer, winning big hurdle races at Punchestown and Auteuil before flourishing on the Flat; equally capable on winter ground, as he showed as a top juvenile two seasons ago (second in the Triumph).

My Old Gold (Ire)

9 b m Gold Well - Tenbo (Sexton Blake)

Nicky Richards					Tor Side Racing
PLACINGS: 211/32212/51221-					RPR **144+**c

Starts	1st	2nd	3rd	4th	Win & Pl
10	3	5	1	-	£46,845

	4/19	Prth	3m Cls1 List Ch gd-sft	£19,933
123	1/19	Weth	3m Cls3 Nov 110-127 Ch Hcap gd-sft	£7,408
112	4/18	Carl	3m1f Cls3 102-127 Hdl Hcap soft	£7,798

Lightly raced for her age and did well in her first season over fences last term, finishing with a smooth victory in a Listed mares' chase at Perth; trainer expects her to stay beyond 3m and sees her as one for big staying handicap chases.

My Sister Sarah (Ire)

5 ch m Martaline - Reste Ren Or (Goldneyev)

Willie Mullins (Ir)					Barnane Stud
PLACINGS: 112106-1					RPR **137+**h

Starts	1st	2nd	3rd	4th	Win & Pl
7	4	1	-	-	£56,250

128	5/19	Punc	3m 125-138 Hdl Hcap gd-yld	£31,892
	1/19	Fair	2m2f Nov Hdl good	£8,602
	10/18	Punc	2m4f Mdn Hdl good	£7,359
	8/18	Rosc	2m1½f NHF 4yo good	£5,451

Won three of first four races last season and later

got back to winning ways at Punchestown; small filly who had been intimidated at Cheltenham and Fairyhouse according to her trainer but notably she was the pick of Ruby Walsh among trainer's seven in mares' novice at Cheltenham.

Nadaitak

5 b g Teofilo - Tanfidh (Marju)

Ben Pauling					The Megsons
PLACINGS: 412109-					RPR **145+**h

Starts	1st	2nd	3rd	4th	Win & Pl
6	2	1	-	1	£22,972

	1/19	Donc	3m1½f Cls1 Nov Gd2 Hdl good	£17,085
	11/18	Donc	2m5f Cls4 Nov Hdl good	£4,094

Thorough stayer who ran away with a Grade 2 novice hurdle at Doncaster last season by 22 lengths, though perhaps flattered as only three rivals ran below par; no impression in the Albert Bartlett at Cheltenham and little better on his handicap debut at Aintree.

Native River (Ire)

9 ch g Indian River - Native Mo (Be My Native)

Colin Tizzard					Brocade Racing
PLACINGS: 113321/21113/11/234-					RPR **172**c

Starts	1st	2nd	3rd	4th	Win & Pl
24	11	3	6	1	£946,696

	3/18	Chel	3m2¹/₂f Cls1 Gd1 Ch soft	£369,822
	2/18	Newb	2m7½f Cls1 Gd2 Ch soft	£28,475
	2/17	Newb	2m7½f Cls1 Gd2 Ch soft	£28,475
155	12/16	Chep	3m5½f Cls1 Gd3 139-155 Ch Hcap soft	£85,425
155	11/16	Newb	3m2f Cls1 Gd3 140-166 Ch Hcap gd-sft	£113,900
	4/16	Aint	3m1f Cls1 Nov Gd1 Ch gd-sft	£56,319
	11/15	Newb	2m7½f Cls1 Nov Gd2 Ch gd-sft	£20,284
	11/15	Extr	3m Cls2 Nov Ch soft	£12,974
	2/15	Extr	2m1f Cls1 Nov List Hdl gd-sft	£11,390
	11/14	Newc	2m6f Cls2 Nov Hdl soft	£11,261
	10/14	Strf	2m6f Cls5 Mdn Hdl good	£2,599

Gutsy winner of a thrilling Cheltenham Gold Cup from Might Bite in 2018 but not quite at the same level last season, failing to score despite running to a high level; runner-up to Bristol De Mai in the Betfair Chase but was then unsuited by the sharp track when staying on for a remote third in the King George; unable to dominate in the Gold Cup after a slow start before staying on for fourth.

Newtide (Ire)

6 br g Getaway - C'Est Fantastique (Hernando)

Kim Bailey					Lady Dulverton
PLACINGS: 2/41341-					RPR **142+**h

Starts	1st	2nd	3rd	4th	Win & Pl
5	2	-	1	2	£13,230

125	4/19	Ffos	3m Cls3 112-127 Hdl Hcap soft	£6,238
	12/18	Hayd	2m7f Cls4 Mdn Hdl soft	£5,198

Progressive novice hurdler last season; off the mark at Haydock when stepped up to staying trips for the first time and bolted up in a 3m handicap at Perth in April, relishing soft ground; held in high regard at home and set to go novice chasing.

Native River (right) and
Bristol De Mai jump side
by side at Haydock

Next Destination (Ire)

7 b g Dubai Destination - Liss Alainn (Flemensfirth)

Willie Mullins (Ir)   Malcolm C Denmark

PLACINGS: 1/142/11131/   RPR **152**h

Starts	1st	2nd	3rd	4th	Win & Pl
8	5	1	1	1	£151,778

4/18	Punc	3m Nov Gd1 Hdl yield	£52,212
1/18	Naas	2m4f Nov Gd1 Hdl sft-hvy	£46,991
12/17	Navn	2m4f Nov Gd2 Hdl heavy	£21,432
11/17	Naas	2m3f Mdn Hdl sft-hvy	£6,844
1/17	Fair	2m NHF 5-7yo soft	£4,070

Won four out of five in novice hurdles two
seasons ago, including two Grade 1 races;
looked short of pace when a fast-finishing third
in the Ballymore at Cheltenham and duly relished
the step up to 3m when winning at Punchestown
next time; likely to go novice chasing having
missed last season through injury.

Not Another Muddle

8 b g Kayf Tara - Spatham Rose (Environment Friend)

Gary Moore   Saloop

PLACINGS: 2/2125/11/3152-   RPR **145**c

Starts	1st	2nd	3rd	4th	Win & Pl
11	4	4	1	-	£37,059

131	2/19	Sand	1m7¹/₂f Cls3 118-131 Ch Hcap soft	£7,507
120	1/18	Leic	2m Cls4 Nov 96-122 Ch Hcap soft	£6,442
	12/17	Plum	2m3¹/₂f Cls3 Nov Ch soft	£6,657
	1/17	Font	2m3f Cls4 Nov Hdl soft	£4,224

Missed more than a year after winning first two
chases two seasons ago but soon resumed
progress when returning towards the end of last
season; won at Sandown on second run back

and did well to finish fifth in the Grand Annual
after making several mistakes.

Not Many Left (Ire)

6 b g Oscar - Lasado (Jurado)

Jessica Harrington (Ir)   Robcour

PLACINGS: 1/435132/4132-F   RPR **153+**h

Starts	1st	2nd	3rd	4th	Win & Pl
11	2	2	3	2	£52,074

137	1/19	Hntg	3m1f Cls2 116-142 Hdl Hcap gd-sft	£12,512
	1/18	Navn	2m4f Mdn Hdl heavy	£7,087

Progressive staying hurdler last season; slightly
unlucky when third in the Pertemps Final at
Cheltenham (hit the front too soon) having won
a qualifier at Huntingdon; held his own when
stepped up in grade and would have been placed
at Punchestown but for falling at the last.

Notebook (Ger)

6 b g Samum - Nova (Winged Love)

Henry de Bromhead (Ir)   Gigginstown House Stud

PLACINGS: F5/122120-2   RPR **143**h

Starts	1st	2nd	3rd	4th	Win & Pl
6	1	4	-	-	£23,722

	1/19	Tram	2m Mdn Hdl soft	£6,659

Well beaten in last season's Ballymore Novices'
Hurdle at the Cheltenham Festival but finished
second in good novice hurdles at Thurles and
Punchestown either side of that; impressive
point-to-point winner and expected to do better
over fences.

Now McGinty (Ire)

8 b g Stowaway - Western Whisper (Supreme Leader)

Stuart Edmunds — The Garratt Family

PLACINGS: 343/33P00112/2U2128- — RPR **147**c

Starts	1st	2nd	3rd	4th	Win & Pl
21	3	4	4	3	£48,785

	1/19	Chep	2m7¹/₂f Cls3 Nov Ch gd-sft	£7,343
120	3/18	Wwck	2m5f Cls4 97-120 Hdl Hcap soft	£4,419
110	3/18	Wwck	2m5f Cls4 94-117 Hdl Hcap heavy	£4,549

Showed smart form in staying novice chases; won a red-hot contest at Chepstow (next three all won next time) and pushed Mister Malarky close when second in the Reynoldstown; far from disgraced when eighth behind Topofthegame in the RSA at Cheltenham.

O O Seven (Ire)

9 b g Flemensfirth - Kestral Heights (Eagle Eyed)

Nicky Henderson — Christopher Hanbury

PLACINGS: 213154/3450P3/1908-1 — RPR **156**c

Starts	1st	2nd	3rd	4th	Win & Pl
25	8	3	3	2	£172,553

147	5/19	Punc	2m4f 130-153 Ch Hcap yld-sft	£53,153
147	12/18	Donc	3m Cls2 133-147 Ch Hcap good	£15,640
148	1/17	Hntg	2m4f Cls3 Nov 129-148 Ch Hcap gd-sft	£6,498
	11/16	Chel	2m4¹/₂f Cls2 Nov Ch good	£15,698
	2/16	Muss	3m Cls2 Hdl soft	£14,389
	12/15	Sand	2m Cls3 Nov Hdl soft	£6,498
	11/15	Hntg	2m Cls5 Mdn Hdl gd-sft	£2,599
	12/14	Hntg	2m Cls6 NHF 4-6yo gd-sft	£1,560

Classy handicap chaser who bounced back to form when winning at Punchestown in May after breaking blood vessels in the Topham; had also won over 3m at Doncaster but didn't seem to stay the trip on soft ground after running well for a long way in the Ultima at Cheltenham.

Off You Go (Ire)

6 b g Presenting - Ozzy Oscar (Oscar)

Charles Byrnes (Ir) — John P McManus

PLACINGS: 406311/18123- — RPR **155+**h

Starts	1st	2nd	3rd	4th	Win & Pl
11	4	1	2	1	£154,644

143	2/19	Leop	2m 120-148 Hdl Hcap gd-yld	£66,441
134	10/18	Gway	2m¹/₂f 106-134 Hdl Hcap yield	£14,695
123	2/18	Leop	2m 122-147 Hdl Hcap soft	£52,212
107	12/17	Limk	2m4f 98-120 Hdl Hcap heavy	£6,581

Lightly raced but sharply progressive in handicaps over the last two seasons, winning a second Ladbrokes Hurdle at Leopardstown in February off a 20lb higher mark than when successful in 2018; second and third when tried at Grade 2 level subsequently, both times over further.

Ok Corral (Ire)

9 b g Mahler - Acoola (Flemensfirth)

Nicky Henderson — John P McManus

PLACINGS: 1/2/12125/11P- — RPR **156+**c

Starts	1st	2nd	3rd	4th	Win & Pl
10	5	3	-	-	£66,063

	1/19	Wwck	3m Cls1 Nov List Ch good	£14,238
	12/18	Plum	3m1¹/₂f Cls3 Nov Ch soft	£7,522
	2/18	Kemp	2m5f Cls4 Nov Hdl soft	£4,094
	5/17	Kemp	2m Cls4 Nov Hdl good	£3,249
	2/15	Kemp	2m Cls5 Mdn NHF 4-6yo soft	£2,274

Finished second in the Albert Bartlett in 2018 and not far off that level when novice chasing last term; disappointed in the National Hunt Chase but had easily won a hot Listed novice chase at Warwick to go off just 4-1 for that race; very lightly raced for his age.

Ok Corral (white cap) is lightly raced and open to improvement

Old Guard

8 b g Notnowcato - Dolma (Marchand De Sable)

Paul Nicholls   The Brooks Family & J Kyle

PLACINGS: 7/713154174/2232634-   RPR **158**h

Starts		1st	2nd	3rd	4th	Win & Pl
34		8	4	5	7	£363,723
	2/18	Font	2m3f Cls1 Gd2 Hdl gd-sft			£45,560
149	12/17	Newb	2m4¹/₂f Cls2 123-149 Hdl Hcap gd-sft			£25,992
	10/17	Kemp	2m Cls1 List Hdl good			£17,165
	10/16	Extr	2m1¹/₂f Cls4 Ch good			£6,498
	12/15	Chel	2m1f Cls1 Gd2 Hdl soft			£74,035
145	11/15	Chel	2m¹/₂f Cls1 Gd3 128-147 Hdl Hcap gd-sft			£56,950
137	10/15	Chel	2m¹/₂f Cls3 116-139 Cond Hdl Hcap good			£6,256
	11/14	Newb	2m¹/₂f Cls3 Hdl 3yo soft			£6,498

Four-time winner in Graded/Listed company over hurdles and continued to run well at that level last season, finishing second in the Ascot Hurdle and West Yorkshire Hurdle; most effective at around 2m4f and yet to fully convince with his stamina over further.

On The Blind Side (Ire)

7 b g Stowaway - Such A Set Up (Supreme Leader)

Nicky Henderson   A D Spence

PLACINGS: 1/1116/41P2-   RPR **149+**c

Starts		1st	2nd	3rd	4th	Win & Pl
8		4			1	£58,808
	1/19	Kemp	3m Cls4 Nov Ch gd-sft			£4,614
	12/17	Sand	2m4f Cls1 Nov Gd2 Hdl gd-sft			£17,085
	11/17	Chel	2m5f Cls1 Nov Gd2 Hdl gd-sft			£17,165
	10/17	Aint	2m4f Cls4 Mdn Hdl gd-sft			£5,005

Looked a potential star when winning two Grade 2 novice hurdles in late 2017 but has had little go right since; did well to beat bet365 Gold Cup winner Talkischeap when off the mark over fences at Kempton last season but was never travelling when pulled up in the RSA.

One For Arthur (Ire)

10 b g Milan - Nonnetia (Trempolino)

Lucinda Russell   Two Golf Widows

PLACINGS: 1P/1335243/1511/UU6-   RPR **143**c

Starts		1st	2nd	3rd	4th	Win & Pl
148		7	3	5	1	£668,938
	4/17	Aint	4m2¹/₂f Cls1 Gd3 143-161 Ch Hcap gd-sft			£561,300
137	1/17	Wwck	3m5f Cls1 Gd3 129-152 Ch Hcap soft			£34,170
127	10/16	Kels	3m2f Cls3 109-135 Ch Hcap gd-sft			£11,047
	10/15	Kels	2m7¹/₂f Cls4 Nov Ch good			£4,549
	3/15	Ayr	3m¹/₂f Cls4 Nov Hdl soft			£3,899
120	2/15	Ayr	3m¹/₂f Cls4 Nov 94-120 Hdl Hcap soft			£3,574
	1/15	Hayd	2m3f Cls4 Nov Hdl 4-7yo heavy			£3,899

Impressive winner of the Grand National in 2017, crowning a hugely progressive season; missed the following campaign through injury and twice unseated on his comeback last term but showed plenty of his old spark when sixth back at Aintree for the National.

One For Rosie

6 gr g Getaway - Whisky Rose (Old Vic)

Nigel Twiston-Davies   Paul & Clare Rooney

PLACINGS: 1/13123-   RPR **145**h

Starts		1st	2nd	3rd	4th	Win & Pl
6		3	1	2	-	£35,394
	2/19	Wwck	2m3f Cls4 Nov Hdl 4-7yo good			£4,419
	11/18	Carl	2m4f Cls4 Nov Hdl good			£4,549
	10/17	Bang	2m¹/₂f Cls6 NHF 4-6yo good			£1,949

Won two of first three over hurdles last season before a fine second under topweight in the EBF Final at Sandown; beaten less than six lengths behind Reserve Tank when moved up to Grade 1 level at Aintree; trainer expects improvement when stepped up in trip.

Ornua (Ire)

8 ch g Mahler - Merry Heart (Broken Hearted)

Henry de Bromhead (Ir)   John J Phelan & Syed Momin

PLACINGS: 36/11P30/3112122F1-P   RPR **159+**c

Starts	1st	2nd	3rd	4th	Win & Pl
17	6	3	3	-	£136,552

4/19	Aint	2m Cls1 Nov Gd1 Ch good	£56,130
10/18	Rosc	2m¹/₂f Nov Gd3 Ch good	£20,885
7/18	NAbb	2m¹/₂f Cls3 Nov Ch good	£11,148
6/18	Wxfd	2m Ch good	£6,814
5/17	Clon	2m¹/₂f Hdl good	£6,581
5/17	DRoy	2m Mdn Hdl good	£5,791

Front-running chaser who won four times in a busy novice campaign last season, most notably in a Grade 1 at Aintree; likely that will prove a weak race for the grade (runner-up Us And Them beaten much further in other top chases) but type to do well in small-field Graded races.

Pairofbrowneyes (Ire)

10 b g Luso - Frankly Native (Be My Native)

Willie Mullins (Ir)   Fibbage Syndicate

PLACINGS: 352232206/801F/001F-   RPR **158+**c

Starts	1st	2nd	3rd	4th	Win & Pl
31	6	4	6	2	£216,341

146	3/19	Naas	3m 128-151 Ch Hcap yld-sft	£53,153
137	3/18	Gowr	2m7f 120-140 Ch Hcap heavy	£52,212
122	12/15	Limk	2m3¹/₂f 112-140 Ch Hcap heavy	£23,256
116	11/15	Cork	2m1f 103-131 Ch Hcap heavy	£12,093
114	11/14	Punc	2m 114-125 Hdl Hcap soft	£12,188
	1/14	Fair	2m4f Mdn Hdl sft-hvy	£4,600

Has won the last two editions of the Leinster National only to then fall early on when well fancied for the Irish Grand National both times; much improved and lightly raced since moving to Willie Mullins in early 2018 and could yet have another big handicap chase in him.

Paisley Park (Ire)

7 b g Oscar - Presenting Shares (Presenting)

Emma Lavelle   Andrew Gemmell

PLACINGS: 2/1220/11111-   RPR **172+**h

Starts	1st	2nd	3rd	4th	Win & Pl
10	6	3	-	-	£361,565

3/19	Chel	3m Cls1 Gd1 Hdl gd-sft	£182,878
1/19	Chel	3m Cls1 Gd2 Hdl gd-sft	£33,762
12/18	Asct	3m¹/₂f Cls1 Gd1 Hdl soft	£56,950
147	11/18	Hayd	3m¹/₂f Cls1 Gd3 125-147 Hdl Hcap good	£56,950
140	10/18	Aint	2m4f Cls2 116-140 Hdl Hcap good	£17,204
	12/17	Hrfd	2m3¹/₂f Cls4 Nov Hdl soft	£4,549

Came from nowhere to emerge as last season's dominant staying hurdler, winning five out of five; scrambled home in the Long Walk Hurdle

at Ascot before taking form to a new level in two runs at Cheltenham, including when a decisive winner of the Stayers' Hurdle.

Paloma Blue (Ire)

7 br g Stowaway - Court Leader (Supreme Leader)

Henry de Bromhead (Ir)   C Jones

PLACINGS: 12/321340/416-6   RPR **146+**c

Starts	1st	2nd	3rd	4th	Win & Pl
12	3	2	2	2	£58,687

12/18	Leop	2m1f Ch good	£9,540
12/17	Leop	2m Mdn Hdl yield	£7,371
1/17	Fair	2m NHF 5-7yo soft	£4,731

High-class novice hurdler (beaten only three lengths in the Supreme in 2018) but didn't quite make the grade over fences last season; impressive when beating subsequent Aintree winner Moon Over Germany but finished a well-beaten sixth in the Racing Post Arkle.

Penhill

8 b g Mount Nelson - Serrenia (High Chaparral)

Willie Mullins (Ir)   Tony Bloom

PLACINGS: 161114112/12/   RPR **162**h

Starts	1st	2nd	3rd	4th	Win & Pl
11	7	2	-	1	£388,650

3/18	Chel	3m Cls1 Gd1 Hdl soft	£192,707
3/17	Chel	3m Cls1 Nov Gd1 Hdl good	£71,188
12/16	Limk	3m Nov Gd2 Hdl sft-hvy	£19,305
10/16	Tipp	2m Nov Gd3 Hdl soft	£14,697
9/16	List	2m Nov Hdl yield	£9,949
7/16	Gway	2m¹/₂f Nov Hdl gd-yld	£11,305
5/16	Tram	2m Mdn Hdl good	£4,522

Did remarkably well to win the 2018 Stayers' Hurdle after a long injury layoff, showing a terrific turn of foot in a slowly run race, but remains fragile having then missed last season as well; also won at Cheltenham in 2017 but has twice failed to follow up at Punchestown.

Pentland Hills (Ire)

4 b g Motivator - Elle Galante (Galileo)

Nicky Henderson   Owners Group 031

PLACINGS: 111-   RPR **148+**h

Starts	1st	2nd	3rd	4th	Win & Pl
3	3	-	-	-	£130,586

4/19	Aint	2m1f Cls1 Gd1 Hdl 4yo gd-sft	£56,155
3/19	Chel	2m1f Cls1 Gd1 Hdl 4yo gd-sft	£70,338
2/19	Plum	2m Cls4 Mdn Hdl good	£4,094

Unbeaten hurdler who won all three runs in just six weeks last season, including the Triumph

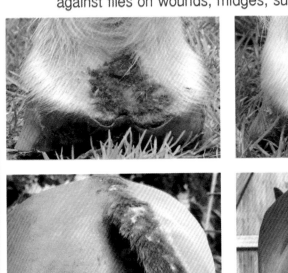

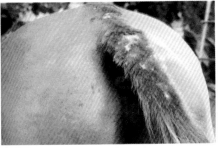
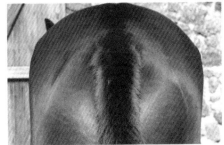
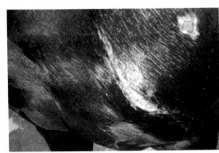
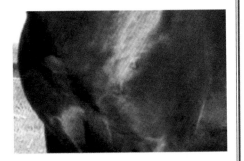

Hurdle; didn't get enough credit for that win (perhaps due to modest Flat form, though had won two of last three) and proved point by following up when only third favourite at Aintree.

Petit Mouchoir (Fr)

8 gr g Al Namix - Arnette (Denham Red)

Henry de Bromhead (Ir) Gigginstown House Stud

PLACINGS: /23F113/12324/6304-4 RPR **157**h

Starts	1st	2nd	3rd	4th	Win & Pl
22	5	4	5	4	£331,477

10/17	Punc	2m Ch yld-sft	£7,634
1/17	Leop	2m Gd1 Hdl good	£55,470
12/16	Leop	2m Gd1 Hdl yield	£43,382
11/15	Thur	2m Mdn Hdl 4yo soft	£5,349
4/15	Punc	2m NHF 4-5yo gd-yld	£45,736

Dual Grade 1 winner in 2016-17, including the Irish Champion Hurdle, but couldn't quite match that level in top 2m hurdles last season and twice disappointed when tried over further; had gradually lost his way after a promising start to his chase career two seasons ago.

Politologue (Fr)

8 gr g Poliglote - Scarlet Row (Turgeon)

Paul Nicholls J Hales

PLACINGS: 11214F/111241/14422- RPR **171**c

Starts	1st	2nd	3rd	4th	Win & Pl
23	10	6	-	4	£653,876

11/18	Asct	2m5f Cls1 Gd2 Ch gd-sft	£39,865
4/18	Aint	2m4f Cls1 Gd1 Ch soft	£140,985
12/17	Kemp	2m Cls1 Gd2 Ch soft	£52,854
12/17	Sand	1m7½f Cls1 Gd1 Ch gd-sft	£85,827
11/17	Extr	2m1½f Cls1 Gd2 142-162 Ch Hcap soft	£37,192
2/17	Kemp	2m4½f Cls2 Ch gd-sft	£12,512
12/16	Asct	2m5f Cls1 Nov Gd2 Ch gd-sft	£18,224
11/16	Hayd	2m5½f Cls2 Nov Ch soft	£16,245
2/16	Extr	2m1f Cls1 Nov List Hdl heavy	£11,524
6/15	Autl	2m2f Hdl 4yo soft	£17,860

High-class from 2m to 2m5f; unable to add to

Grade 1 tally last term (had previously won the Tingle Creek and Melling) but came close to a big upset when second to Altior in the Champion Chase; didn't stay 3m in the King George and bled when a distant second in the Melling.

Posh Trish (Ire)

6 b m Stowaway - Moscow Demon (Moscow Society)

Paul Nicholls Highclere Thoroughbred Racing

PLACINGS: 1/11030/121118- RPR **141**+h

Starts	1st	2nd	3rd	4th	Win & Pl
11	6	1	1	-	£57,654

12/18	Tntn	2m1½f Cls1 Nov List Hdl gd-sft	£11,390
12/18	Winc	1m7½f Cls4 Nov Hdl gd-sft	£4,549
12/18	Newb	2m1½f Cls1 Nov List Hdl soft	£14,860
10/18	Chep	2m3½f Cls4 Nov Hdl good	£4,809
11/17	Chel	2m1½f Cls1 List NHF 4-6yo soft	£11,390
10/17	Aint	2m1f Cls4 NHF 4-6yo gd-sft	£3,754

Smart mare who won four of her first five over hurdles, including two Listed mares' novice races at Newbury and Taunton; below her best when only eighth in the mares' novice at the Cheltenham Festival (sent off just 3-1); point-to-point winner and should stay further.

Potters Corner (Ire)

9 b g Indian Danehill - Woodford Beauty (Phardante)

Christian Williams All Stars Sports Racing & J Davies

PLACINGS: /132d61/2342/9P1FF1-5 RPR **144**+c

Starts	1st	2nd	3rd	4th	Win & Pl
18	5	2	3	1	£123,356
135					
120					

3/19	Uttx	4m2f Cls1 List 128-154 Ch Hcap heavy	£84,655
12/18	Winc	3m1f Cls3 100-124 Ch Hcap gd-sft	£12,996
4/16	Ffos	2m4f Cls4 Nov Hdl soft	£3,249
9/15	Chep	2m3½f Cls5 Mdn Hdl good	£2,274
9/14	Chep	2m Cls6 NHF 4-6yo good	£1,560

Richly deserving winner of last season's Midlands National at Uttoxeter having fallen when in

All eyes are on Posh Trish as she scores at Newbury last season

contention in the Somerset National and Eider Chase previously; thorough stayer who relished heavy ground that day but also acts on good.

Precious Cargo (Ire)
6 b g Yeats - Kilbarry Classic (Classic Cliche)

Nicky Henderson | Thomas Barr

PLACINGS: 120/116- | RPR **138+**h

Starts	1st	2nd	3rd	4th	Win & Pl
6	3	1	-	-	£13,554
	3/19	Sand	2m Cls4 Nov Hdl soft		£5,198
	1/19	Kemp	2m Cls4 Nov Hdl gd-sft		£4,094
	1/18	Ayr	2m Cls5 NHF 4-6yo heavy		£2,274

Won first two races over hurdles last season but only sixth of seven when stepped up to Grade 1 level at Aintree (sent off just 4-1); described as 'just messing about' over hurdles by his trainer, who thinks he could be a Cheltenham Festival horse as a novice chaser.

Present Man (Ire)
9 b g Presenting - Glen's Gale (Strong Gale)

Paul Nicholls | Mr & Mrs Mark Woodhouse

PLACINGS: 21U1141P/11043/184P- | RPR **155**c

Starts	1st	2nd	3rd	4th	Win & Pl
25	8	5	1	4	£157,125
144	11/18	Winc	3m1f Cls1 List 122-144 Ch Hcap good		£34,170
142	11/17	Winc	3m1f Cls1 List 130-154 Ch Hcap soft		£34,170
	10/17	Kemp	2m5f Cls4 Nov Hdl good		£3,899
	4/17	Asct	2m5f Cls3 Nov Ch good		£9,747
	12/16	Donc	3m Cls1 Nov Gd2 Ch good		£19,933
132	11/16	Asct	2m5f Cls3 114-138 Ch Hcap gd-sft		£16,245
125	10/16	Winc	2m4f Cls3 119-127 Ch Hcap gd-fm		£6,498
	11/14	Winc	1m7¹/₂f Cls6 NHF 4-6yo gd-sft		£1,625

Has won the last two runnings of the Badger Ales Trophy at Wincanton but hasn't achieved much else in that time; given wind surgery after a couple of disappointing subsequent efforts last term but did no better when pulled up in the bet365 Gold Cup on his final run.

Presenting Percy
8 b g Sir Percy - Hunca Munca (Presenting)

Pat Kelly (Ir) | Philip J Reynolds

PLACINGS: 741154116/131121/18- | RPR **149**c

Starts	1st	2nd	3rd	4th	Win & Pl
19	10	2	1	2	£284,510
	1/19	Gowr	3m Gd2 Hdl soft		£23,919
	3/18	Chel	3m¹/₂f Cls1 Nov Gd1 Ch good		£100,132
	1/18	Gowr	3m Gd2 Hdl heavy		£23,496
145	12/17	Fair	3m5f 117-145 Ch Hcap soft		£25,214
	10/17	Gway	2m6¹/₂f Ch heavy		£10,003
146	3/17	Chel	3m Cls1 List 137-147 Hdl Hcap good		£54,103
130	2/17	Fair	2m4f 108-138 Hdl Hcap heavy		£13,667
115	11/16	Punc	2m Nov 90-121 Hdl Hcap soft		£7,235
	10/16	Gway	2m Mdn Hdl 4-5yo yield		£5,879
	4/16	Baln	2m1f NHF 4-7yo heavy		£4,296

Brilliant winner of the RSA Chase in 2018 (second Cheltenham Festival victory); Gold Cup favourite throughout last season but given a unique preparation as connections avoided quick ground (had sole prep run over hurdles) and only eighth at Cheltenham when found to be lame.

Quel Destin (Fr)
4 ch g Muhtathir - High Destiny (High Yield)

Paul Nicholls | Martin Broughton & Friends

PLACINGS: 54/F12111115- | RPR **137**h

Starts	1st	2nd	3rd	4th	Win & Pl
11	6	1	-	1	£133,223
	2/19	Hayd	1m7¹/₂f Cls2 Hdl 4yo gd-sft		£12,996
	12/18	Chep	2m Cls1 Gd1 Hdl 3yo soft		£37,018
	12/18	Donc	2m¹/₂f Cls1 Gd2 Hdl 3yo good		£28,135
	11/18	Chel	2m¹/₂f Cls2 Hdl 3yo good		£18,006
	10/18	Kemp	2m Cls3 Hdl 3yo good		£6,498
	5/18	Autl	1m7f Hdl 3yo heavy		£19,115

Only fifth in last season's Triumph Hurdle but had looked like Britain's leading juvenile hurdler prior to that, winning five in a row including the Grade 1 Finale Hurdle at Chepstow; coped well with soft ground that day but equally effective on good; has scope to improve.

Quick Grabim (Ire)
7 b g Oscar - Top Her Up (Beneficial)

Willie Mullins (Ir) | Geraldine Worcester

PLACINGS: 2170/2F/1141-45 | RPR **146+**h

Starts	1st	2nd	3rd	4th	Win & Pl
12	4	2	-	2	£93,053
	12/18	Fair	2m Nov Gd1 Hdl good		£46,991
	10/18	Tipp	2m Nov Gd3 Hdl good		£17,568
	9/18	List	2m Mdn Hdl soft		£8,177
	12/16	Leop	2m NHF 4-7yo yield		£4,748

Won three of his first four races over hurdles last season, including the Grade 1 Royal Bond, although that race failed to work out; held up by training problems subsequently and well beaten on comeback runs at Punchestown and Auteuil.

Ramses De Teillee (Fr)
7 gr g Martaline - Princesse D'Orton (Saint Cyrien)

David Pipe | John White & Anne Underhill

PLACINGS: 326/322121279/5122P- | RPR **158**c

Starts	1st	2nd	3rd	4th	Win & Pl
18	3	7	2	1	£90,736
140	12/18	Chep	2m7¹/₂f Cls2 127-142 Ch Hcap heavy		£12,660
	1/18	Chep	2m7¹/₂f Cls3 Nov Ch heavy		£7,343
122	11/17	Chep	2m7¹/₂f Cls4 Nov 103-122 Ch Hcap heavy		£3,899

Progressive young staying chaser who won at Chepstow last season (all three victories over fences at that course) before finishing second in the Welsh National and the Grand National Trial at Haydock; never able to get involved when pulled up in the Grand National.

MY **FIVE** TO **WATCH**
Tom Park

●Chacun Pour Soi ●Champ ●Cyrname
●Klassical Dream ●Samcro

Reserve Tank (right) pulled off a festival double over hurdles last season and looks an exciting prospect for novice chases

Rather Be (Ire)

8 b g Oscar - Irish Wedding (Bob Back)

Nicky Henderson — Matt & Lauren Morgan

PLACINGS: 29/112U18/1U12/B59P- — RPR **139**c

Starts	1st	2nd	3rd	4th	Win & Pl
18	6	3	-	-	£85,096
	2/18	Fknm	2m¹/₂f Cls3 Nov Ch soft		£7,408
	12/17	Towc	2m Cls3 Nov Ch gd-sft		£6,330
136	4/17	Aint	2m4f Cls1 Gd3 130-146 Hdl Hcap good		£39,389
	12/16	Hntg	2m3¹/₂f Cls4 Nov Hdl gd-sft		£3,249
	10/16	Hrfd	2m Cls4 Nov Hdl 4-6yo good		£3,899
	12/15	Ludl	1m6f Cls4 NHF 4-5yo soft		£3,899

Well fancied for several big handicap chases last season having been beaten a head in the novice handicap at the 2018 Cheltenham Festival but yet to deliver; unlucky when brought down in the BetVictor Gold Cup (going well) but disappointing subsequently.

Rathhill (Ire)

6 b g Getaway - Bella Venezia (Milan)

Nicky Henderson — John P McManus

PLACINGS: 2/14- — RPR **138**h

Starts	1st	2nd	3rd	4th	Win & Pl
2	1	-	-	1	£7,473
	12/18	Newb	2m¹/₂f Cls4 Mdn Hdl soft		£4,809

Held in very high regard at home and was sent off favourite for last season's Tolworth Hurdle after an impressive hurdling debut at Newbury; disappointing fourth at Sandown when too green according to his trainer and missed the rest of the season.

Rathvinden (Ire)

11 b g Heron Island - Peggy Cullen (Presenting)

Willie Mullins (Ir) — R A Bartlett

PLACINGS: 3/P/2113112BU14/13-0 — RPR **163**c

Starts	1st	2nd	3rd	4th	Win & Pl
21	9	3	3	1	£313,693
	2/19	Fair	3m1f Gd3 Ch gd-yld		£23,919
	3/18	Chel	4m Cls1 Nov Gd2 Am Ch soft		£74,950
	10/17	Tipp	2m4f Nov Gd3 Ch heavy		£17,083
	9/17	List	2m4f Nov Ch heavy		£11,038
	8/17	Gway	2m2f Nov Gd3 Ch yield		£25,214
	7/17	Wxfd	3m1f Ch good		£6,581
	12/13	Cork	2m Mdn Hdl soft		£5,610
	11/13	Cork	2m NHF 4-7yo sft-hvy		£5,610
	6/13	Dpat	2m2f NHF 4-7yo gd-fm		£3,927

Laid out for last season's Grand National and ran a fine race to finish third behind Tiger Roll at Aintree; came to chasing very late after injury problems but won the National Hunt Chase in 2018 and looked to have progressed again when winning the Bobbyjo Chase impressively.

Real Steel (Fr)

6 b g Loup Breton - Kalimina (Monsun)

Willie Mullins (Ir) — Sullivan Bloodstock

PLACINGS: 2/1F50P4/F1162-1 — RPR **159+**c

Starts	1st	2nd	3rd	4th	Win & Pl
13	4	2		1	£109,938
151	5/19	Punc	2m5f Nov 130-151 Ch Hcap gd-yld		£53,153
	2/19	Thur	2m2f Ch good		£14,405
	1/19	Fair	2m5¹/₂f Ch yield		£7,769
	11/17	Thur	2m Mdn Hdl 4yo soft		£5,791

Progressive novice chaser last season, winning three times; also took Grade 1 record to 0-6 but came closest when second to Voix Du Reve in the Ryanair Gold Cup and followed up by winning a good novice handicap at Punchestown off top weight on his final start.

Reikers Island (Ire)

6 b g Yeats - Moricana (Konigsstühl)

Philip Hobbs   James Drummond

PLACINGS: 4231F15/3146P-   RPR **147**+c

Starts	1st	2nd	3rd	4th	Win & Pl
8	2	-	1	1	£24,606
124	12/18	Winc	3m1f Cls3 102-126 Ch Hcap good		£16,245
	3/18	Font	2m5½f Cls4 Nov Hdl soft		£4,094

Young chaser who lost his way towards the end of last season but had made an exciting start over fences, winning a good handicap at Wincanton by six lengths on his second run; might well have followed up when favourite for the Mandarin at Newbury but for a final-fence blunder that almost saw his rider unseated.

Reserve Tank (Ire)

5 b g Jeremy - Lady Bellamy (Black Sam Bellamy)

Colin Tizzard   The Reserve Tankers

PLACINGS: 37111-1   RPR **151**+h

Starts	1st	2nd	3rd	4th	Win & Pl
6	4	-	1	-	£119,447
	5/19	Punc	2m4f Nov Gd1 Hdl gd-yld		£53,153
	4/19	Aint	2m4f Cls1 Nov Gd1 Hdl good		£56,130
	3/19	Kemp	2m5f Cls4 Nov Hdl gd-sft		£4,260
	2/19	Sand	2m Cls4 Nov Hdl soft		£5,198

Massive improver in second half of last season, winning four successive novice hurdles including a Grade 1 double at Aintree and Punchestown; strong likelihood those won't prove particularly strong races for the grade but still looks a fine prospect for fences.

Harry Skelton celebrates as Roksana wins the Mares' Hurdle at Cheltenham

Rhinestone (Ire)

6 b g Montjeu - Apticanti (Aptitude)

Joseph O'Brien (Ir)   John P McManus

PLACINGS: 2129/142P-					RPR **146+**h
Starts	1st	2nd	3rd	4th	Win & Pl
8	2	3	-	1	£51,012
11/18	Naas	2m Mdn Hdl gd-yld			£8,177
12/17	Thur	2m NHF 4-7yo heavy			£5,528

Long held in high regard (sent off just 5-1 when ninth in the 2018 Champion Bumper) and ran his best race when pushing Commander Of Fleet to half a length in a Grade 1 at Leopardstown last season; disappointed at Cheltenham for a second time when pulled up in the Albert Bartlett.

Riders Onthe Storm (Ire)

6 br g Scorpion - Endless Moments (Saddlers' Hall)

Tom Taaffe (Ir)

Mrs Paul Shanahan, Mrs John Magnier & J Carthy

PLACINGS: 45/521260/431FP-					RPR **142+**c
Starts	1st	2nd	3rd	4th	Win & Pl
13	2	2	1	2	£36,215
2/19	Punc	2m Nov Ch gd-yld			£10,267
1/18	Navn	2m Nov Hdl heavy			£8,722

Showed huge promise when beating Impact Factor in a novice chase at Punchestown last term but finished his season on a low note when pulled up behind that rival at Fairyhouse (sent off favourite); fell early when 10-1 for the novice handicap at the Cheltenham Festival.

River Wylde (Ire)

8 b g Oscar - Clarin River (Mandalus)

Ian Williams   Grech & Parkin

PLACINGS: 23/1011135/12/FP6-					RPR **157+**c
Starts	1st	2nd	3rd	4th	Win & Pl
13	5	1	2	-	£57,670
11/17	Uttx	2m Cls3 Ch gd-sft			£6,330
2/17	Kemp	2m Cls1 Nov Gd2 Hdl good			£17,085
1/17	Ludl	2m Cls4 Nov Hdl soft			£3,899
12/16	Ludl	2m Cls4 Mdn Hdl gd-sft			£3,899
5/16	Wwck	2m Cls6 NHF 4-6yo gd-sft			£1,949

Finished third in the Supreme Novices' Hurdle in 2017 but has suffered bad fortune with injuries since making a winning start over fences the following season, running just four times and struggling in hot handicaps last spring; bought for £58,000 at the Grech & Parkin dispersal sale.

Road To Respect (Ire)

8 ch g Gamut - Lora Lady (Lord America)

Noel Meade (Ir)   Gigginstown House Stud

PLACINGS: 1432211/12143/13235-					RPR **171**c
Starts	1st	2nd	3rd	4th	Win & Pl
24	7	6	6	2	£490,196
	11/18	DRoy	3m Gd1 Ch gd-yld		£73,097
	12/17	Leop	3m Gd1 Ch yield		£75,641
	10/17	Punc	3m1f Gd3 Ch soft		£20,171
	4/17	Fair	2m4f Nov Gd1 Ch gd-yld		£50,427
145	3/17	Chel	2m5f Cls1 Gd3 133-158 Ch Hcap good		£59,798
	11/16	Naas	2m3f Ch yld-sft		£6,105
	2/16	Thur	2m6¹/₂f Mdn Hdl heavy		£4,522

Dual Grade 1 winner in Ireland, most recently in the Champion Chase at Down Royal early last season, but just tends to come up short in the very best chases; just pipped by Bellshill in the Irish Gold Cup before coming down in trip to finish third in the Ryanair Chase.

Robinsfirth (Ire)
10 b g Flemensfirth - Phardester (Phardante)

Colin Tizzard   Christine Knowles & Wendy Carter

PLACINGS: 1/4/124/21U/421/21-   RPR **159**+c

Starts		1st	2nd	3rd	4th	Win & Pl
13		5	4	-	3	£129,886
148	2/19	Hayd	3m4¹/₂f Cls1 Gd3 130-156 Ch Hcap good			£56,950
142	12/17	Chel	3m2f Cls1 Gd3 127-148 Ch Hcap soft			£25,628
	1/17	Extr	2m3f Cls3 Ch soft			£7,798
	12/14	Extr	2m1f Cls4 Nov Hdl gd-sft			£3,574
	4/13	Winc	1m7¹/₂f Cls6 NHF 4-6yo good			£1,625

Fragile but talented staying chaser who has run just twice since 2017, finishing second in last season's Peter Marsh Chase before winning the Grand National Trial back at Haydock; very lightly raced for his age and open to further improvement after just eight runs over fences.

Rock The Kasbah (Ire)
9 ch g Shirocco - Impudent (In The Wings)

Philip Hobbs   Mrs Diana L Whateley

PLACINGS: 0/1324126/1P2/616BP-   RPR **158**c

Starts		1st	2nd	3rd	4th	Win & Pl
27		9	6	2	1	£208,157
147	11/18	Chel	3m3¹/₂f Cls1 Gd3 134-160 Ch Hcap good			£33,762
142	10/17	Chep	2m7¹/₂f Cls2 134-160 Ch Hcap gd-sft			£19,494
	2/17	Chep	2m7¹/₂f Cls3 Nov Ch soft			£6,498
	10/16	Chep	2m3¹/₂f Cls2 Nov Ch good			£19,494
144	1/16	Asct	2m3¹/₂f Cls3 125-151 Hdl Hcap soft			£28,475
136	11/15	Hayd	2m3f Cls2 121-139 Hdl Hcap soft			£25,024
	3/15	Newb	2m4¹/₂f Cls3 Nov Hdl gd-sft			£5,848
	11/14	Font	2m3f Cls4 Nov Cond Hdl soft			£3,119
	10/14	Ffos	2m Cls6 Mdn NHF 4-6yo soft			£1,643

Inconsistent but talented staying chaser who has won good handicaps at Chepstow and Cheltenham in the last two seasons; kept fresh for the Grand National in the spring but struggling when brought down at Aintree and pulled up in the bet365 Gold Cup.

Rocky's Treasure (Ire)
8 b g Westerner - Fiddlers Bar (Un Desperado)

Kim Bailey   J Perriss

PLACINGS: 3411/3PP5/411121352-   RPR **155**+c

Starts		1st	2nd	3rd	4th	Win & Pl
17		6	2	3	2	£78,316
	12/18	Donc	3m Cls1 Nov Gd2 Ch good			£22,780
	11/18	Weth	3m Cls4 Nov Ch good			£6,758
	10/18	Fknm	3m Cls3 Nov Ch good			£8,789
	10/18	Kels	2m7¹/₂f Cls4 Nov Ch good			£6,628
125	4/17	Ffos	3m Cls3 115-134 Hdl Hcap good			£5,523
117	2/17	Donc	3m¹/₂f Cls3 108-131 Hdl Hcap good			£5,697

Made a terrific start to chasing career last season when beaten only by Santini in first five runs over fences, making all in a Grade 2 at Doncaster by 17 lengths; slightly disappointing he didn't win again, though ran well when second under a big weight in a Cheltenham handicap.

Roksana (Ire)
7 b m Dubai Destination - Talktothetail (Flemensfirth)

Dan Skelton   Mrs Sarah Faulks

PLACINGS: 4/31112/312-   RPR **156**h

Starts		1st	2nd	3rd	4th	Win & Pl
9		4	2	2	1	£163,169
	3/19	Chel	2m4f Cls1 Gd1 Hdl soft			£70,563
130	3/18	Newb	2m4¹/₂f Cls1 Nov Gd2 115-135 Hdl Hcap soft			£22,780
	12/17	Font	3m Cls4 Nov Hdl heavy			£3,249
	11/17	Plum	2m4¹/₂f Cls4 Nov Hdl good			£3,249

Fortuitous winner of last season's Mares' Hurdle at Cheltenham after Benie Des Dieux's final-flight fall but proved herself a high-class mare in her own right when second in a 3m Grade 1 at Aintree behind If The Cap Fits; set for a light campaign geared towards same two races.

Ronald Pump
6 ch g Schiaparelli - Fruit Yoghurt (Hernando)

Matthew J Smith (Ir)   Laois Limerick Syndicate

PLACINGS: 08374R/4404911411-   RPR **146**+h

Starts		1st	2nd	3rd	4th	Win & Pl
16		4	-	1	5	£56,656
136	4/19	Fair	3m Nov 112-136 Hdl Hcap gd-yld			£29,234
123	3/19	Fair	3m 108-130 Hdl Hcap soft			£9,989
108	1/19	Fair	3m 81-108 Hdl Hcap good			£6,659
102	12/18	Cork	2m4f Nov 80-102 Hdl Hcap sft-hvy			£5,996

Massive improver last season, winning four of his last five races and climbing 43lb in the handicap; most effective when stepped back up to 3m and won a valuable novice handicap final over the trip at Fairyhouse; acts on any ground.

Rouge Vif (Fr)
5 b g Sageburg - Rouge Amour (Cadoudal)

Harry Whittington   Kate & Andrew Brooks

PLACINGS: 1/5212113-   RPR **143**+h

Starts		1st	2nd	3rd	4th	Win & Pl
8		4	2	1	-	£57,319
	3/19	Kels	2m2f Cls1 Nov Gd2 Hdl gd-sft			£28,475
	1/19	Newc	2m¹/₂f Cls4 Nov Hdl soft			£4,094
	12/18	Sthl	1m7¹/₂f Cls4 Mdn Hdl gd-sft			£4,094
	3/18	Ludl	2m Cls4 NHF 4-6yo soft			£4,809

Won three novice hurdles last season, most notably when making all in a Grade 2 at Kelso; fair third behind Felix Desjy when stepped up to Grade 1 level but not felt to be at his best on that soft ground (previous win on soft had come when struggling to land odds of 4-11).

Royal Rendezvous (Ire)
7 b g King's Theatre - Novacella (Beyssac)

Willie Mullins (Ir)   Dr S P Fitzgerald

PLACINGS: 4F1/5111-P   RPR **140**+h

Starts		1st	2nd	3rd	4th	Win & Pl
5		3	-	-	-	£20,410
	10/18	Gway	2m¹/₂f Mdn Hdl yield			£7,632
	10/18	Tipp	2m NHF 4-7yo good			£7,087
	8/18	Dpat	2m3f NHF 4-7yo gd-yld			£5,451

Won by 16 lengths on hurdling debut last season, adding to two bumper victories, but was out for seven months before being pulled up at Punchestown on his return in May; described by his trainer as having huge potential.

Saint Calvados (Fr)

6 b g Saint Des Saints - Lamorrese (Pistolet Bleu)

Harry Whittington			Kate & Andrew Brooks

PLACINGS: 1116/1114/1337-   RPR **159**c

Starts	1st	2nd	3rd	4th	Win & Pl
12	7	-	2	1	£152,437

	11/18	Naas	2m Gd3 Ch yield	£17,688
	2/18	Wwck	2m Cls1 Nov Gd2 Ch soft	£22,780
147	1/18	Newb	2m¹/₂f Cls3 Nov 135-147 Ch Hcap soft	£7,343
143	12/17	Newb	2m¹/₂f Cls3 Nov 127-143 Ch Hcap heavy	£8,656
	3/17	Autl	2m2f Hdl 4yo v soft	£28,718
	12/16	Cagn	2m1¹/₂f Hdl 3yo soft	£15,882
	11/16	Fntb	2m2f Hdl 3yo heavy	£8,118

Came up short in top company last season but has won all four races over fences below Grade 1 level, including a Grade 3 at Naas last season (Footpad beaten when falling at the last); unable to build on that, finishing off with a seventh in the Champion Chase.

Saldier (Fr)

5 b g Soldier Hollow - Salve Evita (Monsun)

Willie Mullins (Ir)			Mrs S Ricci

PLACINGS: 1531/F-   RPR **146+**h

Starts	1st	2nd	3rd	4th	Win & Pl
5	2	-	1	-	£66,306

	4/18	Punc	2m Gd1 Hdl 4yo yld-sft	£52,212
	2/18	Gowr	2m Mdn Hdl 4yo heavy	£7,359

Smart Flat horse (competed up to Group 2

level in 2017) who got better with practice after starting his hurdling career late two seasons ago; finished fifth in the Triumph Hurdle on just his second run and comprehensively reversed that form when winning at Punchestown; missed last season through injury.

Sam Spinner

7 b g Black Sam Bellamy - Dawn Spinner (Arctic Lord)

Jedd O'Keeffe			Caron & Paul Chapman

PLACINGS: 12/1211/21153/UU428-   RPR **165**h

Starts	1st	2nd	3rd	4th	Win & Pl
16	6	4	1	1	£243,312

	12/17	Asct	3m¹/₂f Cls1 Gd1 Hdl gd-sft	£56,950
139	11/17	Hayd	2m7f Cls1 Gd3 130-156 Hdl Hcap heavy	£56,950
	2/17	Catt	2m3¹/₂f Cls4 Nov Hdl 4-7yo soft	£3,899
	1/17	Catt	2m3¹/₂f Cls4 Nov Hdl gd-sft	£3,899
	11/16	Newc	2m¹/₂f Cls4 Nov Hdl gd-sft	£6,498
	2/16	Catt	1m7¹/₂f Cls6 Mdn NHF 4-6yo soft	£1,949

Developed into a top staying hurdler two seasons ago but has been largely disappointing since his win in the Long Walk Hurdle in 2017; bounced right back to his best when second behind Paisley Park in last season's Stayers' Hurdle only to run below par again at Aintree.

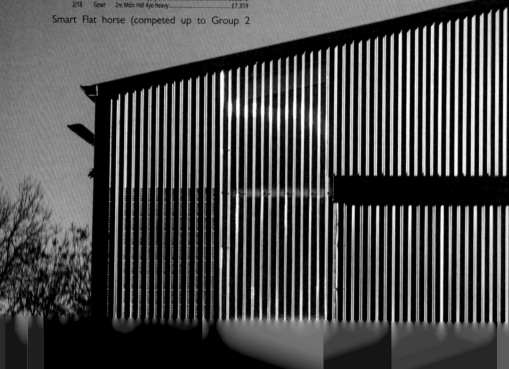

Samcro (Ire)

7 ch g Germany - Dun Dun (Saddlers' Hall)

Gordon Elliott (Ir)   Gigginstown House Stud

PLACINGS: 1/1111/1111F/225-   RPR **163**h

Starts 11	1st 7	2nd 2	3rd -	4th -	Win & Pl £211,728
	3/18	Chel	2m5f Cls1 Nov Gd1 Hdl soft		£71,188
	2/18	Leop	2m Nov Gd1 Hdl soft		£52,212
	11/17	Navn	2m4f Nov Gd3 Hdl sft-hvy		£21,432
	10/17	Punc	2m Mdn Hdl yld-sft		£6,844
	4/17	Fair	2m NHF 4-7yo gd-yld		£8,424
	12/16	Navn	2m List NHF 4-7yo sft-hvy		£12,436
	11/16	Punc	2m NHF 4yo soft		£4,522

Ireland's big hope last season after an impressive novice campaign (won the Ballymore at Cheltenham) in 2017-18 but failed to make the grade in top 2m hurdles; possibly affected by physical issues (found to have a lung infection) and now likely to go up in trip over fences.

Sams Profile

5 b g Black Sam Bellamy - Lucylou I (Bob Back)

Mouse Morris (Ir)   Michael O'Flynn & John F O'Flynn

PLACINGS: 13/1225-2   RPR **150+**h

Starts 6	1st 1	2nd 3	3rd 1	4th -	Win & Pl £50,027
	11/18	Cork	2m Mdn Hdl 4yo yield		£7,359

Smart novice hurdler last season; finished second behind Battleoverdoyen and Reserve Tank in 2m4f Grade 1 races, though beaten 15 lengths into fifth in the Ballymore at Cheltenham; point-to-point winner and likely to go novice chasing.

Samcro stretches his legs as he builds up to a campaign that will see him running in novice chases

San Benedeto (Fr)

8 ch g Layman - Cinco Baidy (Lure)

Paul Nicholls   P J Vogt

PLACINGS: 13/224542/363460173-   RPR **159**c

Starts	1st	2nd	3rd	4th	Win & Pl
40	10	7	9	4	£320,111

147	3/19	Newb	2m4f Cls1 Gd3 154 Ch Hcap gd-sft	£28,475
	4/17	Aint	2m Cls1 Nov Gd1 Ch good	£56,793
150	4/17	Asct	2m1f Cls2 Nov 124-150 Ch Hcap good	£29,675
145	3/17	Donc	2m¹/₂f Cls2 128-145 Ch Hcap soft	£18,768
140	2/17	Muss	2m Cls3 127-141 Ch Hcap good	£14,296
	6/16	Worc	2m4f Cls4 Nov Ch good	£4,549
	5/16	Sedg	2m3¹/₂f Cls4 Nov Ch gd-fm	£4,029
130	11/15	Winc	2m4f Cls3 114-134 Hdl Hcap heavy	£7,596
	5/15	Strf	2m¹/₂f Cls4 Nov Hdl good	£3,249
	3/15	Winc	1m7¹/₂f Cls4 Nov Hdl good	£3,249

Gained an overdue win in last season's Greatwood Gold Cup at Newbury having run well in defeat since previous victory in a Grade 1 novice chase at Aintree in April 2017; proved stamina having done much of his racing over 2m and should have more options just below the top level.

Santini

7 b g Milan - Tinagoodnight (Sleeping Car)

Nicky Henderson   Mr & Mrs R Kelvin-Hughes

PLACINGS: 1/1131/132-   RPR **166**+c

Starts	1st	2nd	3rd	4th	Win & Pl
7	4	1	2	-	£166,106

12/18	Newb	2m7¹/₂f Cls1 Nov Gd2 Ch soft	£22,780
4/18	Aint	3m¹/₂f Cls1 Nov Gd1 Hdl soft	£56,224
1/18	Chel	2m4¹/₂f Cls1 Nov Gd2 Hdl heavy	£18,224
12/17	Newb	2m4¹/₂f Cls3 Nov Hdl soft	£6,498

Lightly raced gelding who won a Grade 1 novice hurdle in 2018 and very nearly managed the same feat as a novice chaser last season; found 3m at Kempton too sharp when third behind La Bague Au Roi but stepped up on that when a half-length second in a red-hot RSA Chase.

Saturnas (Fr)

8 b g Davidoff - Sayuri (Acatenango)

Willie Mullins (Ir)   Wicklow Bloodstock

PLACINGS: 1210/2186/052-   RPR **154**+c

Starts	1st	2nd	3rd	4th	Win & Pl
11	3	3	-	-	£100,707

1/18	Fair	2m1f Ch soft	£9,267
12/16	Leop	2m Nov Gd1 Hdl yield	£36,875
11/16	Naas	2m Mdn Hdl yld-sft	£5,426

Won a Grade 1 as a novice hurdler at the end of 2016 but failed to reach similar heights over fences the following season; got back on track when a neck second in the 2018 Kerry National only to miss the rest of last term through injury.

Scaramanga (Ire)

4 b g Mastercraftsman - Herboriste (Hernando)

Paul Nicholls   Malcolm C Denmark

PLACINGS: 3212-   RPR **129**+h

Starts	1st	2nd	3rd	4th	Win & Pl
4	1	2	1	-	£14,757

3/19	Tntn	2m¹/₂f Cls4 Mdn Hdl gd-sft	£5,133

Useful and progressive juvenile hurdler last season; got off the mark by nine lengths at Taunton and looked unlucky when second on handicap debut at Ascot (favourite for a fiercely competitive race) having been given plenty to do.

Sceau Royal (Fr)

7 b g Doctor Dino - Sandside (Marchand De Sable)

Alan King   Simon Munir & Isaac Souede

PLACINGS: /114369/12111/14232-   RPR **169**c

Starts	1st	2nd	3rd	4th	Win & Pl
25	11	5	2	2	£325,740

11/18	Chel	2m Cls1 Gd2 Ch good	£42,203
1/18	Donc	2m¹/₂f Cls1 Nov Gd2 Ch soft	£19,933
12/17	Sand	1m7¹/₂f Cls1 Nov Gd1 Ch gd-sft	£29,810
11/17	Wwck	2m Cls3 Nov Ch 4-5yo gd-sft	£9,384
10/17	Wwck	2m Cls4 Nov Ch good	£5,198
149	11/16	Winc	1m7¹/₂f Cls1 Gd2 133-149 Hdl Hcap good	£35,772
10/16	Chel	2m¹/₂f Cls2 Hdl 4yo good	£21,977
1/16	Hntg	2m Cls2 Hdl 4yo soft	£12,512
12/15	Chel	2m1f Cls2 Hdl 3yo soft	£12,628
11/15	Wwck	2m Cls4 Hdl 3yo gd-sft	£3,249
3/15	Bord	2m¹/₂f Hdl 3yo v soft	£7,814

Proved himself a high-class 2m chaser last season; won the Shloer Chase at Cheltenham before finishing third in the Champion Chase and chasing home Altior in the Celebration Chase; well placed to take advantage of that horse's potential step up in trip.

Secret Investor

7 b g Kayf Tara - Silver Charmer (Charmer)

Paul Nicholls   Hills Of Ledbury (Aga)

PLACINGS: 12/22721/1122411-   RPR **155**+c

Starts	1st	2nd	3rd	4th	Win & Pl
13	5	6	-	1	£84,982

4/19	Ayr	2m4¹/₂f Cls1 Nov Gd2 Ch good	£25,979
3/19	Winc	2m4f Cls4 Nov Ch good	£5,523
10/18	Chep	2m3¹/₂f Cls1 Nov Gd2 Hdl gd-sft	£22,780
5/18	Kemp	3m¹/₂f Cls4 Nov Hdl good	£4,194
4/18	Strf	2m6f Cls4 Nov Hdl gd-sft	£6,758

Completed a hat-trick in last season's Persian War Novices' Hurdle and gradually reached a similar level over fences after initial jumping problems; much better in that department when winning a Grade 2 at Ayr on his final run; loses novice status at end of October.

Settie Hill (USA)

6 b g Cape Blanco - Claire Soleil (Syncline)

Nicky Henderson   Michael Buckley & Lord Vestey

PLACINGS: 1/82/1U1-   RPR **139**h

Starts	1st	2nd	3rd	4th	Win & Pl
6	3	1	-	-	£11,971

6/18	NAbb	2m5¹/₂f Cls4 Nov Hdl good	£5,003
5/18	Sthl	2m4¹/₂f Cls5 Nov Mdn Hdl good	£3,119
4/17	MRas	2m¹/₂f Cls6 NHF 4-6yo good	£1,560

Looked a fine prospect when sent hurdling last term and would have landed an early-season hat-trick but for a late fall at Market Rasen; has recovered from season-ending setback that followed subsequent win at Newton Abbot in June.

Sharjah (Fr)

6 b g Doctor Dino - Saaryeh (Royal Academy)

Willie Mullins (Ir)   Mrs S Ricci

PLACINGS: 11F7846/31311B-   RPR **168+**h

Starts	1st	2nd	3rd	4th	Win & Pl
13	5	-	2	1	£300,735

146	12/18	Leop	2m Gd1 Hdl gd-yld	£65,265
	11/18	Punc	2m Gd1 Hdl good	£52,212
	8/18	Gway	2m 135-146 Hdl Hcap soft	£156,637
	11/17	Gowr	2m Nov Hdl 4yo heavy	£8,161
	9/17	Gowr	2m Mdn Hdl 4yo heavy	£6,844

One of the surprise packages of last season when landing a Grade 1 double in the Morgiana and Ryanair Hurdles; had gone off the boil as a novice after a bad fall but got back on track with victory in the Galway Hurdle; unlucky to be brought down early in the Champion Hurdle.

Shattered Love (Ire)

8 b m Yeats - Tracker (Bustino)

Gordon Elliott (Ir)   Gigginstown House Stud

PLACINGS: 1107/11211125/2209P-   RPR **159+**c

Starts	1st	2nd	3rd	4th	Win & Pl
22	9	6	1		£267,843

3/18	Chel	2m4f Cls1 Nov Gd1 Ch soft	£85,425
12/17	Leop	3m Nov Gd1 Ch yld-sft	£42,863
12/17	Cork	2m¹/₂f Nov Gd3 Ch heavy	£20,763
11/17	Clon	2m2f Ch soft	£7,371
10/17	Fair	2m5f Ch gd-yld	£6,318
2/17	Fair	2m2f Nov Gd3 Hdl sft-hvy	£18,397
12/16	Thur	2m Nov List Hdl soft	£15,827
10/16	Tipp	2m Mdn Hdl yld-sft	£4,522
3/16	Naas	2m NHF 4-7yo sft-hvy	£4,522

High-class mare who won two Grade 1 novice chases two seasons ago, including the JLT at Cheltenham; unable to win in open company last season and form tailed off, even after wind surgery midway through the season, though ran well for a long way when ninth in the Gold Cup.

Silver Streak (Ire)

6 gr g Dark Angel - Happy Talk (Hamas)

Evan Williams   L Fell

PLACINGS: 432114/12U6/1122235-   RPR **157**h

Starts	1st	2nd	3rd	4th	Win & Pl
17	5	5	2	2	£265,488

139	10/18	Ffos	2m Cls2 139-159 Hdl Hcap gd-sft	£28,152
132	5/18	Hayd	1m7¹/₂f Cls1 Gd3 130-156 Hdl Hcap good	£56,950
122	10/17	Chep	2m Cls2 120-135 Hdl 4yo Hcap gd-sft	£12,996
116	3/17	Muss	1m7¹/₂f Cls4 100-122 Hdl Hcap good	£4,549
96	12/16	Tntn	2m¹/₂f Cls5 74-102 Hdl Hcap good	£3,899

Won the Swinton Hurdle and Welsh Champion

Sceau Royal (right) battles with Altior in last season's Champion Chase

Hurdle last season before bridging the gap to Graded company, finishing second in two Grade 2 contests and a fine third in the Champion Hurdle at Cheltenham; failed to stay 2m4f when fifth in the Aintree Hurdle.

Singlefarmpayment

9 b g Milan - Crevamoy (Shardari)

Tom George   **N T Griffith & H M Haddock**

PLACINGS: P/321B2/2F5P52/4208-   RPR **152**c

Starts		1st	2nd	3rd	4th	Win & Pl
26		3	9	1	3	£113,710
125	12/16	Chel	3m1¹/₂f Cls2 Nov Ch good			£15,640
	1/16	Chel	3m Cls2 125-144 Hdl Hcap heavy			£12,512
	12/15	Sthl	3m Cls4 Nov Hdl soft			£3,899

Hugely consistent in top staying handicaps at Cheltenham in recent seasons but has compiled a remarkable record of near misses; beaten a head by Cogry last season to go with short-head defeats in each of the previous two campaigns; still handicapped to win a big one.

Sire Du Berlais (Fr)

7 b g Poliglote - Royale Athenia (Garde Royale)

Gordon Elliott (Ir)   **John P McManus**

PLACINGS: 3130/248/8618-   RPR **154+**h

Starts		1st	2nd	3rd	4th	Win & Pl
11		2	1	2	1	£76,491
145	3/19	Chel	3m Cls1 Gd3 134-148 Hdl Hcap gd-sft			£56,270
	5/16	Comp	2m1f Hdl 4yo v soft			£7,765

Landed a big gamble when winning last season's Pertemps Final, staying on strongly to get up late; hadn't previously won in two seasons for Gordon Elliott but had only stepped up to 3m for

the first time when qualifying with an eyecatching sixth at Leopardstown.

Siruh Du Lac (Fr)

6 b g Turgeon - Margerie (Le Balafre)

Nick Williams   **John White & Anne Underhill**

PLACINGS: 324/P113/1111-   RPR **151+**c

Starts		1st	2nd	3rd	4th	Win & Pl
11		6	1	2	1	£145,397
141	3/19	Chel	2m4¹/₂f Cls1 Gd3 135-156 Ch Hcap gd-sft			£61,897
134	1/19	Chel	2m4¹/₂f Cls1 Gd3 131-151 Ch Hcap gd-sft			£42,203
129	12/18	Extr	2m3f Cls3 124-137 Ch Hcap soft			£16,245
123	11/18	Newb	2m4f Cls3 116-137 Ch Hcap good			£8,058
118	12/17	Extr	2m3f Cls4 100-120 Ch Hcap soft			£7,148
112	11/17	Bang	2m4¹/₂f Cls4 93-122 Ch Hcap soft			£3,899

Hugely progressive chaser over the last two seasons, winning six out of eight over fences including all four last term as he climbed 27lb in the handicap; last two victories came at Cheltenham, including the Plate in March; should get further.

Sizing John

9 b g Midnight Legend - La Perrotine (Northern Crystal)

Jessica Harrington (Ir)   **Ann & Alan Potts Limited**

PLACINGS: 13/211223/321111/17/   RPR **173**c

Starts		1st	2nd	3rd	4th	Win & Pl
20		5	3	3	1	£776,805
	12/17	Punc	2m4f Gd1 Ch heavy			£42,863
	4/17	Punc	3m1¹/₂f Gd1 Ch gd-yld			£126,068
	3/17	Chel	3m2¹/₂f Cls1 Gd1 Ch good			£327,463
	2/17	Leop	3m1¹/₂f Gd1 Ch soft			£72,436
	1/17	Thur	2m4f Gd3 Ch yld-sft			£22,692
	11/15	Punc	2m Nov Gd2 Ch sft-hvy			£21,163
	10/15	Punc	2m Ch soft			£7,488
	12/14	Leop	2m Nov Gd1 Ch heavy			£43,333
	11/14	Naas	2m Mdn Hdl 4yo yield			£5,750

Cheltenham Gold Cup win the highlight of

a stunning treble in 2017 as he also won at Leopardstown and Punchestown, proving himself the dominant staying chaser of the season; has barely run since flopping at Leopardstown that year but trainer retains the faith.

Snugsborough Hall (Ire)

8 b g Beneficial - Saddlers Arc (Saddlers' Hall)

Liam Cusack (Ir)   Rising Sun Partnership

PLACINGS: 04/1P203F/5623311C-1   RPR **145**+c

Starts		1st	2nd	3rd	4th	Win & Pl
20		4	2	3	1	£68,971
127	5/19	Punc	2m 127-150 Ch Hcap yield			£34,550
	3/19	Leop	2m1f Nov Ch soft			£12,189
	2/19	Clon	2m4f Ch gd-yld			£6,659
96	5/17	Punc	2m4¹/₂f 80-102 Hdl Hcap good			£5,791

Sharply progressive novice chaser last season and made it three wins in his last four races when winning a competitive handicap at Punchestown by 11 lengths (going well when carried out at Fairyhouse in between); raised 16lb for that win but still on the upgrade.

Sofia's Rock (Fr)

5 b g Rock Of Gibraltar - Princess Sofia (Pennekamp)

Dan Skelton   Mezzone Family

PLACINGS: 131-5   RPR **141**+h

Starts		1st	2nd	3rd	4th	Win & Pl
4		2	-	1	-	£12,790
	3/19	Ludl	2m Cls4 Nov Hdl gd-sft			£5,198
	9/18	Worc	2m Cls4 Nov Mdn Hdl good			£4,159

Smart Flat horse (peak mark of 100) and took well to hurdles last season, winning two of his first three races; thrown in at the deep end for his handicap debut in the Swinton at Haydock

and ran a cracker to be beaten less than four lengths having gone off fast in front.

Some Chaos (Ire)

8 b g Brian Boru - Iruna Iris (Golden Tornado)

Michael Scudamore   Mason Scudamore Racing

PLACINGS: 335/137794/112511-   RPR **149**+c

Starts		1st	2nd	3rd	4th	Win & Pl
11		4	1	1	1	£58,879
138	3/19	Kels	3m2f Cls2 120-146 Ch Hcap good			£31,280
127	2/19	Winc	3m1f Cls3 126-136 Ch Hcap good			£9,357
109	11/18	MRas	3m Cls4 Nov 109-121 Ch Hcap good			£7,473
102	10/18	Bang	2m4¹/₂f Cls4 Nov 81-106 Ch Hcap good			£4,614

Massive improver last season following change of yard and switch to fences, winning four times and rising 43lb in the handicap; signed off with biggest success at Kelso in a valuable handicap; gained all four wins on good ground and trainer would have reservations on soft.

Soul Emotion (Fr)

6 b g Martaline - Second Emotion (Medaaly)

Nicky Henderson   Mr & Mrs J D Cotton

PLACINGS: 1435/PF11/5-   RPR **145**h

Starts		1st	2nd	3rd	4th	Win & Pl
9		3	-	1	1	£52,044
137	4/18	Sand	2m4f Cls2 126-143 Hdl Hcap gd-sft			£21,896
125	3/18	Sand	2m4f Cls3 118-134 Hdl Hcap soft			£9,384
	5/16	Comp	2m Hdl 3yo v soft			£7,765

Joined Nicky Henderson from France two seasons ago and won both subsequent starts in 2m4f handicap hurdles at Sandown before missing last season; could go further over hurdles but seems likely to go chasing (fell and pulled up in two attempts in France).

Sire Du Berlais (right) swoops late to land last season's Pertemps Final

Southfield Stone

6 gr g Fair Mix - Laureldean Belle (Supreme Leader)

Paul Nicholls   Mrs Angela Hart & Mrs Angela Yeoman

PLACINGS: 3/1113217-   RPR **145+**h

Starts	1st	2nd	3rd	4th	Win & Pl
8	4	1	2	-	£38,472

2/19	Kemp	2m Cls1 Nov Gd2 Hdl good	£17,085
12/18	Tntn	2m¹/₂f Cls4 Nov Hdl good	£5,133
11/18	Tntn	2m¹/₂f Cls4 Nov Hdl good	£5,133
11/18	Tntn	2m¹/₂f Cls4 Mdn NHF 4-6yo gd-fm	£3,249

Useful novice hurdler last season, winning three times following bumper success; gained biggest win when beating Angels Breath in a Grade 2 at Kempton, though that form didn't work out as well as expected; best of two runs at Grade 1 level came when third in the Tolworth.

Speaker Connolly (Ire)

6 b g Court Cave - Kylebeg Dancer (General Monash)

Alan Fleming (Ir)   Barry Connell

PLACINGS: 58601P/98613UF-   RPR **143+**c

Starts	1st	2nd	3rd	4th	Win & Pl
13	2	-	1	-	£27,491

119	12/18	Leop	2m5f 102-123 Ch Hcap good	£10,903
	3/18	Wxfd	2m Mdn Hdl heavy	£6,269

Took time to get to grips with fences last season but bolted up on his handicap debut at Leopardstown despite still not jumping fluently; good third next time but making no impression when unseating in the Kim Muir at Cheltenham and fell back over hurdles at Wexford.

Speredek (Fr)

8 b/br g Kapgarde - Sendamagic (Sendawar)

Nigel Hawke   Kapinhand

PLACINGS: 6/PP111/1212P8/24F6-   RPR **161**c

Starts	1st	2nd	3rd	4th	Win & Pl
24	7	4	1	3	£126,848

135	1/18	Sand	1m7¹/₂f Cls2 127-150 Ch Hcap heavy	£18,768
129	11/17	Extr	2m1f Cls3 120-134 Hdl Hcap soft	£7,799
129	3/17	Ludl	2m Cls2 129-142 Ch Hcap soft	£12,512
122	2/17	Sand	1m7¹/₂f Cls3 113-135 Ch Hcap soft	£7,507
115	2/17	Tntn	2m2f Cls4 Nov 106-120 Ch Hcap soft	£5,697
107	3/16	Extr	2m7f Cls4 93-114 Hdl Hcap gd-sft	£3,249
	3/15	Carl	2m1f Cls6 NHF 4-6yo soft	£1,560

Smart 2m chaser who was second in a valuable handicap at Ascot last season having finished second to Un De Sceaux in the Clarence House Chase earlier in 2018; won over 2m7f over hurdles but yet to complete in four runs beyond 2m2f over fences (pulled up three times).

Spiritofthegames (Ire)

7 b g Darsi - Lucy Walters (King's Ride)

Dan Skelton   N W Lake

PLACINGS: 11421/12357/14335-   RPR **154**c

Starts	1st	2nd	3rd	4th	Win & Pl
14	4	2	3	2	£83,671

	10/18	Chep	2m3¹/₂f Cls1 Nov List Ch good	£16,465
129	11/17	Ling	2m3¹/₂f Cls3 112-132 Hdl Hcap soft	£7,596
	3/17	Tntn	2m3f Cls4 Nov Hdl good	£4,549
	10/16	Ayr	2m4¹/₂f Cls5 Mdn Hdl gd-sft	£2,729

Didn't win again after impressive chasing debut at Chepstow last season but maintained consistent record in top handicaps; twice finished third at

Southfield Stone gets ready for take-off before winning the Dovecote Novices' Hurdle at Kempton

Cheltenham, including behind Siruh Du Lac in the Plate, having also been placed in the Betfair and Lanzarote Hurdles in 2018.

Springtown Lake (Ire)
7 b g Gamut - Sprightly Gal (Old Vic)

Philip Hobbs				Tim Syder
PLACINGS: 202/1F2310/1245P-				RPR **150**c

Starts 13	1st 3	2nd 2	3rd 1	4th 1	Win & Pl £39,199

137	11/18	Sand	2m4f Cls3 Nov 120-137 Ch Hcap soft.................£9,384
	1/18	Leic	2m4¹/₂f Cls3 Nov Hdl 4-7yo heavy.......................£8,356
	10/17	Worc	2m4f Cls5 Mdn Hdl good.....................................£2,859

Useful novice chaser last season and ran a fair race when fifth in the novice handicap at the Cheltenham Festival; below his best when twice tried over 3m but perhaps unsuited by good ground at Aintree (has won on good but better on soft according to trainer).

Steely Addition (Ire)
7 b g Craigsteel - Blond's Addition (Lord America)

Philip Hobbs				Step By Step
PLACINGS: 1334/F118/3141-				RPR **153**+c

Starts 11	1st 4	2nd -	3rd 3	4th 2	Win & Pl £24,362

	3/19	Hrfd	3m1f Cls4 Nov Ch good......................................£4,614
137	12/18	Chep	2m7¹/₂f Cls3 Nov 122-137 Ch Hcap heavy...........£7,408
123	11/17	Chep	2m7¹/₂f Cls3 106-125 Hdl Hcap soft.....................£5,523
116	10/17	Winc	2m5¹/₂f Cls4 89-119 Hdl Hcap good....................£3,899

Strong stayer who produced a big performance when winning a novice handicap chase at Chepstow on heavy ground last season (runner-up won next time off 7lb higher, pair clear); below par back there next time and didn't need to run to his best to win at 1-2 at Hereford.

Step Back (Ire)
9 ch g Indian River - Stepitoutmary (Roselier)

Mark Bradstock				Cracker & Smodge Partnership
PLACINGS: /5121/119/2311/76P3-				RPR **142**c

Starts 10	1st 3	2nd 1	3rd 2	4th -	Win & Pl £113,556

135	4/18	Sand	3m5f Cls1 Gd3 135-161 Ch Hcap gd-sft...........£84,405
	4/18	Fknm	3m Cls4 Nov Ch gd-sft.......................................£5,592
	2/17	Ludl	3m Cls4 Mdn Hdl gd-sft.....................................£3,899

Brilliant 15-length winner of the bet365 Gold Cup at Sandown in 2018; trained for the Grand National last season but lost far too much ground by jumping right-handed and was pulled

up; good step back in the right direction when third in the bet365 Gold Cup.

Summerville Boy (Ire)
7 b g Sandmason - Suny House (Carroll House)

Tom George				R S Brookhouse
PLACINGS: 122311/474-6				RPR **155**h

Starts 10	1st 3	2nd 2	3rd 1	4th 2	Win & Pl £138,250

	3/18	Chel	2m¹/₂f Cls1 Nov Gd1 Hdl heavy........................£71,188
	1/18	Sand	2m Cls1 Nov Gd1 Hdl heavy.............................£28,475
	5/17	Klny	2m1f NHF 5-7yo soft..£5,265

Won the Tolworth and Supreme Novices' Hurdle two seasons ago; nowhere near that level last season but diagnosed with a leg fracture after first two runs and did slightly better on second run back in the spring when not beaten far at Punchestown; likely to go novice chasing.

Supasundae
9 b g Galileo - Distinctive Look (Danehill)

Jessica Harrington (Ir)				Ann & Alan Potts Limited
PLACINGS: 12412/321221/22271-2				RPR **159**+h

Starts 26	1st 8	2nd 9	3rd 2	4th 2	Win & Pl £756,642

	4/19	Aint	2m4f Cls1 Gd1 Hdl soft...................................£141,325
	4/18	Punc	2m Gd1 Hdl soft..£143,584
	2/18	Leop	2m Gd1 Hdl soft..£75,000
148	3/17	Chel	2m5f Cls1 Gd3 136-156 Hdl Hcap gd-sft..........£54,103
	12/16	Punc	2m4f Hdl soft..£9,044
	12/15	Leop	2m Mdn Hdl heavy..£7,488
	12/14	Asct	1m7¹/₂f Cls1 List NHF 4-6yo soft......................£11,390
	3/14	Weth	2m Cls6 NHF 4-6yo good...................................£1,711

Classy and versatile hurdler who has won three Grade 1 races and finished second in seven over the last two seasons; ideally suited by 2m4f, winning the Aintree Hurdle over that trip last term, but has won big races over 2m and finished second in the 2018 Stayers' Hurdle.

Superb Story (Ire)
8 b g Duke Of Marmalade - Yes My Love (Anabaa)

Harry Fry				A Holt, J Robinson, A Taylor & S Miller
PLACINGS: 1444/121/P1/				RPR **148**h

Starts 9	1st 4	2nd 1	3rd -	4th 3	Win & Pl £115,768

145	1/17	Muss	1m7¹/₂f Cls2 119-145 Hdl Hcap good...............£25,992
138	3/16	Chel	2m1f Cls1 Gd3 138-152 Hdl Hcap good............£51,255
120	10/15	Weth	2m Cls3 119-133 Hdl Hcap good.........................£5,523
	1/15	Muss	1m7¹/₂f Cls3 Hdl 4yo gd-sft.................................£9,747

Lightly raced hurdler who suffered a tendon injury when being prepared for the 2017 Champion

Follow us
@RacingPost

Hurdle and only made it on to the track again on the Flat this summer; had flourished in handicaps, most notably when winning the 2016 County Hurdle for Dan Skelton.

Takingrisks (Ire)

10 b g Golden Tornado - Downtown Rosie (Good Thyne)

Nicky Richards   Frank Bird

PLACINGS: 214P/2F4213/5123611-   RPR **146**+c

Starts	1st	2nd	3rd	4th	Win & Pl
25	7	5	3	4	£207,875
135	4/19	Ayr	4m Cls1 Gd3 134-152 Ch Hcap good		£122,443
129	3/19	Ayr	3m¹/₂f Cls2 127-144 Ch Hcap heavy		£18,838
122	11/18	Ayr	3m¹/₂f Cls3 118-138 Hdl Hcap good		£13,256
127	3/18	Ayr	3m Cls3 119-137 Ch Hcap heavy		£9,586
130	2/17	Kels	2m6¹/₂f Cls3 Nov 119-130 Ch Hcap heavy		£6,330
122	3/16	Carl	3m1f Cls3 98-122 Hdl Hcap good		£5,848
	12/15	Kels	2m6¹/₂f Cls5 Mdn Hdl heavy		£2,599

Veteran chaser who hit career-best form last spring, notably when winning the Scottish Grand National at Ayr; appreciated running beyond 3m2f for the first time as he outstayed main rivals despite a notably early blunder; highly versatile with wins on good and heavy ground.

Talkischeap (Ire)

7 b g Getaway - Carrigmoorna Oak (Milan)

Alan King   Charles Dingwall

PLACINGS: 011233/1141P/321251-   RPR **160**+c

Starts	1st	2nd	3rd	4th	Win & Pl
15	5	3	3	1	£124,658
145	4/19	Sand	3m5f Cls1 Gd3 134-160 Ch Hcap good		£84,405
	1/19	Donc	3m Cls4 Nov good		£4,614
133	2/18	Newb	3m Cls2 123-145 Hdl Hcap good		£12,512
	5/17	Wwck	2m3f Cls4 Nov Hdl good		£5,198
	5/17	Font	2m3f Cls5 Mdn Hdl gd-fm		£2,599

Ran well against top novice chasers early last season (twice placed behind La Bague Au Roi) and made a mockery of lenient handicap mark when running away with the bet365 Gold Cup at Sandown; 12lb rise will demand more but remains unexposed over marathon trips.

Terrefort (Fr)

6 gr g Martaline - Vie De Reine (Mansonnien)

Nicky Henderson   Simon Munir & Isaac Souede

PLACINGS: /5226/13131121/432P-   RPR **162**c

Starts	1st	2nd	3rd	4th	Win & Pl
18	5	5	3	1	£215,692
	4/18	Aint	3m1f Cls1 Nov Gd1 Ch soft		£56,337
	2/18	Sand	2m4f Cls1 Nov Gd1 Ch soft		£31,323
137	1/18	Hntg	2m4f Cls3 Nov 120-137 Ch Hcap soft		£7,798
	9/17	Claf	2m2f Hdl 4yo heavy		£9,436
	8/17	Claf	2m3¹/₂f Ch 4yo heavy		£14,769

Dual Grade 1 winner as a novice chaser two seasons ago but didn't quite make the grade in open company last term; not beaten far when third behind Frodon in the Cotswold Chase but easily brushed aside by Clan Des Obeaux next time and pulled up in the Ryanair.

The Bay Birch (Ire)

8 b m Beneficial - Tournant Vic (Old Vic)

Matt Sheppard   Tony Scrivin

PLACINGS: 57212112/1603UP1711-   RPR **147**+c

Starts	1st	2nd	3rd	4th	Win & Pl
36	7	4	3	3	£98,117
137	4/19	Hayd	2m5¹/₂f Cls2 110-137 Ch Hcap good		£31,455
128	3/19	Bang	3m Cls3 102-128 Ch Hcap soft		£7,408
125	2/19	Wwck	3m Cls3 105-127 Ch Hcap good		£9,747
	5/18	Uttx	2m4f Cls3 Nov Hdl good		£6,583
115	4/18	Extr	2m3f Cls3 Nov 112-125 Ch Hcap heavy		£10,397
100	3/18	Towc	2m4f Cls4 100-115 Ch Hcap heavy		£5,783
94	2/18	Towc	2m4f Cls4 Nov 77-100 Ch Hcap soft		£5,194

Massive improver in second half of last season, winning three out of four over fences from February and April to climb 20lb in the weights; thrives at that time of year having also won three times during those months in 2018; set to run in bigger handicaps as well as pursuing black type in mares' chases.

The Glancing Queen (Ire)

5 b m Jeremy - Glancing (Kayf Tara)

Alan King   Dingwall, Farrell, Hornsey & Murray

PLACINGS: 1/1351-   RPR **121**+b

Starts	1st	2nd	3rd	4th	Win & Pl
4	2	-	1	-	£42,905
	4/19	Aint	2m1f Cls1 Gd2 NHF 4-6yo soft		£25,322
	11/18	Chel	2m1¹/₂f Cls1 List NHF 4-6yo good		£12,379

Won the Grade 2 mares' bumper at Aintree's Grand National meeting last season having run a huge race against geldings when fifth in the Champion Bumper at Cheltenham; held in very high regard by her trainer and expected to thrive over hurdles.

The Two Amigos

7 b g Midnight Legend - As Was (Epalo)

Nicky Martin   Bradley Partnership

PLACINGS: 50424/611111/O1211F-   RPR **147**+c

Starts	1st	2nd	3rd	4th	Win & Pl
12	3	2	-	2	£44,838
134	1/19	Plum	3m4¹/₂f Cls3 108-134 Ch Hcap gd-sft		£19,018
124	12/18	Extr	3m6¹/₂f Cls3 105-127 Ch Hcap soft		£16,245
109	10/18	NAbb	3m2f Cls4 Nov 107-122 Ch Hcap heavy		£5,425

Prolific point-to-point winner who made a successful switch to racing under rules last season, winning three handicap chases; showed abundant stamina when victorious over 3m6½f

Talkischeap pulls away from the opposition before winning last season's bet365 Gold Cup

on soft ground at Exeter; fell when 7-1 for the Grand National Trial at Haydock.

The Worlds End (Ire)

8 b g Stowaway - Bright Sprite (Beneficial)

Tom George   McNeill Family

PLACINGS: 3111F1/84474/1316P9-   RPR **159**+c

Starts	1st	2nd	3rd	4th	Win & Pl
18	7	-	2	3	£130,789
12/18	Chel	3m1½f Cls2 Nov Ch good			£15,857
10/18	Chep	2m7½f Cls3 Ch good			£7,408
4/17	Aint	3m½f Cls1 Nov Gd1 Hdl good			£56,141
2/17	Hayd	2m7f Cls1 Nov Gd2 Hdl gd-sft			£16,972
1/17	Chep	2m3½f Cls4 Nov Hdl soft			£3,249
12/16	Chep	2m3½f Cls3 Mdn Hdl gd-sft			£6,498
4/16	Chep	2m Cls6 NHF 4-6yo soft			£1,949

Yet to build on Grade 1 novice hurdle win at Aintree in April 2017 despite continuing to hint at big potential; unsuited by soft ground for much of following season (last three wins on good) and let down by jumping in top novice chases last term after two wide-margin wins in smaller races.

The Young Master

10 b g Echo Of Light - Fine Frenzy (Great Commotion)

Neil Mulholland   Mike Burbidge & The Old Masters

PLACINGS: F06F9/U63P6U8/11P32-   RPR **149**c

Starts	1st	2nd	3rd	4th	Win & Pl
40	9	3	4	1	£267,938
135	11/18	Chel	3m1f Cls3 116-139 Am Ch Hcap good		£15,598
130	10/18	Chep	2m7½f Cls2 130-150 Ch Hcap good		£22,155
148	4/16	Sand	3m5f Cls1 Gd3 144-159 Ch Hcap good		£84,405
144	12/14	Asct	3m Cls1 List 135-161 Ch Hcap gd-sft		£56,270
121	10/14	Chel	3m1f Cls3 107-125 Am Ch Hcap good		£7,195
	9/14	Worc	2m7f Cls4 Ch good		£4,327
110	1/14	Sedg	3m3f Cls4 100-112 Hdl Hcap heavy		£3,899
103	1/14	Fknm	2m7½f Cls4 102-108 Hdl Hcap heavy		£3,249
94	11/13	Font	2m5½f Cls5 Nov 69-95 Hdl Hcap heavy		£1,949

Veteran staying chaser who enjoyed a resurgent campaign last season, winning at Chepstow and Cheltenham; suggested he could still be competitive off higher marks when third in the Kim Muir and second in the bet365 Gold Cup in the spring.

Third Wind

5 b/br g Shirocco - Act Three (Beat Hollow)

Hughie Morrison   Mouse Hamilton-Fairley

PLACINGS: 30/1211-   RPR **137**+h

Starts	1st	2nd	3rd	4th	Win & Pl
6	3	1	1	-	£53,686
131	3/19	Sand	2m4f Cls1 Nov Gd3 123-138 Hdl 4-7yo Hcap soft	£42,203
	2/19	Tntn	2m3f Cls4 Nov Hdl soft		£5,133
	12/18	Plum	2m4½f Cls4 Mdn Hdl soft		£4,094

Won three out of four in novice hurdles last season, including a successful handicap debut in a fiercely competitive EBF Final at Sandown; got up on the line in a stiff test over 2m4f that day and promises to stay further; could go novice chasing.

Thistlecrack

11 b g Kayf Tara - Ardstown (Ardross)

Colin Tizzard   John & Heather Snook

PLACINGS: 211111/11112/54/32P-   RPR **174**c

Starts	1st	2nd	3rd	4th	Win & Pl
24	13	3	2	1	£732,630
12/16	Kemp	3m Cls1 Gd1 Ch good			£119,026
11/16	Newb	2m7½f Cls1 Nov Gd2 Ch gd-sft			£20,167
11/16	Chel	3m½f Cls2 Nov Ch gd-sft			£16,025
10/16	Chep	2m7½f Cls3 Nov Ch gd-sft			£7,798
4/16	Aint	3m½f Cls1 Gd1 Hdl soft			£84,405
3/16	Chel	3m Cls1 Gd1 Hdl good			£170,850
1/16	Chel	3m Cls1 Gd2 Hdl heavy			£34,170
12/15	Asct	3m½f Cls1 Gd1 Hdl gd-sft			£56,950
11/15	Newb	3m Cls1 Gd2 Hdl soft			£25,628
4/15	Aint	3m½f Cls1 Gd1 Hdl gd-sft			£56,437
2/15	Asct	1m7½f Cls2 Nov Hdl soft			£9,384
1/15	Winc	1m7½f Cls4 Nov Hdl heavy			£3,899
4/14	Winc	1m7½f Cls6 NHF 4-6yo good			£1,625

Hasn't quite hit the heights anticipated when remarkably winning the 2016 King George as a novice, with injuries hampering subsequent progress; still showed high-class form last season when second in the King George but never a factor when pulled up in the Gold Cup.

Thomas Darby (Ire)

6 b g Beneficial - Silaoce (Nikos)

Olly Murphy   Mrs Diana L Whateley

PLACINGS: 112312-   RPR **154**h

Starts	1st	2nd	3rd	4th	Win & Pl
6	3	2	1		£48,856

1/19	Tntn	2m½f Cls4 Nov Hdl gd-sft	£5,133
10/18	Chel	2m½f Cls3 Mdn Hdl good	£9,285
5/18	Hntg	2m Cls5 Am Mdn NHF 4-6yo good	£2,274

Took a long time to build on promise of hurdling debut (beat Elixir De Nutz at Cheltenham) but ran a stormer when back there for the Supreme Novices' Hurdle, finishing second to Klassical Dream; had refused to settle when a beaten favourite at Ascot and Kempton in between.

Thomas Patrick (Ire)

7 b g Winged Love - Huncheon Siss (Phardante)

Tom Lacey   David Kellett

PLACINGS: P1/0021281411/2P8P4-   RPR **156**c

Starts	1st	2nd	3rd	4th	Win & Pl
15	4	3	-	2	£77,085

139	4/18	Aint	3m1f Cls1 Gd3 129-155 Ch Hcap soft	£42,203
131	3/18	Newb	3m2f Cls3 129-140 Ch Hcap soft	£12,762
	2/18	Chep	2m7½f Cls4 Nov Ch heavy	£4,614
114	11/17	Extr	2m7f Cls4 98-117 Hdl Hcap soft	£4,224

Sent off just 3-1 for the Ladbrokes Trophy last season having followed a hugely progressive novice campaign with a close second on his return behind Elegant Escape but was pulled up at Newbury and never recovered his form; dropped to just 1lb above last winning mark.

Thyme Hill

5 b g Kayf Tara - Rosita Bay (Hernando)

Philip Hobbs   The Englands & Heywoods

PLACINGS: 123-   RPR **132**b

Starts	1st	2nd	3rd	4th	Win & Pl
3	1	1	1	-	£14,895

10/18	Worc	2m Cls5 NHF 4-6yo good	£2,274

Best of the British-trained runners in the Champion Bumper at Cheltenham when third behind Envoi Allen and Blue Sari, stepping up on previous neck defeat at the track; should prove a leading novice hurdler.

Tiger Roll (Ire)

9 b g Authorized - Swiss Roll (Entrepreneur)

Gordon Elliott (Ir)   Gigginstown House Stud

PLACINGS: 2221331P/2P511/4111-   RPR **174+**c

Starts	1st	2nd	3rd	4th	Win & Pl
34	12	5	3	4	£1,365,745

159	4/19	Aint	4m2½f Cls1 Gd3 142-164 Ch Hcap gd-sft	£500,000
	3/19	Chel	3m6f Cls2 Ch soft	£40,235
	2/19	Navn	2m5f Gd2 Hdl yield	£23,919
150	4/18	Aint	4m2½f Cls1 Gd3 142-161 Ch Hcap heavy	£500,000
	3/18	Chel	3m6f Cls2 Ch soft	£40,261
	3/17	Chel	4m Cls1 Nov Gd2 Am Ch gd-sft	£71,952
138	10/16	Limk	3m 131-144 Ch Hcap yield	£43,382
	6/16	Kbgn	2m4f Nov Ch good	£6,331
	5/16	Baln	2m1f Ch good	£5,200
	10/14	Chel	2m1½f Cls2 Hdl 4yo gd-sft	£18,768
	3/14	Chel	2m1f Cls1 Gd1 Hdl 4yo good	£68,340
	11/13	MRas	2m1½f Cls4 Hdl 3yo soft	£3,899

Went down in folklore when becoming the first horse since Red Rum to win back-to-back Grand Nationals last season; had already looked a big improver when winning Cheltenham's Cross Country Chase by 22 lengths as well as a Grade 2 over hurdles.

Tiger Tap Tap (Ger)

4 ch g Jukebox Jury - Tomato Finish (Starborough)

Willie Mullins (Ir)   Mrs S Ricci

PLACINGS: 249-   RPR **135**h

Starts	1st	2nd	3rd	4th	Win & Pl
3	-	1	-	1	£7,039

Came closer than any other horse to beating the brilliant but ill-fated Sir Erec when a neck second on hurdling debut at Leopardstown last season; unable to build on that in two subsequents runs, including when only ninth in the Triumph Hurdle.

Timoteo (Fr)

6 b g Diamond Green - Goldnella (Goldneyev)

Alan King   Million In Mind Partnership

PLACINGS: 5/3255242/87511-   RPR **142+**c

Starts	1st	2nd	3rd	4th	Win & Pl
13	2	3	1	1	£30,458

124	3/19	Kemp	2m Cls3 Nov 119-132 Ch Hcap gd-sft	£8,654
117	3/19	Strf	2m1f Cls4 Nov 103-117 Ch Hcap gd-sft	£4,809

Launched chasing career in fine style with two wins in the space of five days in March and clearly impressed his trainer, who paid £55,000 to buy him off the Million In Mind partnership in May; had been kept to hurdles previously on return from 18-month layoff.

Tobefair

9 b/br g Central Park - Nan (Buckley)

Debra Hamer				Down The Quay Club

PLACINGS: 1/11110/493/849P221-   RPR **147+**h

Starts	1st	2nd	3rd	4th	Win & Pl
24	8	3	1	3	£87,700
142	4/19	Chel	3m Cls2 120-144 Hdl Hcap good	£12,380
134	2/17	Newb	3m Cls2 115-139 Hdl Hcap soft	£12,512
126	1/17	Wwck	3m2f Cls2 115-138 Hdl Hcap soft	£12,512
120	12/16	Chep	2m7¹/₂f Cls3 110-129 Hdl Hcap good	£6,498
116	11/16	Ffos	3m Cls3 115-132 Hdl Hcap good	£6,498
109	9/15	Chep	2m7¹/₂f Cls4 93-120 Hdl Hcap good	£3,249
95	7/15	Worc	2m7f Cls5 Nov 74-100 Hdl Hcap gd-fm	£2,599
81	6/15	Worc	2m7f Cls5 Nov 73-99 Hdl Hcap gd-fm	£2,599

Out of sorts for nearly two years before showing career-best form at the end of last season, winning well at Cheltenham after a close second in the Pertemps Final; had won seven in a row prior to the Pertemps in 2017 but had chase campaigns aborted in each of the last two seasons.

Top Notch (Fr)

8 b/g Poliglote - Topira (Pistolet Bleu)

Nicky Henderson				Simon Munir & Isaac Souede

PLACINGS: /3111123/31141/310P-   RPR **167+**c

Starts	1st	2nd	3rd	4th	Win & Pl
27	14	4	4	1	£398,870
	1/19	Kemp	2m4¹/₂f Cls1 List Ch good	£23,048
	4/18	Sand	2m6¹/₂f Cls1 Gd2 Ch gd-sft	£31,470
	12/17	Tntn	2m5¹/₂f Cls1 Gd2 Ch gd-sft	£28,475
	11/17	Asct	2m5f Cls1 Gd2 Ch gd-sft	£39,865
	2/17	Sand	2m4f Cls1 Nov Gd1 Ch soft	£28,475
	12/16	Asct	2m5f Cls2 Ch gd-sft	£15,640
	11/16	Plum	2m1f Cls3 Nov Ch heavy	£6,498
	11/16	Wwck	2m Cls3 Nov Ch 4-5yo soft	£9,384
	2/16	Kels	2m2f Cls3 Hdl heavy	£16,245
	2/15	Hayd	1m7¹/₂f Cls2 Hdl 4yo soft	£9,747
	1/15	Asct	1m7¹/₂f Cls3 Hdl 4yo soft	£6,498
	12/14	Newb	2m¹/₂f Cls3 Hdl 3yo gd-sft	£6,498
	4/14	Engh	2m¹/₂f Hdl 3yo v soft	£19,200
	3/14	Bord	2m¹/₂f Hdl 3yo heavy	£8,400

Prolific chaser who has won his last seven chases below Grade 1 level, including a hat-trick of Grade 2 wins two seasons ago; spent much of last season looking for Grade 1 opportunities over hurdles but flopped in the Stayers' Hurdle after a promising third in the Long Walk.

Top Ville Ben (Ire)

7 b g Beneficial - Great Decision (Simply Great)

Philip Kirby				Harbour Rose Partnership

PLACINGS: 2F4/6321PF8F/115F13-   RPR **156**c

Starts	1st	2nd	3rd	4th	Win & Pl
20	7	2	2	1	£57,376
	3/19	Weth	3m Cls3 Nov Ch soft	£8,151
	12/18	Weth	3m Cls4 Nov Ch gd-sft	£5,059
	11/18	Hexm	3m Cls4 Nov Ch soft	£6,108
130	12/17	Hayd	2m7f Cls3 115-132 Hdl Hcap heavy	£6,498
	2/17	Towc	1m7¹/₂f Cls4 Nov Hdl heavy	£3,899
	1/17	Leic	1m7¹/₂f Cls4 Nov Hdl gd-sft	£5,198
	12/16	Ludl	1m6f Cls4 NHF 4-5yo gd-sft	£3,899

Wide-margin winner of three small-field novice chases in the north last season and proved himself in stronger company when third behind top-class Lostintranslation and Topofthegame; all those performances on flat, left-handed track and sole flop came at contrasting Ascot.

Topofthegame (Ire)

7 ch g Flemensfirth - Derry Vale (Mister Lord)

Paul Nicholls				Chris Giles & Mr& Mrs P K Barber

PLACINGS: 1/142/F412/2212-   RPR **167+**c

Starts	1st	2nd	3rd	4th	Win & Pl
11	3	5	-	2	£240,041
	3/19	Chel	3m1¹/₂f Cls1 Nov Gd1 Ch soft	£98,473
142	2/18	Sand	2m7¹/₂f Cls1 Gd3 123-147 Hdl Hcap soft	£56,270
	12/16	Asct	2m7¹/₂f Cls3 Mdn Hdl gd-sft	£7,798

Has been a work in progress for some time (initial novice chase campaign was even aborted two seasons ago) but got it right when it mattered by winning the RSA Chase at Cheltenham; that looks red-hot form but remains his only win in five attempts over fences.

Tornado Flyer (Ire)

6 b g Flemensfirth - Mucho Macabi (Exceed And Excel)

Willie Mullins (Ir)				TFP Partnership

PLACINGS: 131/1P-4   RPR **141**h

Starts	1st	2nd	3rd	4th	Win & Pl
6	3		1	1	£76,379
	12/18	Punc	2m4f Mdn Hdl good	£7,087
	4/18	Punc	2m¹/₂f Gd1 NHF 4-7yo yield	£52,212
	1/18	Fair	2m NHF 5-7yo soft	£5,451

Top-class bumper performer two seasons ago, winning a Grade 1 at Punchestown after coming third at Cheltenham; novice hurdle campaign limited by injury (picked up a knock when pulled up on his second run) but finished a fair fourth on his return back at Punchestown.

Torpillo (Fr)

4 ch g Alanadi - Astherate (Balko)

Nigel Twiston-Davies				Simon Munir & Isaac Souede

PLACINGS: 1/1140-   RPR **136+**h

Starts	1st	2nd	3rd	4th	Win & Pl
5	3	-		1	£28,459
	1/19	Sand	2m Cls3 Hdl 4yo soft	£6,498
	12/18	Sand	2m Cls2 Hdl 3yo heavy	£12,512
	4/18	Nanc	2m1f Hdl 3yo soft	£8,496

One-time Triumph Hurdle favourite last season, showing plenty of ability when making all for wide-margin wins at Sandown on soft and heavy ground on first two runs in Britain; below that level twice subsequently, including when well beaten in the Fred Winter.

MY FIVE TO WATCH
Steve Mason

● Chacun Pour Soi ● Emitom
● Humble Hero ● Klassical Dream
● Secret Investor

Tout Est Permis (Fr)

6 gr g Linda's Lad - Kadalbleue (Kadalko)

Noel Meade (Ir) — Gigginstown House Stud

PLACINGS: 215/1273F4558/71118-   RPR **155**+c

Starts	1st	2nd	3rd	4th	Win & Pl
20	5	3	1	2	£119,364

			Win & Pl
1/19	Thur	2m4½f Gd2 Ch good	£23,919
138 11/18	Navn	3m 122-150 Ch Hcap good	£52,212
128 10/18	Gway	2m6½f 111-128 Ch Hcap soft	£14,150
9/17	Gowr	2m2f Ch sft-hvy	£7,371
12/16	Limk	2m Mdn Hdl 3yo heavy	£5,653

Big improver following move to Noel Meade last season, running out a clearcut winner of the Troytown at Navan; successfully stepped up to Grade 2 level at Thurles next time, getting up close home on drop to 2m4f; didn't stay when well beaten in the Irish National.

Tower Bridge (Ire)

6 b g High Chaparral - Walkamia (Linamix)

Joseph O'Brien (Ir) — John P McManus

PLACINGS: 4/1104153/5322-   RPR **148**c

Starts	1st	2nd	3rd	4th	Win & Pl
12	3	2	2	2	£97,793

			Win & Pl
2/18	Leop	2m6f Nov Gd1 Hdl soft	£52,212
7/17	Bell	2m½f NHF 4-7yo good	£6,055
5/17	Baln	2m½f NHF 4yo good	£5,265

Grade 1 winner over hurdles before finishing fifth and third at Cheltenham and Aintree; retains novice status over fences having failed to win last season but ran well in defeat, notably when second in the novice handicap at the Cheltenham Festival behind runaway winner A Plus Tard.

Traffic Fluide (Fr)

9 b g Astarabad - Petale Rouge (Bonnet Rouge)

Gary Moore — Galloping On The South Downs Partnership

PLACINGS: /3/46632/4575011/21-   RPR **161**c

Starts	1st	2nd	3rd	4th	Win & Pl
24	6	3	4	3	£213,108

			Win & Pl
149 11/18	Asct	3m Cls1 Gd3 134-149 Ch Hcap good	£56,950
140 4/18	Chel	2m5f Cls1 Gd2 135-160 Ch Hcap good	£34,170
4/18	Plum	2m4f Cls4 Nov Hdl heavy	£5,003
135 3/15	Sand	1m7½f Cls3 Nov 122-140 Ch Hcap good	£6,498
129 2/15	Plum	2m1f Cls3 Nov 129-145 Ch Hcap gd-sft	£7,988
10/14	Stra	2m4f Ch 4yo heavy	£8,800

Benefited from a step up in trip and drop in grade last season when winning the Silver Cup at Ascot (only previous runs over 3m at Grade 1 level); laid out for the Grand National only to miss Aintree after a setback; trainer reports him back in training and likely to be aimed at the National again.

Truckers Lodge (Ire)

7 b g Westerner - Galeacord (Accordion)

Paul Nicholls — Gordon & Su Hall

PLACINGS: 311/42/1441221-2   RPR **140**h

Starts	1st	2nd	3rd	4th	Win & Pl
11	4	4	-	3	£34,433

			Win & Pl
3/19	Extr	2m7f Cls4 Nov Hdl gd-sft	£4,224
123 12/18	Chep	2m7½f Cls3 110-129 Hdl Hcap heavy	£6,758
5/18	Sthl	2m4½f Cls5 Mdn Hdl good	£3,444
4/17	Chep	2m Cls6 NHF 4-6yo good	£1,949

Big improver when stepped up to around 3m last season, finishing first (by ten lengths) and second in a couple of handicaps at Chepstow before winning a novice at Exeter; close second on chasing debut in May over 3m2f and expected to get much further.

Tudor City (Ire)

7 b g Yeats - She's Our Mare (Commanche Run)

Tony Martin (Ir)   John Breslin

PLACINGS: 2/P22219/005/2582-21   RPR **147**+h

Starts	1st	2nd	3rd	4th	Win & Pl
20	2	7	-	1	£234,719
139	8/19	Gway	2m 132-147 Hdl Hcap good		£159,459
	4/17	Fair	2m Mdn Hdl gd-yld		£7,897

Smart dual-purpose performer who got up late to win the Galway Hurdle this summer; had been knocking on the door in similar races last season (twice finished second in good races at Fairyhouse) and likely to be aimed at more big 2m handicaps.

Umbrigado (Ire)

5 br g Stowaway - Dame O'Neill (Dr Massini)

David Pipe   John White & Anne Underhill

PLACINGS: 2/1116-   RPR **140**h

Starts	1st	2nd	3rd	4th	Win & Pl
4	3	-	-	-	£11,261
	2/19	Extr	2m2½f Cls4 Nov Hdl gd-sft		£4,549
	12/18	Sthl	1m7½f Cls5 Mdn Hdl soft		£3,119
	11/18	Uttx	2m Cls5 NHF 4-6yo good		£2,274

Beaten only once under rules when just under

ten lengths behind Reserve Tank in a Grade I at Aintree; had won three times prior to that, impressively defying a penalty at Exeter; could go novice chasing and trainer has already earmarked the Cheltenham Festival.

Un De Sceaux (Fr)

11 b g Denham Red - Hotesse De Sceaux (April Night)

Willie Mullins (Ir)   Edward O'Connell

PLACINGS: 22/161112/11211/25-1   RPR **173**+c

Starts	1st	2nd	3rd	4th	Win & Pl
32	23	5	-	-	£1,519,268
	4/19	Punc	2m Gd1 Ch yield		£159,459
	4/18	Punc	2m Gd1 Ch yld-sft		£143,584
	4/18	Fair	2m4f Gd2 Ch heavy		£41,770
	1/18	Asct	2m1f Cls1 Gd1 Ch soft		£86,430
	12/17	Cork	2m½f Gd2 Ch heavy		£30,256
	3/17	Chel	2m5f Cls1 Gd1 Ch good		£170,850
	1/17	Chel	2m½f Cls1 Gd1 Ch soft		£40,053
	12/16	Sand	1m7½f Cls1 Gd1 Ch gd-sft		£84,405
	5/16	Autl	2m5½f Gd2 Hdl v soft		£57,904
	1/16	Asct	2m1f Cls1 Gd1 Ch soft		£71,188
	4/15	Punc	2m Nov Gd1 Ch yield		£53,488
	3/15	Chel	2m Cls1 Gd1 Ch gd-sft		£85,425
	1/15	Leop	2m1f Nov Gd1 Ch yld-sft		£37,209
	12/14	Fair	2m Ch soft		£6,900
	4/14	Autl	2m3½f Gd2 Hdl heavy		£65,625
	3/14	Autl	2m3½f Gd3 Hdl v soft		£50,625
	2/14	Gowr	2m Gd2 Hdl heavy		£21,667
	1/14	Navn	2m Hdl soft		£10,833
	12/13	Thur	2m Hdl soft		£8,695
	4/13	Punc	2m Nov Hdl heavy		£11,890
	2/13	Punc	2m Mdn Hdl sft-hvy		£4,207
	10/12	Sbri	1m4f NHF 4yo v soft		£4,167
	2/12	Mchl	1m4f NHF 4yo gd-sft		£4,167

Remarkable veteran chaser who looked as good as ever last season, taking his Grade I tally to ten when winning Punchestown's Champion Chase for the second successive year in April; ideally suited by 2m with plenty of cut, though still effective over further.

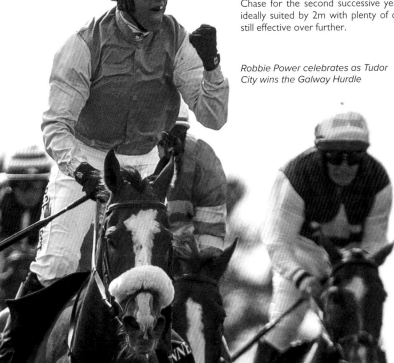

Robbie Power celebrates as Tudor City wins the Galway Hurdle

Unowhatimeanharry heads to victory at the Punchestown festival

Uncle Alastair

7 b g Midnight Legend - Cyd Charisse (Kayf Tara)

Nicky Richards   Paul & Clare Rooney

PLACINGS: 11/F11133/2-   RPR **145+**c

Starts	1st	2nd	3rd	4th	Win & Pl
9	5	1	2	-	£22,383

1/18	Ayr	2m Cls4 Nov Hdl heavy	£4,809
12/17	Ayr	2m4¹/₂f Cls4 Nov Hdl heavy	£3,899
12/17	Carl	2m4f Cls4 Nov Hdl 4-6yo soft	£5,198
2/17	Ayr	2m Cls6 NHF 4-6yo soft	£1,625
1/17	Weth	2m Cls5 NHF 4-6yo gd-sft	£2,274

Won five of first six races under rules (fell when going well on other run) before just coming up short in better novice hurdles; made a promising start over fences last season when second to Vinndication only to suffer an injury; trainer feels he has the world at his feet.

Unowhatimeanharry

11 b g Sir Harry Lewis - Red Nose Lady (Teenoso)

Harry Fry   John P McManus

PLACINGS: 1/11131/1230/31F80-1   RPR **156+**h

Starts	1st	2nd	3rd	4th	Win & Pl
33	13	2	9	2	£639,461

5/19	Punc	3m Gd1 Hdl gd-yld	£159,459
11/18	Newb	3m Cls1 Gd2 Hdl soft	£28,609
11/17	Aint	2m4f Cls2 Hdl soft	£28,152
4/17	Punc	3m Gd1 Hdl gd-yld	£126,068
1/17	Chel	3m Cls1 Gd2 Hdl soft	£34,170
12/16	Asct	3m¹/₂f Cls1 Gd1 Hdl gd-sft	£56,950
11/16	Newb	3m Cls1 Gd2 Hdl soft	£28,475
3/16	Chel	3m Cls1 Nov Gd1 Hdl good	£68,340
138 2/16	Extr	2m7f Cls2 124-139 Hdl Hcap heavy	£11,617
12/15	Chel	3m Cls1 Nov Gd2 Hdl soft	£17,165
123 11/15	Newb	2m4¹/₂f Cls4 Nov 109-123 Hdl Hcap soft	£6,498
123 11/15	Chel	2m5f Cls3 118-125 Cond Hdl Hcap gd-sft	£7,507
2/13	Font	2m1¹/₂f Cls6 NHF 4-6yo soft	£1,625

Dominant staying hurdler three seasons ago, winning four out of five with sole defeat coming at odds-on in the Stayers' Hurdle; often out of sorts since then but still showed signs of life last season, most notably when winning fourth Grade 1 at Punchestown in April.

Us And Them (Ire)

6 b g Stowaway - Manorville (Flemensfirth)

Joseph O'Brien (Ir)   Burnham Plastering & Dry Lining

PLACINGS: 24/31120/4122222-U   RPR **157**c

Starts	1st	2nd	3rd	4th	Win & Pl
15	3	7	1	2	£141,128

11/18	Navn	2m1f Ch good	£9,267
12/17	Punc	2m Nov Hdl heavy	£9,477
11/17	Cork	2m Mdn Hdl 4yo sft-hvy	£6,844

Won only once last season but ran consistently well in top company, finishing second in four Grade 1 races including the Racing Post Arkle (albeit beaten 13 lengths by Duc Des Genievres); yet to run beyond 2m1f but stayed on notably well at Cheltenham and Aintree.

Valtor (Fr)

10 b g Nidor - Jossca (Badolato)

Nicky Henderson   Simon Munir & Isaac Souede

PLACINGS: 9784/P4653332/671P0-   RPR **161+**c

Starts	1st	2nd	3rd	4th	Win & Pl
50	7	5	9	7	£439,260

148 12/18	Asct	3m Cls1 List 133-157 Ch Hcap soft	£56,950
10/16	Autl	2m7¹/₂f Gd3 Ch v soft	£57,904
0 6/16	Autl	2m6f Ch Hcap heavy	£31,434
4/15	Autl	2m6f Ch v soft	£24,186
10/14	Autl	2m5¹/₂f Ch 5yo v soft	£22,000
9/14	Redn	1m7f NHF 4-5yo good	£4,167
6/13	Ques	2m2¹/₂f Ch 4yo soft	£5,463

Surprised even his trainer when a 33-1 winner of the Silver Cup at Ascot on his British debut last season; hadn't won in last 15 starts in France before being bought as a Grand National horse

and struggled in two subsequent runs, including when well beaten at Aintree.

Vinndication (Ire)

6 b g Vinnie Roe - Pawnee Trail (Taipan)

Kim Bailey					Moremoneythan
PLACINGS: 1111/1135-				RPR **156**+c	

Starts	1st	2nd	3rd	4th	Win & Pl
8	6	-	1	-	£71,418

12/18	Asct	2m5f Cls1 Nov Gd2 Ch soft	£19,933
11/18	Carl	2m4f Cls3 Nov Ch soft	£7,473
2/18	Hntg	2m3½f Cls1 Nov List Hdl soft	£17,085
1/18	Asct	2m5½f Cls3 Nov Hdl 4-7yo soft	£6,758
12/17	Leic	2m4½f Cls3 Nov Hdl soft	£6,498
11/17	Ludl	2m Cls4 NHF 4-6yo good	£3,249

Won first six races under rules, including two novice chases last season; came up short when

stepped up in grade but still ran well when third in the Scilly Isles and fifth in the JLT at Cheltenham (first run going left-handed); likely to step up to 3m.

Vintage Clouds (Ire)

9 gr g Cloudings - Rare Vintage (Germany)

Sue Smith					Trevor Hemmings
PLACINGS: 22F3F7/124233/1P2F6-				RPR **151**c	

Starts	1st	2nd	3rd	4th	Win & Pl
143	11/18	Hayd	3m1½f Cls2 130-144 Ch Hcap good	£31,714
132	10/17	Aint	3m1f Cls3 Nov 120-133 Ch Hcap gd-sft	£9,097
	11/15	Hayd	2m3f Cls3 Nov Hdl 4-7yo soft	£6,498
	1/15	Weth	2m Cls6 NHF 4-6yo soft	£1,643

Has won only twice in three seasons over fences

but has been placed in a string of top staying handicaps; second in the Ultima at Cheltenham last season (had been third in 2018) but fell at the first in the Grand National and was only sixth when favourite for the Scottish version.

Vision D'Honneur (Fr)

5 b g Vision D'Etat - Hembra (Croco Rouge)

Gordon Elliott (Ir)   Gigginstown House Stud

PLACINGS: 4139-F   RPR **139**h

Starts	1st	2nd	3rd	4th	Win & Pl
5	1	-	1	1	£18,171
	1/19	Punc	2m Mdn Hdl good		£7,492

Lost his way slightly in the spring but had gone off just 12-1 for last season's Supreme Novices' Hurdle at Cheltenham after a couple of eyecatching runs; impressively won a maiden at Punchestown and finished third behind Klassical Dream in a Grade 1 at Leopardstown.

Vision Des Flos (Fr)

6 b g Balko - Marie Royale (Turgeon)

Colin Tizzard   Ann & Alan Potts Limited

PLACINGS: 1/3421622/U2352310-6   RPR **151**h

Starts	1st	2nd	3rd	4th	Win & Pl
17	3	5	3	1	£196,829
	2/19	Font	2m3f Cls1 Gd2 Hdl gd-sft		£45,560
	2/18	Extr	2m1f Cls1 Nov List Hdl heavy		£14,238
	4/17	Punc	2m NHF 4-5yo gd-yld		£50,427

Progressed well last season, benefiting from going up in trip after wind surgery midway through the campaign; likely to finish second in a 3m Grade 1 at Punchestown until a final-flight blunder and had beaten If The Cap Fits in the National Spirit Hurdle at Fontwell two starts earlier.

Voix Du Reve (Fr)

7 br g Voix Du Nord - Pommbelle (Apple Tree)

Willie Mullins (Ir)   Andrea & Graham Wylie

PLACINGS: 2/89000/1103113FU1-4   RPR **155**+c

Starts	1st	2nd	3rd	4th	Win & Pl
24	7	3	3	1	£163,577
	4/19	Fair	2m4f Nov Gd1 Ch gd-yld		£53,153
	11/18	Punc	2m Nov Gd2 Ch good		£23,235
	10/18	Gway	2m2f Ch yield		£7,632
	7/18	Bell	2m4f Hdl gd-fm		£7,087
	5/18	Klny	2m4f Hdl good		£9,812
	11/15	Engh	2m1½f Hdl 3yo v soft		£17,860
	9/15	Nanc	2m1f Hdl 3yo v soft		£7,814

Highly tried in novice chases last season and landed a Grade 1 win in the Ryanair Gold Cup at Fairyhouse, relishing step up to 2m4f having looked just short of top class over 2m (and again when fourth at Punchestown); going well when unseated three out in the JLT at Cheltenham.

Waiting Patiently (Ire)

8 b g Flemensfirth - Rossavon (Beneficial)

Ruth Jefferson   Richard Collins

PLACINGS: 221/111/111/U23-   RPR **165**c

Starts	1st	2nd	3rd	4th	Win & Pl
12	7	3	1	-	£222,164
	2/18	Asct	2m5f Cls1 Gd1 Ch soft		£85,827
	1/18	Kemp	2m4½f Cls1 List Ch gd-sft		£22,780
	11/17	Carl	2m4f Cls1 List Ch gd-sft		£17,085
	1/17	Hayd	2m4f Cls1 Nov Gd2 Ch soft		£18,546
	12/16	Newc	2m1½f Cls3 Nov Ch soft		£6,498
123	11/16	Sedg	2m1½f Cls3 Nov 115-130 Ch Hcap soft		£6,498
	1/16	Sedg	2m4f Cls4 Nov Hdl gd-sft		£3,798

Looked to have the world at his feet when winning the Ascot Chase in 2018, making it six out of six over fences, but hasn't gone on since then, albeit in just three runs; was brought down in the King George last season but below his best twice subsequently; said to need soft ground.

Wakanda (Ire)

10 b g Westerner - Chanson Indienne (Indian River)

Sue Smith   Mrs M B Scholey

PLACINGS: P/752P3/2521P0/541P-   PR **152**+c

Starts	1st	2nd	3rd	4th	Win & Pl
35	9	8	2	4	£289,381

146	1/19	Hayd	3m1¹/₂f Cls1 Gd2 140-154 Ch Hcap gd-sft	£42,713
145	1/18	Donc	3m Cls1 List 131-157 Ch Hcap soft	£45,560
151	12/15	Asct	3m Cls1 List 137-158 Ch Hcap gd-sft	£56,950
145	11/15	Newc	2m7¹/₂f Cls1 List 128-153 Ch Hcap soft	£34,170
139	10/15	Weth	2m3¹/₂f Cls1 List 132-145 Ch Hcap soft	£15,661
	1/15	Hayd	2m4¹/₂f Cls1 Nov Gd2 Ch heavy	£17,370
	12/14	Kels	2m7¹/₂f Cls3 Nov Ch soft	£10,128
120	10/14	Hexm	2m4f Cls4 Nov 101-120 Ch Hcap good	£6,844
	7/13	Slig	2m Mdn Hdl 4yo good	£4,207

Has run well in a string of top staying handicaps in recent seasons and won last season's Peter Marsh Chase at Haydock; did that off 146 and won the Sky Bet Chase and finished second in the Rowland Meyrick two seasons ago on only occasions rated lower since 2015.

Walk In The Mill (Fr)

9 b g Walk In The Park - Libre Amour (Lost World)

Robert Walford   Baroness Harding

PLACINGS: 352/1197/513P/31334-   RPR **148**+c

Starts	1st	2nd	3rd	4th	Win & Pl
24	5	4	6	1	£222,114

137	12/18	Aint	3m2f Cls1 Gd3 134-160 Ch Hcap soft	£84,195
131	11/17	Asct	3m Cls3 122-135 Ch Hcap gd-sft	£16,245
126	1/17	Winc	2m4f Cls2 126-144 Ch Hcap soft	£12,558
121	11/16	Extr	2m1¹/₂f Cls3 111-123 Ch Hcap soft	£9,583
	4/15	Fntb	2m3f Ch v soft	£8,558

Comfortable winner of last season's Becher Chase over the Grand National fences and ran a cracker in the National itself when fourth behind Tiger Roll; kept on the go in between with two defeats in novice hurdles; likely to have a similar campaign again.

Walt (Ire)

8 b g King's Theatre - Allee Sarthoise (Pampabird)

Neil Mulholland   Phil Simmonds

PLACINGS: 332/433P/2065121P6-6   RPR **145**c

Starts	1st	2nd	3rd	4th	Win & Pl
23	3	4	6	1	£82,985

134	2/19	Kemp	3m Cls1 Gd3 134-154 Ch Hcap good	£56,950
118	12/18	Tntn	2m7f Cls4 Nov 99-121 Ch Hcap good	£6,108
120	1/17	Font	2m3f Cls3 104-127 Hdl Hcap soft	£5,393

Lost his way in the spring but had been progressive over fences prior to that, winning the valuable 888Sport Handicap Chase at Kempton over Double Shuffle after a wide-margin success at Newbury; has gained both chase victories on good ground.

Warriors Tale

10 b g Midnight Legend - Samandara (Kris)

Paul Nicholls   Trevor Hemmings

PLACINGS: 13253115/U22P/41P0P-   RPR **154**+c

Starts	1st	2nd	3rd	4th	Win & Pl
30	6	7	2	2	£128,660

147	12/18	Aint	2m5f Cls2 130-147 Ch Hcap soft	£49,520
137	3/17	Newb	2m4f Cls2 125-143 Ch Hcap gd-sft	£12,660
130	3/17	Newb	2m4f Cls3 Nov 130-143 Ch Hcap soft	£6,498
	5/16	Prth	3m Cls4 Nov Ch gd-fm	£4,328
110	2/15	Kels	2m6¹/₂f Cls3 110-125 Hdl Hcap gd-sft	£6,498
	1/15	Ayr	2m4¹/₂f Cls5 Mdn Hdl soft	£2,469

Bought by Trevor Hemmings for the Grand National after finishing second in the 2018 Sky Bet Chase but has been pulled up in the last two runnings; looks much better back over distances short of 3m and won over the National fences in last season's Grand Sefton.

Warriors Tale scores at Aintree last December

Wenyerreadyfreddie (Ire)
8 ch g Beneficial - Ware It Vic (Old Vic)

Nicky Henderson | M Landau & J Lightfoot

PLACINGS: 2/321/4P/22117P- | RPR **153+**c

Starts	1st	2nd	3rd	4th	Win & Pl
12	3	4	1	1	£33,251

	11/18	Asct	2m3f Cls3 Nov Ch good	£10,007
130	11/18	Asct	2m3f Cls3 Nov 122-140 Ch Hcap good	£10,007
	3/17	Donc	2m1½f Cls4 Nov Cond Hdl soft	£3,899

Looked a very smart recruit to fences when twice winning at Ascot early last season, hacking up in a novice handicap off 130 and claiming the scalp of Kildisart when conceding 5lb; twice disappointing subsequently, including when looking a non-stayer over 2m6½f.

West Approach
9 b g Westerner - Ardstown (Ardross)

Colin Tizzard | John & Heather Snook

PLACINGS: PP/131356P/3P522966- | RPR **154**h

Starts	1st	2nd	3rd	4th	Win & Pl
30	4	4	6	1	£121,517

	12/17	Extr	2m3f Cls2 Nov Ch soft	£16,025
	10/17	Ffos	2m5f Cls3 Ch soft	£9,097
	5/16	NAbb	2m1f Cls2 Nov Hdl good	£9,495
	1/15	Newb	2m1½f Cls5 NHF 4-6yo heavy	£2,053

Has spent most of the last two campaigns over fences but appreciated a return to hurdles midway through last season, finishing second behind Paisley Park in the Long Walk Hurdle and the Cleeve; sixth when favourite for the bet365 Gold Cup off a potentially good chase mark.

Western Ryder (Ire)
7 b g Westerner - Seesea (Dr Massini)

Warren Greatrex | Albatross Club, Bryan Drew & Friends

PLACINGS: 21253/U114265/53330- | RPR **151**h

Starts	1st	2nd	3rd	4th	Win & Pl
18	4	3	4	1	£97,985

	12/17	Chel	2m1f Cls3 Nov Hdl 4-6yo soft	£7,798
	11/17	Chep	2m Cls4 Nov Hdl heavy	£3,249
	12/16	Asct	1m7½f Cls1 List NHF 4-6yo gd-sft	£17,085
	5/16	Ffos	2m Cls4 NHF 4-6yo good	£3,249

Without a win since two novice hurdles in late 2017 but has proved himself a smart 2m hurdler; ran well under big weights in a couple of valuable handicaps last season but couldn't repeat that form in smaller fields when favourite for a couple of Grade 2 contests.

Whatswrongwithyou (Ire)
8 ch g Bienamado - Greenfield Noora (Topanoora)

Nicky Henderson | 5 Hertford Street Racing Club

PLACINGS: 2/1012/2113/621178- | RPR **144**c

Starts	1st	2nd	3rd	4th	Win & Pl
13	5	2	2	-	£45,090

	2/19	Font	2m2f Cls3 Nov Ch gd-sft	£9,748
	1/19	Ffos	2m Cls4 Nov Hdl soft	£4,614
	2/18	Newb	2m1½f Cls3 Nov Hdl soft	£6,758
	1/18	Newb	2m1½f Cls4 Nov Hdl soft	£4,549
	3/17	Ludl	2m Cls4 NHF 4-6yo soft	£3,899

Useful hurdler (third in the 2018 Imperial

Cup) who won a couple of small-field novice chases last season; aimed at top 2m handicaps subsequently and stayed on into a fair seventh in the Grand Annual (got too far back) before disappointing at Aintree.

Whisper (Fr)
11 b g Astarabad - Belle Yepa (Mansonnien)

Nicky Henderson | Walters Plant Hire

PLACINGS: 1/251/5P8/1122/125/7 | RPR **139**h

Starts	1st	2nd	3rd	4th	Win & Pl
26	11	5	2	2	£402,790

	11/17	Kemp	2m4½f Cls2 Ch good	£12,512
	1/17	Chel	2m5f Cls1 Nov Gd2 Ch soft	£18,224
	12/16	Chel	2m5f Cls2 Nov Ch gd-sft	£15,698
	4/15	Aint	3m½f Cls1 Gd1 Hdl good	£67,582
	4/14	Aint	3m1½f Cls1 Gd1 Hdl gd-sft	£67,524
153	3/14	Chel	2m5f Cls1 Gd3 135-154 Hdl Hcap good	£45,560
140	12/13	Newb	2m4½f Cls2 134-144 Hdl Hcap heavy	£11,574
	4/13	Chel	2m4½f Cls2 Nov Hdl gd-sft	£10,010
	2/13	Ffos	2m4f Cls4 Nov Hdl 4-7yo heavy	£3,574
	12/12	Ffos	2m4f Cls4 Nov Hdl heavy	£2,599
	4/12	Ffos	2m Cls6 NHF 4-5yo good	£1,848

Ran a mighty race when second in the Ladbrokes Trophy in 2017 but flopped in the King George and missed more than a year before low-key return this spring; always considered more of a Grand National type than a Grade 1 horse by his trainer and likely to come down to feasible mark.

Wholestone (Ire)
8 br g Craigsteel - Last Theatre (King's Theatre)

Nigel Twiston-Davies | Simon Munir & Isaac Souede

PLACINGS: 113/42612323/152950- | RPR **156+**h

Starts	1st	2nd	3rd	4th	Win & Pl
23	7	5	2	4	£248,209

	11/18	Aint	2m4f Cls2 Hdl good	£28,152
	1/18	Chel	2m4½f Cls1 Gd2 Hdl heavy	£28,475
	1/17	Chel	2m4½f Cls1 Nov Gd2 Hdl soft	£17,085
	12/16	Chel	3m Cls1 Nov Gd2 Hdl soft	£17,085
	10/16	Chel	3m Cls3 Nov Hdl good	£6,256
	9/16	Wwck	2m5f Cls4 Mdn Hdl good	£3,574
	9/15	Worc	2m Cls6 NHF 4-6yo good	£1,625

Smart staying hurdler who goes particularly well

Whisper (left) battles with Total Recall in the 2017 Ladbrokes Trophy at Newbury

at Cheltenham, with four of his last five wins coming there; not quite at his best last season, coming second when defending his crown in the Relkeel Hurdle and a well-beaten fifth in the Stayers' Hurdle (third in 2018).

Wicklow Brave

10 b g Beat Hollow - Moraine (Rainbow Quest)

Willie Mullins (Ir)					Wicklow Bloodstock

PLACINGS: /71/72/213F4722F-311   RPR **158**h

Starts	1st	2nd	3rd	4th	Win & Pl
34	10	5	4	1	£394,292
	8/19	Gway	2m2f Nov Gd3 Ch good		£26,577
	5/19	Baln	2m1f Ch good		£6,659
	9/18	List	2m Hdl good		£12,246
	4/17	Punc	2m Gd1 Hdl gd-yld		£126,068
138	3/15	Chel	2m1f Cls1 Gd3 134-146 Hdl Hcap soft		£45,560
	2/14	Punc	2m Nov List Hdl heavy		£16,250
	1/14	Cork	2m Mdn Hdl 4-5yo heavy		£6,038
	10/13	Tipp	2m NHF 4-7yo good		£6,030
	9/13	List	2m NHF 4-7yo soft		£7,854
	7/13	Gway	2m NHF 4-7yo good		£4,488

Famous for winning at the top level on the Flat and over hurdles; has also won a County Hurdle and nearly claimed a second Cheltenham Festival victory in last season's Coral Cup; took well to fences this summer and likely to try to complete the set with a Grade 1 chase win.

William Henry (Ire)

9 b g King's Theatre - Cincuenta (Bob Back)

Nicky Henderson					Walters Plant Hire

PLACINGS: 411/2121/P144/P14-   RPR **156**h

Starts	1st	2nd	3rd	4th	Win & Pl
14	6	2	-	4	£130,142
151	3/19	Chel	2m5f Cls1 Gd3 133-153 Hdl Hcap soft		£56,270
145	1/18	Kemp	2m5f Cls1 List 122-145 Hdl Hcap soft		£25,628
	4/17	Chel	2m2f Cls2 Nov Hdl good		£10,010
	12/16	Newb	2m1/2f Cls4 Hdl gd-sft		£4,549
	4/15	Ayr	2m Cls3 NHF 4-6yo good		£6,498
	3/15	Kemp	2m Cls5 NHF 4-6yo good		£2,559

Fragile but talented hurdler who won last season's Coral Cup under 11st 10lb on first run

following wind surgery; beaten 11 lengths into fourth behind If The Cap Fits when stepped up to Grade 1 level at Aintree; pulled up on only run over fences two seasons ago.

Winter Escape (Ire)

8 b g Robin Des Pres - Saddleeruppat (Saddlers' Hall)

Aidan Anthony Howard (Ir)					John P McManus

PLACINGS: 111/050/3/211153-P   RPR **157**+c

Starts	1st	2nd	3rd	4th	Win & Pl
14	6	1	2	-	£92,909
	1/19	Punc	2m4f Nov Gd3 Ch good		£23,653
	11/18	Cork	2m4f Nov Gd3 Ch yield		£20,885
	9/18	Gway	2m2f Ch soft		£7,904
	2/16	Kemp	2m Cls1 Nov Gd2 Hdl gd-sft		£17,085
	2/16	Donc	2m1/2f Cls4 Nov Hdl gd-sft		£3,899
	12/15	Donc	2m1/2f Cls5 Mdn Hdl gd-sft		£2,924

Lost his way for Alan King having once looked an exciting prospect but was rejuvenated by switch to Ireland last season and claimed the notable scalp of A Plus Tard when completing a hat-trick in a Grade 3 at Punchestown in January; regressed again in the spring.

Wonder Laish

7 b g Halling - Wonder Why (Tiger Hill)

Charles Byrnes (Ir)					Martin White

PLACINGS: 1/7110-   RPR **146**+h

Starts	1st	2nd	3rd	4th	Win & Pl
5	3	-	-	-	£69,104
136	12/18	Fair	2m 122-150 Hdl Hcap good		£52,212
119	11/18	Navn	2m 95-123 Hdl Hcap good		£8,995
	9/17	List	2m Mdn Hdl heavy		£7,897

Smart Flat performer (premier handicap winner)

who translated that form to hurdles last season, winning handicaps at Navan and Fairyhouse (beat subsequent Galway Hurdle winner Tudor City); disappointed on only subsequent run in a valuable handicap at Leopardstown.

Yala Enki (Fr)

9 b/br g Nickname - Cadiane (Cadoudal)

Venetia Williams Hills Of Ledbury (Aga)

PLACINGS: 31441/P364F166/1357- RPR **162**c

Starts		1st	2nd	3rd	4th	Win & Pl
36		9	5	5	5	£283,619
150	11/18	Bang	3m Cls2 126-150 Ch Hcap gd-sft			£16,266
146	2/18	Hayd	3m4¹/₂f Cls1 Gd3 138-161 Ch Hcap heavy			£60,067
146	3/17	Kels	3m2f Cls2 125-147 Ch Hcap heavy			£17,545
139	12/16	Hayd	2m7f Cls2 120-139 Ch Hcap soft			£15,640
	2/16	Asct	2m3¹/₂f Cls2 Nov Hdl soft			£15,640
130	1/16	Kemp	2m5f Cls1 List 127-153 Hdl Hcap soft			£22,780
	11/15	Extr	2m5¹/₂f Cls3 Nov Hdl gd-sft			£5,523
	2/14	Fntb	2m Ch 4yo v soft			£9,600
	10/13	Pari	2m1f Ch 3yo gd-sft			£7,415

Very smart handicap chaser who has run well in a string of gruelling tests of stamina in recent seasons; won the Grand National Trial at Haydock in 2018 when favoured by heavy ground; not beaten far when third in the Welsh Grand National last season.

Yalltari

8 gr g Kayf Tara - Lily Grey (Kadalko)

Venetia Williams Venetia Williams Racehorse Syndicates II

PLACINGS: 33/111/21F3- RPR **149**+c

Starts		1st	2nd	3rd	4th	Win & Pl
9		4	1	3		£41,663
137	12/18	Chep	2m7¹/₂f Cls2 Nov 125-140 Ch Hcap soft			£12,913
126	1/18	Uttx	2m4f Cls2 123-137 Hdl Hcap heavy			£9,384
119	1/18	Extr	2m2¹/₂f Cls3 113-132 Hdl Hcap heavy			£7,027
106	12/17	Hrfd	2m Cls4 89-108 Hdl Hcap soft			£4,549

Won last three over hurdles two seasons ago and continued to progress when sent chasing last season, winning a novice handicap at Chepstow; good third when stepped up in class for the Reynoldstown at Ascot, beaten less than five lengths having travelled notably well.

Yorkhill (Ire)

9 ch g Presenting - Lightning Breeze (Saddlers' Hall)

Willie Mullins (Ir) Andrea & Graham Wylie

PLACINGS: 1/41112/86P8/692-0U1 RPR **143**+c

Starts		1st	2nd	3rd	4th	Win & Pl
21		10	2	-	1	£319,602
	8/19	Gway	2m6¹/₂f Ch soft			£15,946
	3/17	Chel	2m4f Cls1 Nov Gd1 Ch good			£89,275
	1/17	Leop	2m3f Nov Gd3 Ch good			£22,692
	12/16	Fair	2m Ch sft-hvy			£6,331
	4/16	Aint	2m4f Cls1 Nov Gd1 Hdl soft			£42,402
	3/16	Chel	2m5f Cls1 Nov Gd1 Hdl good			£68,340
	1/16	Sand	2m Cls1 Nov Gd1 Hdl heavy			£23,048
	12/15	Punc	2m4f Mdn Hdl heavy			£6,419
	4/15	Punc	2m NHF 4-7yo yield			£6,419
	3/15	Gowr	2m2f NHF 4-7yo soft			£4,814

Won nine of his first ten races under rules,

including twice at the Cheltenham Festival, but victory at Galway this summer was his first since the JLT Novices' Chase in 2017; has had plenty go wrong but fascinating to see if his master trainer can build on recent success.

Younevercall (Ire)

8 b g Yeats - Afarka (Kahyasi)

Kim Bailey Youneverknow Partnership

PLACINGS: 31/1F61/17/2181- RPR **158**+h

Starts		1st	2nd	3rd	4th	Win & Pl
12		6	1	1		£66,577
	4/19	Sand	2m5¹/₂f Cls1 Gd2 Hdl good			£31,323
144	11/18	Kemp	2m5f Cls2 122-145 Hdl Hcap good			£11,886
135	11/16	Kemp	2m5f Cls2 128-135 Hdl Hcap good			£11,886
	4/16	Hntg	2m4¹/₂f Cls4 Nov Hdl gd-sft			£3,899
	10/15	Uttx	2m Cls5 Mdn Hdl good			£2,599
	4/15	Sthl	1m7¹/₂f Cls6 NHF 4-6yo good			£1,949

Fragile gelding who has been very lightly raced through injury but has won five of last eight races going back to 2016; stepped up again when winning a Grade 2 at Sandown on final start having reportedly benefited hugely from wind surgery; could go novice chasing.

Zero Ten (Ire)

6 b g Shantou - Hannah Rose (Un Desperado)

Emmet Mullins (Ir) Mrs A F Mee

PLACINGS: P7/16/1112-11 RPR **144**+h

Starts		1st	2nd	3rd	4th	Win & Pl
7		5	1	-	-	£83,644
	7/19	Gway	2m2f Ch good			£9,051
	5/19	Punc	2m4f Hdl yield			£39,865
	3/19	Leop	2m Nov Hdl soft			£11,099
	9/18	Gway	2m1¹/₂f Mdn Hdl soft			£7,087
	7/18	Gway	2m1¹/₂f NHF 4-7yo good			£9,261

Exciting novice chase prospect who won three out of four in novice hurdles last season following Galway bumper win, with sole defeat a close second in a Grade 2 at Fairyhouse over Easter; won again at Galway this summer, this time making a successful chase debut.

Form figures included in this season's key horses include all runs up to September 5, 2019

KEY HORSES LISTED BY TRAINER

Nick Alexander
Lake View Lad

Caroline Bailey
Crosspark

Kim Bailey
Charbel
Dandy Dan
First Flow
Newtide
Rocky's Treasure
Vinndication
Younevercall

Enda Bolger
Ballyoisin
Movewiththetimes

Peter Bowen
Lord Napier

Mark Bradstock
Step Back

Martin Brassil
City Island

Charles Byrnes
Off You Go
Wonder Laish

Mick Channon
Glen Forsa
Mister Whitaker

Rebecca Curtis
Drovers Lane
Joe Farrell
Lisnagar Oscar

Liam Cusack
Snugsborough Hall

Henry Daly
Atlanta Ablaze

Henry de Bromhead
A Plus Tard
Balko Des Flos
Chris's Dream
Dommage Pour Toi
Honeysuckle
Minella Indo
Monalee
Moon Over Germany
Notebook
Ornua
Paloma Blue
Petit Mouchoir

Philip Dempsey
Derrinross

Stuart Edmunds
Maria's Benefit
Now McGinty

Gordon Elliott
Abacadabras
Alpha Des Obeaux
Apple's Jade
Battleoverdoyen
Borice
Braid Blue
Champagne Classic
Chief Justice
Chosen Mate
Coeur Sublime

Cracking Smart
Dallas Des Pictons
Death Duty
Delta Work
Dortmund Park
Dounikos
Duca De Thaix
Eclair De Beaufeu
Envoi Allen
Farclas
Felix Desjy
Galvin
Hardline
Jury Duty
Malone Road
Mengli Khan
Mick Jazz
Samcro
Shattered Love
Sire Du Berlais
Tiger Roll
Vision D'Honneur

Brian Ellison
Definitly Red

James Ewart
Charmant

Pat Fahy
Castlegrace Paddy

Alan Fleming
Speaker Connolly

Harry Fry
Acting Lass
Bags Groove
Get In The Queue
Hell's Kitchen
If The Cap Fits
Momella
Superb Story
Unowhatimeanharry

Tom George
Activial
Black Op
Boyhood
Bun Doran
Clondaw Castle
Double Shuffle
God's Own
Singlefarmpayment
Summerville Boy
The Worlds End

Nick Gifford
Glen Rocco

Chris Gordon
Highway One O One

Warren Greatrex
Bob Mahler
Emitom
Keeper Hill
La Bague Au Roi
Missed Approach
Western Ryder

Debra Hamer
Tobefair

Micky Hammond
Cadmium

Jessica Harrington
Magic Of Light
Not Many Left
Sizing John
Supasundae

Eddie Harty
Coney Island

Nigel Hawke
Speredek

Nicky Henderson
Adjali
Altior
Angels Breath
Apple's Shakira
Beware The Bear
Birchdale
Brain Power
Brave Eagle
Buveur D'Air
Call Me Lord
Casablanca Mix
Champ
Champagne Platinum
Claimantakinforgan
Daphne Du Clos
Dickie Diver
Downtown Getaway
Epatante
Fusil Raffles
Gold Present
Interconnected
Janika
L'Ami Serge
Might Bite
Mister Fisher
O O Seven
Ok Corral
On The Blind Side
Pentland Hills
Precious Cargo
Rather Be
Rathhill
River Wylde
Santini
Settie Hill
Soul Emotion
Terrefort
Top Notch
Valtor
Wenyerreadyfreddie
Whatswrongwithyou
Whisper
William Henry

Philip Hobbs
Defi Du Seuil
Gala Ball
Jerrysback
Reikers Island
Rock The Kasbah
Springtown Lake
Steely Addition
Thyme Hill

Denis Hogan
Moyhenna

Ellmarie Holden
Ex Patriot

Aidan Howard
Winter Escape

Ruth Jefferson
Waiting Patiently

Patrick G Kelly
Presenting Percy

Alan King
Ballywood
Dingo Dollar
Elgin
Good Man Pat
Sceau Royal
Talkischeap
The Glancing Queen
Timoteo

Neil King
Brandon Castle
Lil Rockerfeller

Philip Kirby
Lady Buttons
Top Ville Ben

Tom Lacey
Kateson
Thomas Patrick

Emma Lavelle
De Rasher Counter
Paisley Park

Tony Martin
Anibale Fly
Tudor City

Nicky Martin
Beer Goggles
The Two Amigos

Donald McCain
Cloudy Dream

Noel Meade
First Approach
Road To Respect
Tout Est Permis

Gary Moore
Baron Alco
Benatar
Diakali
Knocknanuss
Larry
Not Another Muddle
Traffic Fluide

Mouse Morris
Sams Profile

Hughie Morrison
Third Wind

Neil Mulholland
The Young Master
Walt

Emmet Mullins
Zero Ten

Seamus Mullins
Chesterfield

Willie Mullins
Acapella Bourgeois
Al Boum Photo
Allaho
Annamix
Aramon
Bacardys

Bachasson
Bapaume
Bellshill
Benie Des Dieux
Blackbow
Blue Sari
Burrows Saint
Carefully Selected
Cash Back
Chacun Pour Soi
Cilaos Emery
Class Conti
Colreevy
Come To Me
Concertista
Douvan
Duc Des Genievres
Easy Game
Eglantine Du Seuil
Eifile
Elimay
Faugheen
Footpad
Getabird
Great Field
Kemboy
Klassical Dream
Laurina
Livelovelaugh
Melon
Min
Mister Blue Sky
Mr Adjudicator
My Sister Sarah
Next Destination
Pairofbrowneyes
Penhill
Quick Grabim
Rathvinden
Real Steel
Royal Rendezvous
Saldier
Saturnas
Sharjah
Tiger Tap Tap
Tornado Flyer
Un De Sceaux
Voix Du Reve
Wicklow Brave
Yorkhill

Amy Murphy
Kalashnikov
Mercian Prince

Olly Murphy
Brewin'Upastorm
Itchy Feet
Thomas Darby

Richard Newland
Caid Du Lin
Le Patriote

Paul Nicholls
Adrien Du Pont
Ask For Glory
Black Corton
Brelan D'As
Brio Conti
Capeland
Captain Cattistock

KEY HORSES LISTED BY TRAINER

Christopher Wood
Clan Des Obeaux
Cyrname
Danny Kirwan
Danny Whizzbang
Dolos
Dynamite Dollars
Ecco
Frodon
Getaway Trump
Give Me A Copper
Grand Sancy
Kapcorse
Le Prezien
Magic Saint
Malaya
Mcfabulous
Mont Des Avaloirs
Old Guard
Politologue
Posh Trish
Present Man
Quel Destin
San Benedeto
Scaramanga
Secret Investor
Southfield Stone
Topofthegame
Truckers Lodge
Warriors Tale

Paul Nolan
Discorama

Fergal O'Brien
Jarveys Plate

Joseph O'Brien
Band Of Outlaws
Darasso
Early Doors
Fakir D'oudairies
Gardens Of Babylon

Le Richebourg
Mortal
Rhinestone
Tower Bridge
Us And Them

Terence O'Brien
Articulum

Jedd O'Keeffe
Sam Spinner

Jonjo O'Neill
Annie Mc
Cloth Cap

Henry Oliver
Kilfilum Cross
Louis' Vac Pouch

Ben Pauling
Bright Forecast
Global Citizen
Kildisart
Le Breuil
Nadaitak

David Pipe
Daklondike
Ramses De Teillee
Umbrigado

Nicky Richards
My Old Gold
Takingrisks
Uncle Alastair

Philip Rowley
Hazel Hill

Lucinda Russell
One For Arthur

Jeremy Scott
Dashel Drasher

Michael Scudamore
Some Chaos

Matt Sheppard
The Bay Birch

Dan Skelton
Azzuri
Beakstown
Born Survivor
Ch'tibello
Cobra De Mai
Destrier
Mohaayed
Molly The Dolly
Roksana
Sofia's Rock
Spiritofthegames

Matthew Smith
Ronald Pump

Sue Smith
I Just Know
Midnight Shadow
Vintage Clouds
Wakanda

Tom Taaffe
Riders Onthe Storm

Colin Tizzard
Elegant Escape
Elixir De Nutz
Fox Norton
Kilbricken Storm

Lostintranslation
Mister Malarky
Native River
Reserve Tank
Robinsfirth
Thistlecrack
Vision Des Flos
West Approach

Nigel Twiston-Davies
Al Dancer
Ballyandy
Ballyhill
Ballymoy
Ballyoptic
Blue Flight
Bristol De Mai
Calett Mad
Count Meribel
Go Conquer
Good Boy Bobby
One For Rosie
Torpillo
Wholestone

Tim Vaughan
Looksnowtlikebrian

Robert Walford
Walk In The Mill

Ted Walsh
Any Second Now

Paul Webber
Indefatigable

Harry Whittington
Bigmartre
Rouge Vif
Saint Calvados

Christian Williams
Potters Corner

Evan Williams
Silver Streak

Ian Williams
First Assignment
King Of Realms

Jane Williams
Monsieur Lecoq

Nick Williams
Agrapart
Siruh Du Lac

Noel Williams
Another Crick

Venetia Williams
Aso
Calipto
Cepage
Geordie B
Yala Enki
Yalltari

Kayley Woollacott
Lalor

Smart operator Lalor scores at Cheltenham last November

INDEX OF HORSES

INDEX OF HORSES

Passing the huge crowds at Cheltenham during last season's Supreme Novices' Hurdle won by Klassical Dream

INDEX OF HORSES